TAKE BACK
THE RIGHT

PHILIP GOLD

CARROLL & GRAF PUBLISHERS
NEW YORK

TAKE BACK THE RIGHT

How the Neocons and the Religious Right Have Betrayed the Conservative Movement

TAKE BACK THE RIGHT:
How the Neocons and the Religious Right Have Betrayed the Conservative Movement

Published by
Carroll & Graf Publishers
An Imprint of Avalon Publishing Group Inc.
245 West 17th Street
11th Floor
New York, NY 10011

AVALON
publishing group incorporated

First Carroll & Graf edition 2004

Library of Congress Cataloging-in-Publication Data is available.

ISBN: 0-7867-1352-6

Designed by Simon M. Sullivan
Printed in the United States of America
Distributed by Publishers Group West

For Erin
and
The Boo

Contents

If you did not learn your lesson to display it in action,
what did you learn it for?

Epictetus
Discourses

Preface

MALACHI. A prophet. A Hebrew prophet, minor even by the standards of the minor prophets. The Book of Malachi. A few brief, dreary, burned-out pages, wrapping up the Christian Old Testament. End of the line for the prophets. Fitting somehow, that the line should end with Malachi, whose name means "my messenger" in Hebrew, but who has so little left to say.

It's a strange work, the Book of Malachi. It's not often read, not often preached. Chapter Four, Verse One, however, has a certain cachet. It provided the theme of the sermon that Marshal Will Kane, aka Gary Cooper, interrupted in *High Noon* when he went to the Hadleyville church looking for men to stand with him against the return of the outlaws who had sworn to kill him.

For behold, a day cometh that shall burn as an oven . . .

The parishioners of Hadleyville, after a brief, resentful debate over who was to blame for the situation, the nature of citizenship and obligation, and the possibility that the threat might be overblown or evanescent, declined the marshal's request and suggested that, for everybody's sake, he leave town before the bad guys arrived. *High Noon* is oft portrayed as the archetypal western, good against evil. In truth, it was the first commercially successful western ever made where the townspeople take the side of evil and the man of virtue, along with his wife, who had stayed with him to fight, turn their backs on those who abandoned them first.

Nowadays, a lot of conservatives are feeling like Marshal Kane. Betrayed by their own. At the very least, they're feeling ignored, debased, and derided by those they've supported and served. It's a not unprecedented phenomenon in the history of conservatism since the fifties. Conservatives like to believe that they speak truth to power. But when power tells truth that they're not interested just now, please to take it somewhere else, when power sneers that, well, you really don't have anywhere else to go now, do you? . . . it's easy to feel like Marshal Kane. Or like Malachi.

And it's certainly a strange book, and a strange film, to be thinking of when you're sitting in your boss's office, discussing current events and arranging the details of your enforced departure after ten years, and your boss—a good and kind and decent gentleman, a respected friend—seems sad, distracted, and upset.

For nearly ten years, until I became one of the first mainstream conservatives publicly to oppose the Iraq war and the neocon agenda, I was associated with the Discovery Institute, a prominent Seattle-based conservative think tank. It is the national center of the "Intelligent Design" movement, which holds that it is possible to study the physical and biological worlds for evidence of design without inquiring into the nature, intent, or competence of the designer. No, it's not just "backdoor creationism." It's more, far more, and they're always delighted when they can get an atheist (preferably with a PhD or two in some hard science or other) to sign on. Some have. But the program is dependent on conservative Christian money. When you've got heavy donors, Christian or secular, they sometimes take an interest in more than the projects they're funding. Further, Discovery has ties to the Bush administration. Ambassador Bruce Chapman, the Institute's founding president and a former Reagan White House staffer, knows and occasionally meets with some senior people. Discovery's board chair, former congressman John Miller, had accepted a high-level position at State. Somewhere, no doubt, eyebrows were being raised about me. Not because I was important, but for precisely the opposite reason. Why, Bruce, the folks with the eyebrows and the checkbooks doubtless wanted to know, are you still keeping that nuisance around?

For months, no, years, I'd been feeling like Malachi. A minor prophet, now weary, now working through the final iterations of an exhausted form. It's over. But this was not the endgame dialogue between a Hebrew prophet and a nation headed for two millennia of disaster. It was between me and a movement I'd embraced, in adolescent ardor, forty years before . . . the biblically requisite number of years to spend in the wilderness.

It hadn't been a wilderness when, sometime around 1963, I'd signed on. At least, it hadn't seemed that way at the time. The thought that it might someday become a wilderness that I would find abhorrent could not have occurred back then. But it certainly occurred to me in 2002. Conservatism had become a wilderness I was no longer willing to sanction or inhabit, or to pretend might still lead to any kind of promised land. The Bush people, the neocons, the Republican Party, the Buchananites, and even—and particularly—the good, bewildered traditionalists, the "paleocons," had made it a wilderness. A wilderness of folly, of abuse, and of irrelevance.

It's hard to end a long relationship when you've nowhere else to go. It's also hard to leave a wilderness. Prophets often go into the wilderness to receive their messages. Sometimes, they get too attached to desolation. Malachi, I think, would have understood. Perhaps the people he preached to also understood. Their ancestors had.

Bruce Chapman, my boss and friend, labored with me through the final exchanges. His office was filled with the memorabilia of a lifetime in politics. That photo of him as a young Harvard undergraduate, shaking hands with Ike, had always amused me. I focused on it, and heard him tell the finance director to write me a check. It was not a large check, and he had no obligation to do it. But it was typically gracious. My public opposition to the administration's course, coupled with my decades of ever-more-defiant excoriation of what had come to be known as "cultural conservatism," could well have damaged the think tank he'd founded. Discovery was the enterprise to which he intended to devote the rest of his professional life. I had no right to harm it.

★   ★   ★

When *High Noon* came out in 1953, it was widely seen as a commentary on McCarthyism, on America's willingness to surrender to right-wing evil. Now it's conservatives who wonder what kind of evil they've surrendered to. Some shake their heads in honest bewilderment. What on earth are those people in DC doing? Others rage without effect about the war, the lies, the deficits, the threats to civil liberties, the arrogance. Strange how often the fierce and righteous prophets of one era become the impotent whiners of the next.

So seems the Book of Malachi. It ends with God's final, weary, yes-we've-heard-it-all-before, standard Old Testament threat:

Lest I come and strike the earth with a curse.

But it's an exhausted threat. And one can almost imagine it otherwise, with God (or Malachi) as Will Kane after the gunfight, tossing his badge at the feet of the crowd in contempt. *It's over.*

And so it was for me, being something of a minor secular prophet in an age of peril and burnout, and having grown weary of the role. A *WorldNetDaily* column about me a couple months before had called me one of the Cassandras of the conservative movement (Cassandra, according to myth, was a prophetess fated always to be right, never to be heeded). Two Cassandras, actually, the column went on. One a man who, for thirty years, had tried without success to explain to conservatives, intellectuals, and politicians alike, what the Culture War was really all about and why they were losing it. The second, a man who had spent much of the nineties warning about inevitable and devastating terrorist attack, and predicted its imminence in a pair of articles published in *Washington Law & Politics* in June and August 2001. But now it was on to Cassandra Number Three—the conservative who, beginning in the spring of 2002, started warning against the whole notion of redeeming Islam by force of arms, and against the Iraq venture in particular. Discreetly at first, then, in September 2002 in what *Seattle Magazine* later described as a "blistering attack": a *Seattle Weekly* article entitled "An Anti-War Movement of One."

But on this particular day, sitting in the boss's office, I wasn't feeling much like Cassandra. Or Malachi. Was I right? I'd learned long ago, whilst serving as a Marine Corps intelligence officer, that it's fine to be 80 percent certain you're 100 percent right, or 100 percent certain that you're 80 percent right. But when you're 100 percent certain that you're 100 percent right, you're probably wrong.

The prophet Malachi seems sure enough that what he has to say is right. Hebrew prophets, after all, had been using the same lines for centuries. He's mastered the format. He works through the same old mix of threats and accusations and appeals. But it's all bereft of real life, rather like listening to those sound-and-fury screamathons on cable news. Sound and fury, signifying nothing—except perhaps the belief that if you say it loud enough people will think you're right. That, plus the belief that noise is what America wants to hear.

Jack Miles, brilliant author of *God: A Biography*, once described God's covenant with Israel as based on "continuous mutual complaint," on the unlimited right of each party to complain about the other. Once, the arguments had been fierce, the loudness filled with meaning. This quiet little pseudofight was not.

I have loved you, says the Lord. Yet you say, In what way have You loved us?

The dialogues imagined in Malachi have always reminded me of a couple approaching divorce at the end of a long marriage. It's over. They know it; they've known it for quite some time. Nothing's going to change. But they're having one last, flat-toned argument, maybe just for the record, maybe because they don't have any clear idea of what else to do. Both parties know their lines, but the lines long ago lost their power to persuade, to indict, to defend, or to hurt.

Your words have been harsh against me, says the Lord. Yet you say, What have we spoken against You?

So in December 2002, Discovery and I, and conservatism and I, said good-bye. It was, by the standards of the trade, a wondrously civil parting. Having been in Beltway think tanks, having known that world well as a journalist, I'd witnessed many such departures. They were mostly ugly, vindictive, and loud enough to penetrate closed doors and percolate down hallways. I was fortunate, but not surprised. Across the decades, the vast majority of conservatives I'd known had been good people, decent and sincere. Ugliness was certainly not in Bruce's nature.

But I was done with all that. And I knew I hadn't departed conservatism just to play apostate—to take up with a Left that, sad to relate, now speaks mostly to, for, and about itself. A Left that sometimes seems to take a perverse pride in its own irrelevance. A Left from which I'd received all those snide and sneering e-mails and phone messages congratulating me on "finally growing up" and "finally coming to my senses," (always the operative word, *finally*)—now get with the rest of our program. And if you're not going to denounce your former associates—sad how often the local media kept finagling for just that—well, don't come looking for jobs or grant money here.

I didn't denounce my former associates. Any thoughts I might have had of doing so in order to curry favor with the Left were forgotten one night when I was at a Seattle "town hall" meeting. Sitting in the audience, I heard myself vilified from the platform as "some jerk in a think tank who quit conservatism because it wasn't conservative enough." At the break, I tried to introduce myself to the gentleman who'd denounced me and invite him out for a drink. He'd already departed.

But if I wasn't headed Left, I also knew I had an obligation to keep on speaking out. So the question arose, What do you say after you say good-bye? The answer is, You take what you know and recraft it. Not as a protester for the sake of protest, or as a gadfly or a nuisance. Not as a renegade conservative who makes a new career of beating up on former colleagues, comrades, and institutions. Rather, as someone who has had a recurring experience that he wishes to continue anew. For years, decades really, when presenting some new and unusual and unexpected combinations of ideas in various media and forms, I'd had people respond, Yes. Yes. Tell us more. Tell us anything we haven't heard a thousand times already. Tell us more.

And also, and far more importantly, Hey, I knew that. Why didn't anybody ever say it before? Thank you. The two responses are not unrelated.

So that was the question: What could I say and do now, and over the next years of my life, that might make a difference in how people see the age that is upon us; how they decide what needs to be done; and how they find the courage to act?

What's the role now of a minor prophet living in an era of peril and burnout? What do you say after you say good-bye?

The Book of Malachi, perhaps more than anything else, is about the failure of discourse. God and Israel, it seems, have lost the ability to speak to each other, to connect, to motivate. They're so far gone. But Malachi still seems to hope that, could they but once again speak words of meaning, not formulaic old banalities, the relationship might still be fixed.

You have wearied the Lord with your words; yet you say, In what way have we wearied him?

We've wearied the Lord, perhaps. We've wearied each other, certainly. But we still have each other, and maybe that's where we ought to start.

Why do we deal treacherously with one another by profaning the covenant of the fathers?

For we have profaned the covenant of our fathers, and not just the fathers of conservatism. We have profaned the covenant based upon our unlimited right to complain, but also based upon love, covenant love, and on the mutual responsibility of citizens. Democracy runs on the right to complain. It also runs on the right to act and the right to care. In this much, at least, Malachi seems relevant. It's as if he's saying, If only we could speak to each other once again, openly and caringly . . . if only we could take a break from our befuddlements and our habits . . . somehow, still and even now, we could make it right.

And that's what this book is about. It is an invitation from a minor secular prophet, no longer weary, to see what we can do about making it right. Ultimately, it's a message of great possibility and faith and hope. It's about avoiding that final, *Lest I come and strike the earth with a curse.* The curse preceded by Malachi's invocation to: "turn the hearts of the fathers to the children, and the hearts of the children to their fathers," as the proper form of avoidance and redemption.

Continuity across the generations: the essence of conservatism. But the continuities, the faithfulness we need now, are not qualities of what conservatism has become. Nor are they likely to emerge from what conservatism is becoming. Our fathers speak to us in many voices. It's time to listen to some that have not been heard much these last few decades, these last couple millennia. That's what this book offers—not just speaking, but also listening anew, in the hope of making a few things right. Hope, offered in the hope that men and women desirous of speaking to each other in words of meaning can still make a few things right.

—Philip Gold

Acknowledgments

THIS BOOK HAS BEEN several decades in the making. I owe a lot to many people. Some of the most important, who are mentioned in the text, do not appear here. Others do not appear here for other reasons. To the following, in no particular order, I offer my gratitude and appreciation.

Ambassador Bruce. Dr. Bob. The formerly-of-Cleveland crew. The Yardley bunch. Miguel and his pretty women (especially Lena). Dr. Mike. Agent Nancy. Editor in chief Philip. Editor Doris, especially toward the end. The rest of Avalon. Professors Dorothy, R. Emmett, and Phyllis. The kids I taught at Georgetown University. Everybody who reads *Washington Law & Politics*. The Boo's generation. And everyone who put up with me.

In memoriam: Dorothy Pickel, Colin Walters, Woody West. Gone too soon.

And finally, to our warriors in Iraq and everywhere else. This war is unnecessary. You never are. Thank you.

Introduction

THESE ARE THE TIMES that ought to be trying our souls. If they aren't, a decent self-respect suggests that perhaps we might ask ourselves, Why not? At the darkest moment of World War II, Winston Churchill, defiant, taunted the enemy. "What kind of a people do they think we are?" Today, the context is different, the perils foreign and domestic not yet nearly so immediate or grave. But the question, this kind of question, remains apt.

What kind of a people do *we* think we are?

A few days before writing these words, I was speaking with my son and one of his friends. I'd just been asked to address their high school's World Affairs Club. My son's friend, in offering the invite, explained that he was doing so in his capacity as club vice president. Everybody in the club, he told me, was a vice president, for college application purposes. But he was the "real" vice president, and as such empowered to set the agenda. I of course accepted happily—who could refuse an offer like that?—and we got to chatting. At some point, I mentioned that their generation was going to inherit a god-awful mess. My son's friend, a keen and thoughtful young man, as are so many of his generation, replied that his father told him the same thing. Apparently, a lot of parents are saying the same thing, and have been for quite some time.

What kind of a people are we, who can say to our children so casually, *Après nous, le déluge*. After us . . .

A deluge. After us, a deluge of endless war and intermittent terror, occasioned by an empire we neither need nor can sustain—an ugly, perverse empire that addresses those whom we conquer physically, and those whom we conquer in other ways, with an arrogant, You'll thank us later. Why have not the last few millennia taught us that people don't like to be conquered and dominated, let alone redeemed, according to the standards of others? Inevitably and often successfully, they resist.

What part of conquest, and of resistance, don't we understand? And why have not the last few millennia also taught us what conquest inevitably does to the conquerors?

And what part of economics don't we understand? Trillions upon trillions in unpayable debt already amassed, including the "unfunded obligations" of Social Security and Medicare. The commonly accepted current statistic is $100,000 of federal debt for each of us. Then there are the trillions more coming at us as national security expenditures. We've already spent well over $1 trillion a year for defense, foreign adventures, and homeland security at all levels. Now add in millions upon millions of jobs gone forever. Then add in millions of aliens pouring in to work for little, far too little, at the low-end jobs that remain, while millions of others—doctors, scientists, engineers—leave lands that need them desperately, in order to enjoy the good life here. America is strip-mining the planet for people as well as resources.

And we're irredeemably indebted to the world we so voraciously consume. Today, America has the trading profile of a nineteenth-century European colony. We export food and raw materials; we let others sell us most of the rest of what we need. Perhaps it's not that stark. Not yet. The world still craves our weapons and our porn (read here, popular culture). It needs and uses our dollars. For half a century, we've been too big to fail, and in many ways, too convenient for other countries to do without. But just as the cemeteries are filled with indispensable men, so is history filled with nations and empires—and ideas— that turned out not to be so indispensable after all. Let the euro replace the dollar as an international medium, especially for oil. Let a globalizing world, so many of whose nations would love to see us fall, find uses for its money other than funding us and buying us. Impossible? Unthinkable? No. What's unthinkable is the notion that we can go on this way forever. As the hotel desk clerk told Grace Kelly, aka Mrs. Will Kane, a lot of people in Hadleyville thought that her husband had "a comeuppance coming."

How often and how easily gratitude turns to resentment. People do not like to be overshadowed, no matter how benign the declared intent of the colossus that does the overshadowing.

And what part of "GIGO" don't we understand? The old computer maxim—Garbage In, Garbage Out—applies no less to the human intellect and spirit. Pornography, mendacity, mediocrity, triviality, greed: These ye have always with you. But never before have human beings been so utterly immersed in gratuitous imagery of sex and violence; so utterly manipulated politically, culturally, spiritually; and so utterly debased by an entity that I've come to think of as GAG-ME, The Great American Garbage-Making Empire. Nor has any culture ever made such a fetish of bewailing it all, of moaning self-righteously about how awful it is that we're engaged in this race to the bottom—and then done nothing about it, except to go on complaining and consuming. Perhaps we believe in a covenant based upon our unlimited right to complain about ourselves, and believe that virtue can be generated by sufficient quantities of complaint. If so, we're only fooling ourselves, and no longer doing a very good job of that. Not now, when we find our culture more and more reduced to entertainment, and our entertainment to porn . . . and our politics to entertainment.

So, what kind of a people do we think we are? Perhaps we are indeed, and have come to think of ourselves as, a people quite content with all of the above, and with all the rest that we know to be so corrosive and so wrong. Just let it last our time. For decades, "Do it for the children" has been an all-purpose political and cultural mantra. But deep down, and when judged by our actions, we don't care. We just don't care. Just let it last our time. When Kane approached Hadleyville's old retired marshal, a mentor and a friend, he got no help. He did, however, get a lecture on how, deep down, "They just don't care."

I do not believe this. I cannot and I will not. We are a great and a good people, and despite the best efforts of our media and educational and entertainment systems, neither an ignorant nor a stupid people. Stupid people did not make America "the crown jewel of the planet," as *New York Times* columnist Bob Herbert (no jingo/jangle conservative, he) once called us. Evil people did not save the world twice in the twentieth century, from the Axis and from the Soviets. Morons don't populate the nation now. It's just that neither goodness nor greatness are automatic, and neither act of God nor act of Congress, neither Supreme Court decision nor executive order, and (least of all) no opinion poll ever, decreed the United States of America immortal.

We know this. We know, deep down, that we are deep in decadence. Not decadent in ways the professional scolds of cultural conservatism would have us believe. Decadent in the literal sense of the Latin root, *de cadere*, of falling away—of falling away, presumably from some previous standard of excellence, but sometimes just falling away. Literary critic Robert Adams once wrote that the essence of decadence, the essence that empowers all the rest, is "the deliberate neglect of the essentials of self-preservation." This we know that we are doing, across the entire span of our civilization. And we do care.

At least, we want to care.

But we know not how to care. We know not how. The issues, the challenges, the outrages are so many and so complex. And we're small, so very small. We know pretty much what needs to be done, if not always how to do it. Any vice president of the World Affairs Club could tell you what's needed. But we're small. And we practice what the economists sometimes call "rational ignorance." We're busy. So we concentrate on what we can accomplish and affect in our private lives and careers—perhaps with a soupçon of recreational protest, a few hours' community service, or a tax-deductible contribution to one of those advocacy or public interest organizations whose membership consists mostly of mailing lists.

Or perhaps it's even worse than that: a decadence far more fundamental and far more deadly. We know not how to care, but not merely because it's all so very complicated, and because we're so very busy and so small. We know not how to care because we've surrendered ourselves and our civilization to those who presume to tell us what our choices are.

Please stop a moment and reflect that maybe, just maybe, the greatest decadence of this civilization derives from the fact that *we have surrendered ourselves to those who presume to tell us what our choices are.*

Politically, whatever happens, the Republocrats (or if you prefer, the Demolicans) will win. Republicans and Democrats in an ugly symbiosis of venality, stasis, and cant. They tell us what our choices are and one way or another, our choices are always them. And we heed them and submit, and move on to the next surrender.

Economically, whatever happens, those most adept at trashing our economy, and their intellectual courtesans, will win. Call it globalization or downsizing or "rightsizing" or any of a dozen other names. They tell us what our choices are, and our choices are always, one way or another, whatever permits the dismantling and export of this nation's economic body and soul to continue. And we heed them and submit, and move on to the next surrender.

Culturally, whatever happens, those engaged in the race to the bottom will win. Criticism only prompts howls of self-righteous rage, and generates priceless publicity for the product, be it a "Piss Christ," * or Britney Frenching Madonna, or Janet Jackson's 2004 Super Bowl halftime "costume reveal." How many of us, I wonder, would care to wear T-shirts proclaiming, PROUD CONSUMER OF TRASH, or have inscribed on their tombstones, SHE CARED ABOUT JLO AND BEN. How many of us would continue to gorge on and subsidize such offerings, were we forced to say aloud before each consumption, This is what they think of me. This tells me who and what they think I am. And by consuming their products, I agree.

An old Madison Avenue adage holds that some of the people making the commercials are fully as stupid and debauched as

---

* *Piss Christ* is a work by Andres Serrano, a photo of a crucifix submerged in urine. Since the eighties, the National Endowment for the Arts has come under fire in the U.S. Senate and elsewhere for using taxpayers' money to fund Serrano and other artists who produce "blasphemous" and "pornographic" works.

the people they think they're talking to. Add here a goodly chunk of the rest of the cultural enterprise, the books and films and music and news media and the rest. They'll tell us what our choices are, in the manner of, Hello, swine. Here's your swill. And we'll heed them and submit, and then move on to the next surrender.

But sometimes, freedom begins when you tell the people who tell you what your choices are: *Enough. No more.* And sometimes freedom flourishes when you tell them that, given a choice between A and B, you'll take C or D or E. And then you go out and find it, or create it.

The title of this book is *Take Back the Right.* To a certain extent, it is about what is commonly known as the political and cultural Right, told as a personal memoir. But it is also about something far more important: our fundamental right to take back our own existence as citizens of this polity, citizens of this economy, citizens of this culture. It is about fully inhabiting our own lives within these realms, and making ourselves effective within them. For today, the most horrific fact about our civilization is not decadence. It is that our civilization *does not need us.*

Our political system, our government, does not need us. It needs us as taxpayers, of course. It needs us as claimants, as special interests, as dependents, even as protesters (the goofier the better). From time to time, it needs us as voters, to meet certain legal requirements and to validate the sham. But political citizens capable of envisioning and making choices other than those prescribed?—this ever-more-imperial republic needs us not.

Nor does our economy need us. It needs us as consumers, of course, and our plastic. It needs workers, preferably disposable and unentitled, to crank out whatever we haven't yet outsourced. It needs the desperate and the near-desperate to hearten and brighten when the government announces that employment is up (What kinds of jobs were added?) and that productivity is rising (What's being produced?) and that maybe the next few trillion of debt won't be so bad, after all. But "economic citizens," capable of understanding the concept of "opportunity cost"—that the true cost of anything is all the alternatives foregone? This ever-more-unsound economy needs us not.

Nor does our culture need us. It needs us as readers, viewers, listeners, of course, and our plastic. It needs critics whose raison d'être is not to discern and to enlighten, but to howl and whine, critics whose very attentions serve to legitimize the excesses and failures. It needs those who believe that the worst of the offal that you see on the screen, or hear on CDs, or read between covers, or browse on the Net, is the way it is with us humans. Consume enough of it and you get to thinking, perhaps this is the only way it can be. But "cultural citizens," who know that the principle of opportunity cost applies to the spirit as well as to the economy? Now, that might wreck the racket.

So sometimes, freedom begins when you choose not to accept, or leave unchallenged, a civilization that thinks it can get along without its citizens. And that, in the largest sense, is what *Take Back the Right* is about.

But this book is also about "taking back" the conservative Right. The words appear in quotes because, simply put, most of what passes for conservatism today isn't worth the bother of redeeming.

Certainly not the neocons, the America-must-lead-because-America-must lead; let's-go-thump-somebody crowd. FDR once remarked that it was a terrible thing to look over your shoulder when you're trying to lead, and discover that nobody's following. The neocons looked over their shoulders, then looked back and changed the spin. Forget the leadership. We're an empire, and that's the way it is, and ought to be. And if reality hasn't quite conformed to their theories, and if they now, as the *New York Times* so aptly puts it, "loudly express their second thoughts," well, it ain't their butts on the line. Or those of their sons and daughters. Some years ago, former defense secretary Robert McNamara, perhaps the chief architect of the Vietnam disaster, decided with his usual arrogance that, by repenting, he would teach America how to repent. We need no such lessons from Mr. McNamara. We need them even less from the neocons.

Certainly not the Religious Right, the Christ-died-so-we-could-tell-you-what-to-do brigades. From time to time, monotheism emits a terrible sin. It has no commonly accepted name, but it might be called "Godolatry." There's only one God, and we've got him, and we know His will, and stand ready to enforce it. That's the only way it can be, the way it ought to be. Did the Founders fear religion? No, not at all. In many ways, they cherished it. Certainly, they depended on "civil religion" to help produce virtuous citizens. But they feared with a dreadful terror what happens when human ambition and ruthlessness take over religion, and when such debased religion becomes the master or the tool of the state.

And certainly not the Religious Right's more secular allies of the "cultural conservatism" movement, the take-back-our-country cliques and claques. This country isn't theirs to take or to take back. It's theirs to share. No less, but no more. And anyway, man cannot live on reruns alone. "Traditional values" are not always right because they are traditional. And how often, when values and principles and ways of life are under consideration, the self-evident also turns out to be the self-serving.

Certainly not the Stop-the-world, we-want-the-others-to-get-off neopopulists and those farther to the hateful and bigoted far

Right. You cannot face the future, as Ike so sagely put it, by marching backward into the past. And in the end, hate marches you only to hell.

And certainly not—I write this sadly—much of the "paleocon" remnant, those traditionalists who believe that the conservative movement can be redeemed by returning to some former vision of "limited government," coupled with a foreign policy that, in John Quincy Adams's one-hit-wonder quip, "goes not abroad in search of monsters to destroy."

The American people, it is clear, have made their peace with Big Government, at least in its less bankrupting forms. They want the welfare state, the safety net. They've yet to show any real unease with the post-9/11 domestic security apparatus that we're building atop the Cold War apparatus, that we built atop the World War II apparatus. And whatever the trendings of the polls, the notion that America has some special role to play in the world remains potent. Coming over on the *Arbella*, John Winthrop reminded his Puritan fellows that the eyes of the world were upon them; they would found a City on a Hill, and show the world what a godly commonwealth looked like. And even though the City on a Hill turned into Boston, Brother Winthrop still trumps Brother Quincy every time . . . at least until the People get around to their sober second thought.

So what, then, is the political and cultural Right to be taken back? Nothing to be "taken back" at all, at least not in the sense of manifestos and agendas, of action items and of talking points. It is something to be created anew, at present more a sensibility and an ethos than a program. It is rooted in a "usable past of the spirit," a "working reverence" for the American Founders and for certain aspects of antiquity that inspired them. And if the Right is to be taken back by creating it anew, it also leads—indeed, it must lead—to some very nonconservative (as the term is presently understood) conclusions. And then it must lead to a set of principles appropriate to the age now upon us.

This "retaken Right" (Why do we still even use such outdated terms as Right and Left, liberal and conservative?) returns to the fundamental sensibility of the American Founders. Not ideological or religious rigidity, but a constant tension between happy awareness of the infinite possibilities of human freedom and somber acceptance of the notion that people are finite and fallible, and that there is such a thing as evil. But it also seeks guidance far beyond the usual conservative invocations of bourgeois morality, Judeo-Christian heritage, or even the classics per se. Here we draw upon a movement that's been underway in America for several decades now, but has yet to find a name or even attract much notice. Conservatives call it the "neoclassical revival" and, to the extent that they consider it at all, they despise it as unwelcome competition. Sociologist James Davison Hunter, who first popularized the term "Culture War" in its American context, sneers it off as "the neoclassical backlash." But it's more. Much more, and we'll be considering it in some detail as key to a conservatism fit for the twenty-first century. Something that began in the torture rooms of the Hanoi Hilton, then spread through the musings of feminist and postfeminist scholars, and now seeps into our popular culture, cannot be dismissed quite so easily.

As for principles appropriate to the twenty-first century, we shall in this book craft them through a process of recombinance. In science, recombinance often means creating something very different from its parts. Every human being is recombinant, a product of his or her parents, but also far more than the mere fusion of parental DNA. History is recombinant, a tale of strange couplings and unlikely progeny. For example, there is nothing in the obvious properties of two gases, oxygen and hydrogen, that tells you that if you mix them just right, you get Evian. Equally, there is nothing inherent in the properties of Jewish religion, pagan philosophy, and Germanic barbarism to tell you that if you mix them just right, you get Christendom. As used here, the term "recombinance" means the process of bringing together the disparate wisdom of this and other eras to yield appropriate guidance. Sometimes, wisdom is found where you least expect it. Sometimes, also, the most unlikely products of recombinance are also the most useful.

Then, the matter of retaking conservatism becomes an exercise in the virtue known to the Founders as prudence: not caution, but the art of applying (or not applying) general principles to specific situations. As the Stoic slave philosopher Epictetus put it, "Of all existing things, some are in our power, and others are not." For a nation as for an individual, it matters to keep them straight.

In short, the conservatism to be taken back, or more aptly, created anew, is based on the spirit of the Founders and of an antiquity they cherished. But a conservatism fit for the twenty-first century is a conservatism whose very leitmotif is recombinance—the mixing of strange and seemingly incompatible truths and ways. It does not yet exist. Perhaps, as citizens together, we can craft a Right worth taking back . . . while hoping fervently that, somewhere on the Left, something similar is happening.

This book, then, is less a practical or polemical manifesto, a "blueprint for change," or an exercise in denunciatory rhetoric, than a conversation among citizens who, whatever our specific disagreements, can no longer abide what our civilization has become, and is doing in the world. All are invited. However, this is a conversation with rules. Four, in particular.

First, it is nonpartisan or, more aptly, transpartisan. There is nothing in here urging anyone to support or not support any candidate or any other aspect of the Republocrat dominion.

Second, I am declaring this conversation a celebrity-free zone. We have neither time nor energy to waste on the Limbaughs, O'Reillys, Coulters, Frankens, Hannity/Colmeses, Sarandon/Robbinses or the rest of the high-viz, overhyped, and overpaid star system. Let's just give ourselves a break. Don't worry. They'll be there when we get back. It's not that they have nothing of value to say. Even a broken clock is right twice a day, and something can be true even if Rush Limbaugh says it. It's that the celebs of the Right exist in symbiosis with the celebs of the Left. Like the Republocrats, they need each other to keep the shtik going. And like them, they presume to tell us what our choices are.

Third, this conversation shall be academically informed but not academic, which is to say, it will not be a history or analysis in any conventional sense. Whilst preparing to write this book, I spent a good bit of time wandering around several university libraries, and was astonished to discover how much was already on the shelves and how poorly it has endured. So much academic writing is so repetitive, redundant, repetitious, and derivative that it's no wonder PhD stands for Piled Higher and Deeper. Nor has the output of America's journalists aged gracefully. If journalism is "history's rough draft," then books by journalists are too often little more than reporters' notebooks dumped between covers. Nor is this book a think tank monograph, certainly not of the once-you-put-it-down-you-can't-pick-it-up, policy wonk variety. But we will point out items either forgotten or yet to receive their due. There's no point in wasting time and space poring over junk when it's possible to do a little bit to make people aware of a few treasures in need of discovery or rediscovery.

Fourth, this conversation must be civil. We're also taking a break from the diatribes, the hissy-fitting, the histrionics, and the screeds. Some years ago, I encountered a bumper sticker proclaiming: REAL MEN DON'T USE PORN. The principle holds for the political as well as the sexual. Too much out there nowadays, Left and Right, verges on the pornographic, at least in the sense of constituting a profound perversion of what should be a precious act: people speaking to each other in words of reason and meaning. In this book, individuals may be criticized without being vilified; sometimes, as a courtesy, they are not named at all. Others are not named in order to respect their privacy. A few are not named because, frankly, I don't care to give them any more publicity than they've already received. Of the more personal reminiscences: only enough to move the tale along.

So, those are the rules. To which I add one sad exception on civility and a comment on format.

I find it impossible to consider with courteous detachment the neocons, those self-styled "public intellectuals" who have desired a generation-long global crisis worthy of what they deem to be their talents, and who have worked so hard to create the current situation. Whether they led or misled or brainwashed or lobotomized President Bush, I know not and I care not. It's their ideas and their style, the grandiose theories and intellectual arrogance of yet another crop of "Best and Brightest" who have gotten us into yet another unnecessary war, that I have come to find abhorrent.

That's the exception to civility. Now to the comment on format.

This book points toward crafting the ethos of a new conservatism for the twenty-first century, a conservatism open to some hitherto very nonconservative ideas. It is meant for those who wish to take up this task on the Right, and as a possible guide for those who wish to take it up on the Left. It is, to repeat, neither a conventional history nor a standard analysis. It is told as a personal tale, a life journey with an idea that has led in some very unusual directions. But this is not a standard memoir, if only because I'm neither important enough nor cute enough to warrant one, and have no dark secrets to spill. Nor is it a linear presentation. It is, quite deliberately, rather quirky. Sometimes the best way to make points is to evoke rather than explain; sometimes perception matters more than conclusion.

Quirky, indeed. But a conversation can develop in many directions. What matters is that, by the end, ideas have gotten across in ways that others can understand them, perhaps adopt them, or failing that, use them to clarify their own.

Chapter 1

THE MYSTERIES OF PITTSBURGH

When he [Clinton Rossiter] explained that the essence of conservatism was aristocracy, an aristocracy of individual accomplishment and social and cultural connection, a status that in America could be chosen, I was enthralled.

—*Philip Gold*

I F YOU WISH TO understand America in the fifties and early sixties, or most any other decade, look to Pittsburgh. Artfully interpreted, the Mysteries of Pittsburgh, to borrow the title of an old Michael Chabon novel, will tell you what you need to know.

A Pittsburgh-centric view of America starts at Point State Park, site of the original Fort Pitt, and also of one of the military disasters for which G. Washington, then a young Virginia militia colonel on British duty, is not often remembered. It wasn't really his fault, and anyway, he was just a reservist. All that remains of the Fort is a blockhouse known, appropriately enough, as The Blockhouse.

Pittsburgh may have made steel, but it was made by water. The Blockhouse still guards the point—Point State Park, actually—where the Monongahela and Allegheny Rivers join to form the

Ohio. Of itself, this is not unusual. Other American cities have been similarly water-themed. Boston, for example, where the Mystic and the Charles Rivers, so it is said, come together to form the Atlantic Ocean. But in the fifties, the Ohio River held an unusual distinction. It was DOA, killed by the filth of its tributaries, the wastage of a steel industry that everybody knew—but few cared to admit—hadn't that much longer to live. Once, the rivers had been necessary to barge in the coal and iron ore, to barge out the product, to dump the offal and the slag. Railroads had augmented the city's competitive advantage of placement. But now the Japanese and Germans were back up, having rebuilt their cratered factories with modern technology. Specialty steels out of Sweden and elsewhere were coming onstream. Electric furnaces helped the American South cobble together a steel industry of its own, and bright young executives worked for USS and J&L and the rest, only long enough to learn the business, then punch out for the entrepreneurial domain.

The response of the industry establishment, both capital and labor: *No reason to talk about it.* Management, by and large, chose not to modernize extensively. The United Steel Workers (to whom I once belonged when I worked a college summer in an artillery-shell factory), in addition to their endless other demands, wanted yearlong sabbatical leaves with pay for twenty-year workers. Strikes were long in the fifties. When strikes coincided with recessions, as they sometimes did, each recovery proved slower than the last. Taken together, business and labor displayed what the Spanish philosopher José Ortega y Gasset described in his classic *The Revolt of the Masses*, as one of the salient characteristics of the Mass Man: belief that civilization and its material base were a kind of self-sustaining second nature, requiring neither nurture nor care. According to legend, John Kennedy put it even more philosophically. My father, he muttered after the industry had broken its pledge to him and raised prices, always told me that steel men are SOBs. Or words to that effect.

But if they were SOBs, or words to that effect, they also showed a certain civic-mindedness. By the early fifties, and by the rising standards of postwar expectations, Pittsburgh was unlivable. Once, belching smokestacks and untreated industrial drainage had signified prosperity. Though the popular ecological mindset was still several decades off, postwar people wanted more than chocolate-brown rivers and air reeking of hydrogen sulfide and less stenchy but more toxic vapors. Memories of the 1948 Donora, Pennsylvania "killer smog" were still, please pardon the word choice, fresh. Executives were refusing to take assignments in Pittsburgh. So were their wives. Corporate headquarters were threatening to move. Some did. So the men who knew, deep down, that their industries were dying, determined to make their final decades a bit more palatable.

The result was the Pittsburgh Renaissance, a remarkable cooperative effort of business and politics, of corporate and local elites working with and through a liberal Democratic machine. The Sewickley and Fox Chapel crowds got together with the city government, and especially with Davey Lawrence, the mayor and future Pennsylvania governor. The unions and the civic organizations got some skin in the game. So did the Catholic Church, under Bishop John Wright. Renaissance was grand. But when progress threatened some cherished old church, the Bishop, at least according to legend, had no trouble getting on the phone to the mayor with a Don't touch that one, Davey. In those pre-Vatican II days, an admonition from a future cardinal carried ecclesiastical as well as urban-renewal significance.

Gradually, Pittsburgh's more purgatorial aspects abated. By the sixties, the air was breathable, the rivers cleansing, and we had a nice new downtown, stretching back eastward from the Point, with a couple quaint old parish churches nestled amid all the new stuff.

But the downtown Renaissance stayed, by and large, downtown. True, the suburbs were looking more and more like the contents of an out-of-control petri dish, blossoming wherever room could be found for a few dozen ranch houses and a strip mall. The town itself, and the surrounding mill towns, remained a pastiche of ethnic enclaves: Italian, Hungarian, Slovenian, Jewish, black, Polish, much else. Contact was neither encouraged nor sought. It wasn't mutual hostility so much as a traditional separateness. Diversity was respected, not celebrated. High school varsity athletics could yield occasional ethnic interactions, here read fistfights, but few merchants were interested in peddling their ethnic wares outside their domains. As for 90 percent of the city, if you didn't have reason to go there, you didn't. This, coupled with two preceding centuries of assiduous nonzoning and a positive aversion to street grids—except for downtown, which had two—meant that you could live a long time in Pittsburgh without really knowing where you were in relation to much of anything else.

As I learned later, during my brief but traumatic career as a taxi driver, that condition was mine. So long as I stayed between the downtown Hilton and the airport, work was profitable, existence serene. But not everybody wanted to go to the Hilton or the airport, and my increasingly frenetic attempts to talk them into it, plus the ordinary getting-lost, resulted in, apparently, a new record: the greatest number ever of irate-passenger phone calls to the Pittsburgh Yellow Cab Company in a three-day period about a single driver. This led my supervisor to suggest that I'd better haul my ass back to college, since I sure wasn't going to make it as a cabbie.

The experience did have one salutary effect. The rest of my undergraduate summers, when they told me that I'd better haul my ass (the usual phrase) back to school because I was never going to make it as an autoworker or a steelworker, I could afford not to be offended. Anyway, factory jobs were far easier than hacking. You stood in one place. The work came to you. And on an assembly line, you could sleep.

Still, there was more to Pittsburgh than the downtown Renaissance and ethnic noncollegiality. There was culture. American culture, typical of the age. *Flashdance*, that quintessentially hope-springs-infernal film about a gorgeous young female welder/club dancer who wants to make it on the Pittsburgh ballet scene, was decades in the future, along with its still-unmade sequel, *The Pittsburgh Ballet Strikes Back*. But there was a pretty good symphony, many European refugees, and a decent Carnegie Library/Museum complex. There was also the Buhl Planetarium with its Zeiss Ikon Multiple Stereo-Optical Overhead Projector, capable of depicting, on the domed ceiling, the heavens as they were over Bethlehem on Christmas Eve, 6-4 B.C., and through the magic of technology, determining which star or confluence of stars may have led the Magi there. This they did every Christmas for the edification of local schoolchildren, who didn't much care so long as it got them out of class for a field trip. At the time, I was so ignorant of Christianity that I thought the Three Wise Men were named Harold Angel, Round John Virgin, and Reggie Angelorum, and so insufferably intellectual that I believed Santa's helpers were officially known as Subordinate Clauses. Still, I found the display intriguing. Also, quite literally, a pain in the neck.

The city offered more. There was the University of Pittsburgh's

Cathedral of Learning, the world's only Gothic skyscraper, soot-blackened and a perennial feature in directories of bizarre architecture. There was Saturday-Nite Studio Wrestling, an event of some importance when Crusher "We're-so-tough-in-Milwaukee-we-got-beer-comin'-outta-da-water-fountains" Lasowski menaced local icon, Ace "Hello-to-all-my-Hungarian-friends" Freeman. Johnny Valentine? You never knew whether you were getting the hero or the villain. Perhaps he wasn't all that sure himself. Johnny Valentine was a volatile sort. Bruno Sammartino? Sturdy. And it was always a media event when Haystacks Calhoun came to town—not because of Haystacks himself, an artless fellow more dependent on girth than guile. It was because the restaurants took down their ALL YOU CAN EAT signs for the duration of his visit. This was reported on the news at both 7:00 and 11:00 P.M.

Izzy Modell, if memory serves, a local alderman, refereed, providing occasional lessons in applied civics to the performers in the ring and in the audience, particularly to Ringside Rosie, a frenetic, geriatric nonbabe. Civics lessons of another kind were available each Wednesday at a local barbershop, when some official—I never knew his name or position—lorded his way in for the usual free haircut. This he received while fixing traffic tickets, an activity that caused him to ostentatiously not notice the numbers couriers passing in and out of the back room. Nor did he or I pay much attention to the manicurist who, from time to time, led customers into the back for their manicures. And I was in my forties before I realized why she never took her tray of instruments back there with her, or why the customers never emerged with their nails and cuticles visibly improved.

There was also Old Frothingslosh, "The Pale Stale Ale with the Foam on the Bottom," creation of a local radio deejay, and the annual Miss Frothingslosh contest. And in the 1960 World

Series, there was Bill Mazeroski's seventh game/ninth inning home run, which administered a well-deserved humiliation to the Yankees and clinched the Pirates' first championship since 1927. Strictly speaking, we may have forfeited the game. If you look closely at the film, it seems that Maz never crosses home plate. The crowd has him up on its shoulders a few feet before. But 1960 had been that kind of season—endless come-from-behind victories, and a sportscaster, Bob Prince, given to shouting, "We had 'em all the way!" after each nail-biting, cuticle-nibbling victory left even the toughest fans in need of manicures. BEAT 'EM BUCS! bumper stickers were printed up in over forty languages and placed on cars both foreign and domestic. Frenzy trumped ethnicity for a season, and if nobody paid much attention to the ugly racism endured by right field phenom Roberto Clemente, well, like Dr. King, he would become a national treasure only later.

The University of Pittsburgh's Posvar Hall now stands on the site of old Forbes Field. Home plate is under glass in the lobby. Perhaps in some mysterious way, the game is still on.

Khrushchev visited in 1959. I saw his motorcade drive by my elementary school, Colfax, where the principal, a Dr. Hedwig Pregler, ran a thingie called The Workshop, for kids with over-endowed crania. I toiled in The Workshop, enjoyed it, and would have been far better off developmentally hanging with the morons, kids who, I suspect, in later years turned out to be far from moronic.

Khrushchev was wearing a white hat. We liked him in spite of ourselves. He liked us. We could tell. During the Cuban missile crisis of October 1962, a session that left a lot of folks in need of manicures, we took comfort in the fact that, since he liked us, he wasn't going to blow us up. After all, he'd been here. And we'd liked him. And we knew that he knew that we'd liked him.

Mr. K. never did blow up Pittsburgh. But nothing that he learned in Pittsburgh could save him, or his evil empire. The Cold War ended in a forfeit when K's successors realized, among other things, that steel was no longer an emblem of national prowess, just one more commodity. And perhaps in some strange way, the Cold War is still going on. We didn't cross home plate on that one, either.

In sum, then, Pittsburgh's a city worth pondering, certainly, by those who wish a deeper understanding of America, its character and culture and political ken. Of course, it didn't seem quite that way to me then, growing up as—the phrase exaggerates, but not by much—the human garbage of the Jewish community.

★   ★   ★

Poor. Shamefully poor. An old, decrepit, dirty, ill-furnished, shameful house, infused with violence and suffused with the kind of emotional abuse that today would be considered horrific, but back then fell into the same category as Clemente's ordeal. *No reason to talk about it.* The daily shame of school, of occupying the status of kid-nobody-would-be-caught-dead-eating-lunch-with. The shame of knowing that by the standards of the era, and especially of the adolescents of that era, it was deserved and more than deserved. The shame of walking the streets, knowing that people knew things about my family, mysteries that I didn't know myself. Ugly, criminal things, sometimes hinted at, sometimes more than hinted at, once or twice observable. Still, by and large, the mysteries prevailed. Mysteries thrive when there's no reason to talk about them.

It is said that if you claim you remember the sixties, you weren't there. Perhaps it might also be said that, if you venerate the fifties as some paradise of morality, decency, and stability, you weren't there either. Or else, you willfully ignored the mysteries, all the things that weren't talked about. The adulteries and alcoholism, the other cheatings and addictions, the all-too-purposeful violence and humiliation directed at those who didn't or who were decreed not to fit in or belong. And also directed, routinely, at those guilty of womanhood or childhood. These too were mysteries, and for far too many of us who lived the era, they remain mysteries still.

Why mention this?

One reason is personal. This is, in part, a personal book, and I've found the last forty years to be about a lot of overcoming. Erik Erikson, the psychiatrist who popularized the term "identity crisis" (and who often wondered whether so many people had them because they thought they were expected to) was fascinated by people who solved their inner dilemmas and torments in ways that spoke to the world, personally and politically. He studied great historical figures, Martin Luther and Gandhi, but the principle applies to us all. A Yiddish proverb puts it more succinctly. *Do not come back from hell with empty hands.*

This book is, in part, something I carried back from hell. Those of us who whup our demons, our depressions and dysfunctions, without recourse to drugs or interminable therapy or, even worse, assumption of the status of Victim, have at least a modest obligation to tell others, similarly situated, why and how it can be done. But that's for a future book. At issue now is a tale that starts with a simple question, but leads to some very complex answers.

Why did I become, at such a young age, such an unlikely conservative? Asked differently: Why do so many Americans, the poor and much of the middle strata (poverty is always relative), the dissed and unimportant and written-off, become conservatives? Why are they so susceptible to conservative appeals? Godfrey Hodgson notes that our populist impulses seem equally suscep- tible to gratification on the Left and on the Right. Sometimes, they even seem interchangeable. But why?

By conservative I do not mean what historian Richard Hofs- tadter once called "the paranoid style in American politics." Nor do I refer to the tawdry organizations that cater to such: the militias and the organized, if such be the word, racists, anti- Semites, misogynists, and xenophobes. I mean a comparatively rational, principled, dignified conservatism. Generations of American historians, social scientists, and shrinks have pon- dered this matter. They have given us—or, more aptly, have sat- isfied themselves with—three standard basic explanations. They are far from untrue, but also far from adequate. They segue into each other easily, but are nonetheless distinguishable. They cer- tainly figured into the goulash of reasons why I was drawn to the movement, but they provide no definitive explanation.

First, there's a peculiarly American individualism, at once hypertrophic and mythical, that instinctively recoils, even today, from Big Government (at least in the abstract) and col- lectivism. By this reckoning, there is something in the Amer- ican tradition, the American character, that draws the poor toward conservatism. By poor, again, I mean not just the penurious—poverty is always comparative—but many of those situated below the current alleged "meritocracy" and the quasi-mythical "new overclass." That something, according to the standard explanation, hinges on the belief that the average person can control his or her own destiny. The notion runs deep. For centuries, if you weren't making it where you were, there was always plenty of land and good fortune a bit farther out. Go west, young (or older) man—even if it meant staying a couple of counties ahead of your creditors and repeating the process until you got it right. And of course, there's America as the immigrants' mythic but far from illusory land of opportunity. No matter where you happen to find yourself, you're still better off, at least possibility-wise, than in whichever old country you came from. Failure, even as late as the Depression, was an individual matter. If the jobs weren't there, that was still your fault. In the fifties, when all that glittered and a lot that didn't turned to currency, if you weren't making it, your head must be on backward. And even now, despite the cult of the victim and the rise of the "underclass" (which is not an aggregation of the poor but a savage, abhorrent antiuniverse)—and the outsourcing of the American economy—the equations of character with independence and of independence with success remain.

The money, like the truth, is out there. You just have to find it. And if you don't, there's always the consolation of that Lee Greenwood song, "Proud to be an American/Where at least I know I'm free."

At least?

It's an "at least" that, for many millions, can matter greatly. At least in theory. And it seems that you don't have to oppose collectivism in any consistent or even very energetic manner to know that you are at least spiritually exempt. In America, "at least" can count for a lot.

Second, and far from unrelated, is the doctrine of "false consciousness."

It drove Marx crazier than he already was. The poor were afflicted, the workers, the proletariat, with their passivity and, as he so memorably phrased it, their damned *wantlessness*. The poor, with their infuriating ignorance of where their real interests lie. The poor, with their lunatic loyalties to country, church, family. Dr. Marx and his followers finally concluded that the problem was insurmountable. Without a revolutionary vanguard to banish the false consciousness of the poor and, en passant, redefine morality and value and reality, nothing was possible beyond a petty "trade union mentality" that emphasized improving the real lives of real people. Dr. Freud and his followers offered to provide similar services·for the soul, stripping away the false consciousness that allegedly blinds us to the nature of our inner suffering. When, in the fifties and sixties, the "fusion of Marx and Freud" was effected by Drs. Fromm, Marcuse, Brown, and others, the doctrine of false consciousness became a cultural and political staple for women, minorities, and all who could wedge themselves into Victim status. Still, a surprisingly large segment of the poor and middle strata remained immune to all the consciousness-raising. They did not succumb to the notion that their lives were based on unreality, if only because people who pay their taxes, raise their kids, and tend to their own welfare don't always appreciate it when somebody tells them how screwed up they really are. I retain a fond 1968 memory of some student radicals showing up outside the car factory where I was welding the summer away, earnestly determined to help the autoworkers overcome their false consciousness. The students came away from their effort neither successful nor unbruised.

I also vividly recall a late-night "consciousness-raising" discussion between myself, a college friend, and his parents. The father, son of Jewish immigrants and a World War II combat vet, was now a professor at a major university. The mother, a Baptist woman who had lost her first husband in the war, had abandoned her own career as a teacher to raise the kids. Both were staunch liberals, both anti-Vietnam. After hours of being lectured and hectored by their son, the mother finally beseeched him in genuine anguish: "What are you blaming us for?" Replied my friend: "The hydrogen bomb and the Roman Catholic Church." That shut my friend's parents up, although perhaps not in the way he'd intended. It also provided a splendid demonstration of sixties radical false consciousness in action. And it was symptomatic of something much deeper and much uglier. "There is in America today," wrote Walter Lippmann, "a distinct prejudice in favor of those who make the accusations." Of course, he wrote that in 1914. Prejudice in favor of the accusers, it might be noted, has been for far too long a staple of our politics and culture.

Third explanation: cultural politics. At its extreme, this entails what historian Fritz Stern so aptly called "the politics of cultural despair." Stern was writing about pre-Nazi German and Austrian culture, about what happens when people feel themselves dispossessed, despised, and discarded by a civilization that once cherished or seemed to cherish them. Ressentiment can lead to ugly thoughts and happenings. From nineteenth-century nativism to Timothy McVeigh, America has known about this. We've made it an art form, as each wave of immigrants Americanizes to the point where they can look down on more recent arrivals. And as is oft proclaimed, "whiteness" in America has had to be earned by the Irish, the Italians, the Slavs, the Jews, and so on, and not always quickly or easily.

Still, by and large, American ressentiment has been comparatively benign. From Henry Adams to Mark Helprin, America has produced a charming and often brilliant stranger-in-my-own-land literature. But by far the most common form of cultural politics has involved being against the things the people you dislike are for. And vice versa. One prime example was Vietnam. It is arguable that popular support for the war would have faded years before it did, had not supporting the war become a form of protest against the protesters. Another example, a bit more complex, involved the failure of the Equal Rights Amendment—the support not generated by millions of citizens, men especially, who favored the concept but were damned if they'd give it to the Shrieking Sisterhood.

I'd love to see a bumper sticker that proclaims, I'M AGAINST WHAT YOU'RE FOR . . . AND I VOTE.

Three interrelated ideas, then, as to why conservatism since the fifties has appealed to some unlikely customers. American individualism. False consciousness. Cultural politics. Dignity. Delusion. Despair. American conservatism has certainly trafficked in them. But conservatism at its best involves something else entirely: a form of aristocracy—a disciplined excellence that is also modest, benign, humane, and sensitive. Unfortunately, that kind of aristocracy has rarely played well in American culture and politics.

I became a conservative forty years ago for the three standard explanations given above. I chose conservatism because I wanted to believe, desperately, that I had or could have control over my destiny. I had a nasty case of false consciousness about my real interests, one that took a lot of government student loans and VA benefits to start to get over. And conservatism told me that the people who despised me, and whom I hated in turn, were wrong. An inauspicious beginning, perhaps, but adequate for a fourteen-year-old. Sufficiently adequate for me to discover at that age that fourth and greater reason, that ethos of responsible aristocracy of the spirit—an ethos that conservatism was even then abandoning.

I could not, of course, have known any of this at the time. I could not have known that the next few decades would bring far more frustration than relief, and far more questioning than commitment. Nor could I have known that what I sought in conservatism I would ultimately find through a process of recombinance—of blending the basic conservative ethos of responsibility and excellence with some highly non-conservative goals and ideas, and of finding some ideas worth sharing.

More specifically still, I could not have known: That from the sixties to the present moment, conservatism would betray itself four times over:

> *By abandonment of its concept of aristocracy and humane regard, and its debasement of the aristocratic virtues.*

> *By its failure to oppose the Vietnam War—a war that it had not started, but that it had, by its own imprudent posturing, done much to bring about.*

> *By its willful refusal to understand the necessity of changes going on in Culture War America and its totalistic opposition to those changes.*

> *And by a neoconservative infestation that, in the name of democracy and defense, has mortgaged our future to that of Islamic civilization, and threatens us with both financial and moral bankruptcy.*

Much of this book is about those betrayals; the rest of it is about something else I could not have known. Specifically, neither I nor anyone else could have imagined that a twenty-first-century conservatism, based on the principles of late antiquity and the Founders, but placed in the service of some radical goals, might prove a wondrous guide to attaining a rational, benign influence in the world, and to creating a society and a culture worth having at home.

It's all very doable. It simply needs to be done.

★   ★   ★

Squirrel Hill, the Jewish section of Pittsburgh, had mysteries of its own. Those gloriously attractive upper-middle-class kids, those happy (How could they not be happy?) families behind the solid doors of their ample, well-tended houses—these were the Lords of Creation, incomprehensible to me and I unknown, unknowable to them. Decades later, whilst immured in the study of Hellenistic philosophy, I learned that the deities of late antiquity, a fascinating pantheon of recombinance, came in two unexpected flavors. The Epicureans posited gods and goddesses utterly unaware of human existence. The Stoics conceived deities who, even if they were aware of human existence, were incapable of responding to it. Both kinds were happy. Neither wanted their happiness disturbed. After all, the reasoning went, had their happiness been disturbed, they would no longer have been gods.

The imagery was evocative. Olympus or Pittsburgh, the situation seemed the same.

I was not jealous. Karl Marx got that much right. The damned wantlessness of the poor. The Lords of Creation and I were, to put it simply and literally, worlds apart. So lacking in the social graces that I could go for days without speaking or being spoken to, so natural did this situation seem, that envy— real, painful, motivating envy—wasn't even conceivable. Had the concept been available, I might have been diagnosed with Asperger's Syndrome, a condition that includes a dreadful inability to process normal social cues. Back then, however, the diagnosis was simpler: fucked up. And there was anger, a deep and abiding pit ache between my stomach and my soul. Sometimes, it flared into hate.

Political discussions, I discovered with surprise, could trigger it intensely. That started in junior high school. Whenever I heard some well-accoutered, popular girl (Brooks Brothers penny loafers, Brooks Brothers knee socks, Brooks Brothers cardigan sweater worn backward) proclaim that "we" must learn how to "forget that we're affluent" in order to understand the "problems" of the poor, all I could think was, OK, here I am. Whenever I heard some guy who'd just gotten a Triumph Spitfire, or more occasionally, a Corvette, for his sixteenth birthday, declaim on how unjust "we" were, exploiting some country or other, all I could think of was, Yeah, but you're taking your share. And whenever I heard some teacher pontificate on how "we" must do this or that to "help" the elderly or the Negroes or the Cubans or the Indians, all I could think of was, What do you mean, we? And when I realized, for the first time, that when liberals said "we," they meant "the government". . . .

I hated the government as some sort of bizarre extension of "we."

This was the lesser hate. The greater hate was that they were keeping me from my God.

There has never been a moment when I've doubted the existence of divinity. In The *Hidden Face of God*, theologian Richard Elliott Friedman speculates that, just as there is something within the human mind that attunes us to the mathematical nature of the physical universe, perhaps there is also something that attunes us to the existence and nature of the spiritual. I was born a Jew. But because of my people—or so I told myself, then and for decades thereafter—I could not connect with my faith.

It wasn't for lack of background or training. In my grandmother's house, where I lived, Yiddish was still a spoken, or more often screamed, language. I learned just enough to eavesdrop on conversations, plus some phrases that I later found useful in the Marines. Observances were Orthodox. I received a standard bar mitzvah. I spent eight years at *cheder*, a four-days-a-week-after-school-and-Sundays school, the Hebrew Institute of Pittsburgh. I also did several summers at the Yeshiva Achei Timimim, the local Lubavitcher lash-up. I hated every moment of it, with an odium and contempt far deeper than that normally engendered by having religion rammed down your throat as a child. The *Shulkhan Arukh*, a manual regulating every aspect of an observant Jew's life, tormented me. The more I tried (not always with commitment) to follow it, the more I loathed its strictures. So too did I hate the teachers, especially when they took up proclaiming that "We Jews are always the scapegoat."

We, again.

The manipulations that accompanied religious education also tormented. I still remember, with an anger that I did not understand until decades later, a Sunday school Jewish history workbook that asked, If you'd lived back then, would you rather be a Pharisee or a Saducee? The obligatory answer, I would rather be a Pharisee, so I could keep the ceremonies and traditions. The complexity of that conflict, the issues involved—how dare they reduce it to twentieth-century ceremonies and traditions? They reduced it in much the same way they reduced the Greeks, presenting them as a bunch of doofuses who ate ham sandwiches, ran around naked in the gym, and worshipped chunks of stone. How the heroic Maccabee liberators morphed into the more-Greek-than-the-Greeks Hasmonean dynasty was a subject carefully elided.

My Lubavitcher days came to a long-anticipated and deliberately-provoked end when the yeshiva suggested that, for a variety of reasons, mostly my insufferable sarcasm, I not return the next summer. Bad enough that I'd taken up describing my knitted *kipa* (skull cap) as an Itsy Bitsy Teeny Weeny Blue and White Embroidered Beanie. This stood in defiant reference to a then-popular novelty song concerning an "Itsy Bitsy Teeny Weeny Yellow Polka Dot Bikini." The *Shulkhan Arukh* clearly prohibited contemplation of such an item, even in the abstract, lest one come to sinful thoughts. Then one hot August day, I was asked in class, "What does the Rumbum say?" about some passage or other. (It's actually, "Rambam," Rabbi Maimonides ben Maimon, a medieval Jewish commentator and sage, but pronounced "Rumbum"). Sweaty, peeved, and thoroughly obnoxious, I replied, "Rum Diddy Bum Bum?" My yeshiva career ended with a well-deserved slap. An incident involving a rabbi's daughter also contributed to my departure. Quite trivial by contemporary standards, but the girl was willing and it got the job done.

Some months later, the Hebrew Institute's director—Fuzzy, as he was known to the students—got tired of my skipping class and/or getting kicked out to go talk to one of the bus drivers. Sam Payne was a black gentleman who'd driven in Patton's Red Ball Express during the war. He had a fine repertoire of mostly true stories, and scandalized the Institute by wearing pink shirts, then considered unacceptably risqué and probably prohibited by the *Shulkhan Arukh*. Normally, Fuzzy didn't much care what you did so long as you didn't disturb the class and your parents came up with the tuition. But I was on scholarship and they had better uses for the money. Fine by me.

So ended my formal instruction, save for one quaint practice. By tradition, if the firstborn of the family is a son, he fasts all day prior to the first Passover ritual banquet, the seder. You can dodge this requirement, at least according to the Pittsburgh variant of this tradition, if you go to the synagogue before sunrise. There you don *tallis*, the ritual prayer shawl, and *tefillin*, "phylacteries," little wooden boxes on leather straps with sacred texts inside. These too had gotten me in trouble at the yeshiva, when I opined that they came from "the phylactery factory." Then you pray with the *minyan*, then loudly and communally study Torah, then break your fast with the only item more forbidden during Passover than bread—whisky. At *minyan* were several old gents who took a certain delight in sending the few high school kids off to class with liquor on their breath. So once a year:

> Homeroom teacher: *What do I smell?*
> Me: *Canadian Club.*
> Homeroom teacher: *Where did you get that?*
> Me: *The synagogue. I was praying.*

Other prayers were more problematical. Jewish services have no offertory. Money must be got in other ways. Local synagogues required that members and nonmembers reserve their seats for the High Holy Days: Rosh Hashanah, the Jewish New Year and ten days later, Yom Kippur, the Day of Atonement. Reservations took money. I had none. And more than once, leaving the Congregation Poale Zedek in humiliation because somebody wanted his seat, I'd ponder yet another of Squirrel Hill's long lost mysteries—what to do when you didn't even have enough money to repent.

One final mystery.

Squirrel Hill, though affluent, was a complex place. I had neighbors with numbers tattooed on their arms. They never spoke of it, though sometimes, late on summer nights with windows open, you could hear them screaming in their sleep. More common were the two-generation psychodramas of immigrant parents, now aging, and their adult children. The subject was always, Can you be a good Jew and (fill in the blanks) do this or not do that? The answer was always, Yes, you can be a good Jew and not keep Kosher/work on the Sabbath/marry a Gentile/ whatever. Listening to those arguments year after year, it occurred to me that the adult children, the Reform Jews were slowly stripping away everything that made Judaism distinctive, and that someday there would be so little left, no one would care.

I certainly didn't care. Not then, at any rate. Nor could I understand that the stripping away was a necessary precondition for future growth, and that what passed for Orthodoxy back then was itself scarcely more than an agglomeration of other people's choices.

Christianity intrigued. No churchgoing. I was sure they wouldn't let me in, or even worse, they'd call my mother. But I did occasionally sneak down to the living room on Sunday mornings to watch the religious programming, *Lamp unto My Feet* and all that. Later, via a newspaper ad, I acquired a New Testament through the Hebrew Christians of Bridgeport, and took their correspondence courses, which arrived in plain brown wrapping. I got through several lessons before I realized that they, too, were interested only in the answers they wanted to hear. So I dropped the course, and stashed my NT where most young adolescents, type-male, of that pre-Internet-porn era kept their *Playboys*: between the mattress and the box spring. The real revelation came the day my grandmother found it.

Haven't we had enough from the Goyim?

Didn't know the old gal could hit that hard.

I'd definitely lost my New Testament, and didn't replace it until 1971, when I found myself in the Quantico Naval Hospital with time to read. Which was pretty much what I'd done every hour, every moment I could while growing up. When my son was fourteen, I made the mistake of mentioning that, when I was his age, my home entertainment complex consisted of a transistor radio and a library card. He smiled indulgently and asked, "Dad, what's a library card?"

And at some point around age fourteen, I discovered that there was conservative stuff to read.

Much of it, the street-corner newsstand variety, was histrionic. Nuke the chicoms. Dig up FDR and replant him, along with the rest of the New Deal, alongside Lenin in Moscow's Red Square Mausoleum. A pox-and-a-half on the New Frontier— Out Where the Waste Begins, conservatives called it. The national debt has just passed whatever it has just passed. Something must be done (at least they didn't say *We* must do something) about the Soviet Postage Stamp Offensive. The Russkies are flooding American hobby shops and philatelic catalogues with endless new commemoratives, selling stamps to collectors at many times their production cost and using the profits to fund the Kremlin Master Plan for World Domination which, by the way, is right exactly precisely on schedule. Get tough with the Commies. Gotta get tough with the Commies. Precisely what getting tough might entail or where it might lead, was left somewhat vague.

Other readings, books such as Russell Kirk's *The American Cause* and James Burnham's *The Suicide of the West*, I found both arrogant and beyond me. As for William F. Buckley Jr., all I can say is: Forty years into the exercise and I'm still never quite sure what he's talking about. Not even two years of high school Latin seemed to help, even though the teacher, a failed Jesuit, kept reminding us that Latin was the language of "Caesars, Popes, and William F. Buckley Jr." This lifelong inability to connect with Mr. Buckley is, it should be noted, a shortcoming I attribute entirely to myself.

Other materials, especially the magazines provided free to public schools for in-class use, probably by some CIA-funded corporation or foundation or other, were more subtle and, in at least one instance, mysterious.

Those late fifties/early sixties teen mags operated on the assumption that adolescents had only two real concerns: "How to Be Popular" and "World Hot Spots." Endless articles proclaimed that the way to be popular was to "Develop a Pleasing Personality." But they never told you what a pleasing personality entailed, and I had absolutely no idea how to go about developing one. World hot spots appeared more direct. There were all those multicolored maps, the Red Menace spreading ever-outward in red, and staunch blue lines linking America to all its staunch blue allies around the world—NATO, SEATO, CENTO, ANZUS, the Rio Accord, the Baghdad Pact, and the rest of John Foster Dulles's grand geostrategic dementia. Neutral nations, especially those guilty of pursuing their own interests and refusing to play the roles allotted them by Washington, DC, were dismissed as immoral, at best. "You're either with us or against us" goes as deep in the American psyche as any other form of false consciousness.

Still, back then it all seemed clear enough, at least in the abstract. The problem came when we had to determine why world hot spots were world hot spots. Usually, we were informed that we had vital interests in some nation or region. What those vital interests were was left mysterious. And so it came to pass one day that we were in civics class, pondering Laos and our unspecified vital interests there, and the teacher asked me which of the three leaders—Souvanna Phouma, Souvannavuong, or Phoumi Nosavan (yes, I still remember their names)—America should support. "Why, the one with the most pleasing personality," I replied.

What a brat.

But the answer may not have been entirely incorrect, in Laos or in any other country where, then or now, we presume to exercise imperial influence and control. And how many of those pleasing personalities, from Ngo Dinh Diem and the Shah of Iran to the current crop of Karzais and Chalabis and other wannabe pleasers, have turned out to be not so pleasing after all.

And then there was Ayn Rand. I loved her uneasily. I read *Anthem* and *The Fountainhead*, and later *Atlas Shrugged*, all more than once. Her heroes were men and women of radiant selfishness and brilliance, damning conventional society, above it, not needing it. Yet they, the purposeful and the egocentric, were the true creators, protectors, and redeemers of civilization. I can still recite whole passages by heart. But unfortunately, I had no more idea of how to acquire radiant selfishness and brilliance than I had of how to acquire a pleasing personality, and no more sense of what to do with it than I had of whom we were supporting in Laos. And I realized, deep down, that something was missing from Rand's absolute insistence on the absolute primacy of the individual. Her god, her sacred word, "I," seemed to me as inadequate, if not as pernicious, as the Squirrel Hill "we."

Then, by accident of fate and the Murray Avenue News Stand, in the early fall of 1963, I came upon historian Clinton Rossiter's *Conservatism in America*. I'd just finished his magnificent *Seedtime of the Republic* in school, and wanted more of what he had to say. When he explained that the essence of conservatism was aristocracy, an aristocracy of individual accomplishment and social and cultural connection, a status that in America can be chosen, I was enthralled. And when he sketched the conservative view of human nature, its limits and its possibilities, I knew what I wanted to be: a conservative aristocrat.

Four decades later, I would discover that "aristocrat" was not and never had been the right word. The proper term was "citizen," in the ancient sense of the person who cultivates *aretē*, an untranslatable Greek word meaning virtue and excellence, in both private and public life. But when you're fourteen and growing up in Pittsburgh, you don't know from *aretē*.

A few months later, JFK's assassination having gotten all our minds off our personal troubles for a while, I was standing at my bedroom window. The room was shabby, filthy, shameful. The transistor radio was playing Johnny and the Hurricanes' "Red River Rock," a song I've ever since equated with humiliating tawdriness. I was staring out at an ugly Pittsburgh winter day. The backyard was mostly mud with grass patches; around the sides were barren bushes with thorns known back then as jaggers. A pair of old rusted-out garbage cans overflowed. Some kids were cutting through the bushes, heedless of the damage they were doing to what was left of my grandmother's garden. I was fifteen, a high school sophomore, and did not know how I was going to survive much more of this.

The guidance counselor had told us that it was time to start planning our futures. I wanted to be a conservative aristocrat. OK. So how does that happen?

I opened a spiral notebook and made a list.

College. I'll go to Yale. Why Yale? There was a popular television comedy back then, *The Many Loves of Dobie Gillis*. One of the main characters was a spoiled rich kid named Chatsworth Osborne Jr. Whenever he screwed up or misbehaved, his dowager mother reminded him sternly that unless he shaped up, he wouldn't go to Yale. "What?" Chatsworth Osborne Jr. usually replied. *"Not go to Yale?"* Very well. If Yale was good enough for Chatsworth Osborne Jr., it was good enough for me.

Notation: Find out where Yale is.

Military service. After graduating from Yale, the Marines. Why the Marines? I'd been reading Leon Uris' best-selling World War II novel, *Battle Cry*. True, the Marines were far less aristocratic than the Navy, where you might die in battle but at least you've had your last meal on a linen tablecloth. But the Marines were damn good fighters and that counted. Anyway, I could use some toughening up.

Notation: Get some exercise.

Career. College professor. Genteel, aristocratic, and lots of time to read and write. Especially, write. I'd discovered, in the accidental way that young people often find their talents, that I was good at it. Teachers would read my compositions out loud in class. The other students seemed not to mind, sometimes even seemed to enjoy it. That helped, along with a strange, barely nascent sense that this was a talent placed within me for some use other than entertaining those who had no other use for me.

I looked down at the list for a moment or two. Ridiculous. Absolutely ridiculous. Then I tore up the sheet and did it.

★   ★   ★

Whatever happened to Pittsburgh?

In August 1987, for the first time in many years, I went back, this time on an expense account, as a journalist driving up from Washington, DC. The assignment: Do a piece on whatever happened to Pittsburgh.

I stayed at the downtown Hilton and was unimpressed. I was, however, amazed at how small the city really was, and how easily you could navigate it once you'd spent a couple minutes with a map. No further mysteries there. And the city was glorious. Not for nothing had Rand McNally, two years before, declared Pittsburgh, "America's most livable city."

The steel industry had collapsed more or less on schedule. Tens of thousands of industrial and related jobs had vanished. High-tech parks and shopping malls had sprouted in their stead, boutiques and trendy restaurants, even a museum dedicated to that Pittsburgh boy-made-good, Andy Warhol. The new downtown skyline was spectacular, the air pristine. And the revitalization of the 1950s was now known as Renaissance I. This high-tech, yuppie revival was Renaissance II. As to where all the former workers had gone, now for the most part middle-aged and unemployable—a mystery. But there was no reason to talk about it. Few of the people I interviewed would.

They told me other things. The politicians told me that, even though Mayor Richard Caliguiri deserved much of the credit for launching the effort, he'd benefited greatly from the revival of the old political/business/civic alliance that had done Renaissance I. And he'd had fine help from Wesley Posvar, chancellor of the University of Pittsburgh, and Richard Cyert, president of Carnegie-Mellon University. These two men, having decided that they couldn't maintain competitive universities in a dead city, had gone out and lured many dozens of high-tech start-ups, with offers of links to university facilities and other goodies. CMU had specialized in number-crunching, Pitt in medicine and biotech.

Chancellor Posvar and President Cyert told me that they'd been happy to get the whole thing started, and had received good help from the city government, after the mayor and the politicians finally caught on.

I went out to my old neighborhood. It had aged, not gracefully. There were, to be sure, some new attractions. A video arcade, a hippie consignment store of sorts, a Kosher Chinese restaurant with pictures of Menachem Schneerson, the *Lubavitcher Rebbe*, in the windows and cheaply printed note cards on each table offering domestic tips from Mrs. Schneerson. Kosher Chinese restaurants are not recommended, even when they offer recipes from the wife of a man whose followers were awaiting the announcement that he, Menachem Schneerson, was the Messiah. The Yeshiva Achei Timimim and the Hebrew Institute of Pittsburgh had modernized and expanded impressively, thanks to bequests. These, I suspected, came from the estates of American-born Jews who'd rediscovered their ancestral faith late in life. The Poale Zedek synagogue, once Orthodox in a nonextreme ethnic way, had gone ultra-observant. I knocked. The door opened. A scruffy young man would not let me past the entryway until I agreed to pray with him. Only those like themselves were admissible. I left.

One mystery still remained: the Lords of Creation who were no longer there. The men and women in those comfy houses and upscale cars, who had endured so much—war, Depression, Holocaust, divorce, God knows what else—and had complained so little about it. An entire generation suffering from what had become known as PTSD, Post-Traumatic Stress Disorder, and all I'd ever really seen of them were their houses and their cars. No reason for them to talk about it. Perhaps America would be a better place today had we not waited so long to understand what The Greatest Generation had endured, as well as acknowledge what they'd accomplished.

Also missing were the children of those comfy houses, among the most privileged of the baby boom. One of them, once, a popular boy, had told me that he respected me because I could write. Later, in a joking, yearbook sort of way, he'd predicted my obituary. Famous Writer Commits Suicide. Turns out, he was the one who killed himself.

I wish I could have known them better. I wish I could have liked them better, found a way, perhaps, to be liked a bit better in turn. They were, all things considered, a good and decent lot. And as Jews they were, irreducibly, my people. And I was, irreducibly, theirs.

Chapter 2

FIRST BETRAYALS

Yes, conservatism needs to change. But it cannot change, cannot be taken back unless and until it faces the truth of its betrayals of self, nation, and planet.

—*Philip Gold*

DON DEVINE IS ONE of the elder statesmen of American conservatism. A former Reagan official (as Director of the Office of Personnel Management, he ran the Civil Service), he has enjoyed a long and distinguished career in public service, practical politics, consulting, academics, and journalism. Tall and slender, blessed with a gravelly, streetwise New York accent, he's an easy man to like and a hard man to dismiss. Currently vice chairman of the American Conservative Union and editor of their online magazine, *Conservative Battle-Line*, he's among the best in the movement. I wish him well.

In 2003, Don Devine began speaking out against the Bush administration's foreign policies. "Conservatism," he told me, "will live or die with empire." A brief trip to Iraq in early 2004 left him impressed with the administration's occupation policies and imbued him with determination to "stay the course." Such special tours for "opinion leaders," carefully arranged and packaged, often have this effect. But no amount of junketing can reconcile him to the administration's domestic policies, especially the rampaging increases in spending and deficits as a way of life. His solution: return to the "Reagan Vision." Forget, or at least minimize, this most un-Gipper-like infatuation with conquest and concentrate instead on returning America to "limited government" and "devolution of power" to the state and local levels.

His prescription struck me as somewhat out of touch. For better or worse (in the long run, worse), the American people have accepted Big Government, along with scores of trillions in unpayable debt. To an ever-increasing percentage of the nation, Ronald Reagan means little more than a name in a history book. I asked him about this. He replied, "Our surveys tell us that this is what people want." Surveys of whom? I wondered. I asked Don about problems such as cultural strife, immigration, discrimination. He replied that people want those problems solved via traditional forms of assimilation and acculturation: in effect, a return to the one-size-fits-all "melting pot" philosophy. I asked him to send me some of his recent writings. He did. One in particular convinced me that conservatism's fifty-year journey was over, and that it will go down in history as a sometimes noble, but ultimately failed, pathetic, and irrelevant movement. For it is not simply that conservatism betrayed itself and the nation four times over. It is also the nature of that betrayal—not just doing what it takes to gain power or making the inevitable compromises, but a suicidal predilection for fighting the battles conservatism wanted to fight, not the battles it needed to fight.

Don Devine's two-page typescript is entitled, "Why I Am a Conservative." It begins with an assertion that, had I not known the man, I would have found arrogant, troublesome, and deluded:

> *I am a conservative because all other political philosophies have failed. And the poor, modern world needs the vision of a positive future that only conservatism can provide.*

Only we are necessary? Only we are right? How many other movements across the millennia have arrogated unto themselves such certainty about themselves and everybody else. But how strange, at this stage of the exercise, still to be making such pronouncements. The claim may not have been without its merits when "all other political philosophies" could be taken to mean fascism, communism, the Soviet menace, the nastier aspects of collectivism. The claim might even have some present value, if meant in the sense that freedom works—that some form of liberal democracy coupled with some form of market economy does more good for more people than anything else yet devised. But as for the notion that we are the highest stage of historical evolution; that history ends with us; that we must think no thought that has not been thought before, conceive nothing new . . .

Don then provides a short précis of conservatism's fifty-year journey from the Creed That Dare Not Speak Its Name to the Creed with Nothing Left to Say. He does not mention the Cold War. The issue is America as a civilization. "As recently as the 1950s," he writes, "liberals could claim 'the end of ideology,' [title of a then-famous book by Daniel Bell] for there was no conservative or even leftist alternative to establishment liberalism." FDR's legatees controlled everything. The East Coast Republican establishment and the "country-club Republicans" grumbled and moaned, but went along. Anyone who spoke seriously of rolling back the New Deal was dismissed and derided as drunk, delirious, demented, or worse. Conservatism, to the extent that it existed, flitted about in little cliques of academics and somewhat larger but still eminently forgettable claques of populists, bigots, and freaks.

Then, writes Don, came "fusionist conservatism," brilliant recombinance of William F. Buckley Jr., Frank Meyer, and the *National Review* crowd:

> *Fusionist conservatism's highest value was liberty, but it was a freedom to be used to pursue traditionally defined and virtuous ends. The conservative alternative was based on freedom: free citizens, free markets, voluntary associations, local governments, unfettered businesses—especially small businesses—and capitalism generally. But freedom was not the end. Judeo-Christian morality, the family, religion, local communities and national patriotism were the values Meyer defined as uniquely Western that both supported freedom and made it meaningful.* The formula was to utilize libertarian means to pursue traditional ends, uniting the previously divided political strands of the right. [Emphasis added.]

Whether things like family, religion, community, and patriotism are uniquely Western may be debated. What Don makes clear is that the concept that kick-started the conservatism of the second half of the twentieth century was the attempt to meld a philosophy that emphasizes the primacy of individual sovereignty and choice with a civilization that's happy to tell people what to think and do: a white, male-dominated, primarily Christian civilization that expects its members, at the very least, to pretend to want to adhere to its norms and aspire to its goals. There might be exceptions, of course, sometimes even cherished and honored deviations—jazz musicians, Beat poets and niks, ivory tower eggheads, your occasional well-meaning pacifist or socialist, maybe even a politician or two. Spice is good. But as for the rest of America:

You're free. Now get with the program.

And yet, this was an American civilization that, at the very moment of conservatism's birth, was already showing the irreparable fissures that would lead to decades of Culture War. It was also a civilization already given to the imperial hubris that would lead to Iraq and beyond. The two were not, and are not, unrelated. The belief that, domestically, only we are right, and the belief that only we are right around the world—in some ways, not that much of a difference.

Still, it was a brilliant recombinance, back then. But it was not a recombinance that could have, or should have, endured. Nor did it accomplish very much, certainly not in any positive sense, certainly not when viewed with historical objectivity. "Barry Goldwater," Don Devine goes on,

> *first awakened a new spirit of freedom politically, but it took the optimism and decency of Ronald Reagan, who was also an early devotee of* National Review, *to provide the inspired leadership that produced the mature conservative movement. . . . Once the conservatives won power, however, they found the job of reforming the welfare state overwhelming and began acceding to it.*

He credits Reagan with reducing nondefense spending from "17.9 to 16.4 percent of GDP," but elides the fact that neither President Reagan nor his congressional minions could even defund the National Endowment for the Arts, let alone abolish a cabinet department or two. Trimming the rate of increase of government spending, even when expressed as a declining percentage of GDP, doth not a rollback of Big Government make.

Nor does Don believe that it established a trend. He notes that, even as conservatives took control of Congress in 1994, they jettisoned fiscal restraint in favor of more Big Government of all kinds, from hyperregulation of the workplace to, most recently, tacking on a few trillion dollars worth of Medicare drug entitlements. Potomac Poison eventually infects them all. Now he considers President Bush, who has increased government spending at a faster rate than any president in history (annual deficits in the half-trillion range are a fixture of Beltway planning), emblematic of a "malaise of the right—a fear that runaway spending was required to keep the masses politically contented." His conclusion:

> *The only possible solution is a return to the original vision of conservatism, one based on overcoming the welfare state, rather than participating in its decline . . .*

and, presumably, in returning power to a people itself returned to traditional values. Ronald Reagan's predecessor, Jimmy Carter, loved to lecture the Republic on "malaise," and on a future of limits, not opportunity. Don Devine's great fear: that unless we return to the faith of our father(s), "Mr. Carter may yet prove to be the superior prophet about America's future."

Lest I come and strike the earth with a curse.

Or a bit more prosaically: If something doesn't work, do more of it. If something hasn't sold for fifty years, keep selling.

I've known Don Devine for years. But only with this essay did I come to see him as a Malachi: a minor prophet in pain, grieving for a movement to which he has dedicated his life, going through the motions, harking back to the covenant of the fathers, because he knows not what else to do. In this, he's far from alone. Over the past couple years, I've gotten literally hundreds of e-mails, mostly from strangers, all pursuing variants of the same theme. I'm a conservative. Have been all my life.

What the hell is going on here? I know what I believe. But does it matter anymore?

Hard questions to answer. But not impossible, if you invoke two basic principles of navigation. If you want to know where you're going, it helps to know where you are. And if you want to know where you are, it helps to know where you've been.

Where have we been? We've been, to repeat a fundamental theme of this book, through four great conservative betrayals.

The first betrayal, the one that empowered the others, came when conservatism abandoned its special sense of aristocracy, that known to the ancients as citizenship and *aretē*, and with it a sense of the world that could get the movement beyond its own programs and grievances. It became, instead, mean-spirited.

The second came when conservatism failed to oppose the Vietnam War in a principled, effective manner, mostly because it had nagged and prattled about "getting tough on the Commies" for so long that no president dared admit that Vietnam didn't matter.

The third came when conservatism turned its back on America during the Culture War, refusing to understand how much had to change, adopting instead a stance of pure opposition, cloaked as a "return" to a pure world that never really existed, save in its proponents' own imaginings. It came when conservatism adopted the attitude, "Whatever the liberals are for, we're against; whatever they're against, we're for." From this flowed a studied unwillingness to face many of America's most grievous sins and shortcomings, an attitude of no-reason-to-talk-about-it that reduced the movement to not much more than defensive bitterness and ideological posturing. Thirty years of failure have rendered cultural conservatism a terminal patient, desperately scanning the chart for any signs of remission. Is church attendance up? Does the latest poll show 2 percent more of Americans oppose abortion than twenty years ago? Are divorce rates at least holding steady? How many politicians invoked God last week? How can we spin this to make it look like we're winning?

Fourth, conservatism surrendered—or, more aptly, has failed to oppose—those who desire to see this country redeem, by force of arms and imperial largesse, an Islamic civilization that, in the end, can only redeem itself. Today, the neocons speak of "Hard Wilsonianism," Woodrow Wilson's old dream of making the world safe for democracy, this time with the force (neocons call it "the will") to back it up. The cost of success, should it ever come, will be enormous. The cost of failure will be far greater. And we've the resources to pay for neither.

Yes, conservatism needs to change. But it cannot change, cannot be taken back unless and until it faces the truth of its betrayals of self, nation, and planet. And not all the self-congratulation on earth, not all the hatred of the evils and shortcomings of its foes, can elide the fact that in one way, conservatism today is a lot like the Islamic world. It is fragmented, it is bitter, it abjures its own creative power. It knows not how to get into the modern world. And in the end, it can only redeem itself.

⭐   ⭐   ⭐

No authoritative history of American conservatism now exists, even if Godfrey Hodgson's *The World Turned Right Side Up* comes close. Nor is a definitive history likely to be produced anytime soon. This book certainly makes no pretense of offering one. It's not that nothing has been written or blogged—the material seems as dauntingly vast as it proves sadly partial and unsatisfactory. For this failure, there are several reasons.

One, obviously, is time. We're still too close. Another is

authorship. Those who study and comment on conservatism often seem to be divided: the movement's veterans and true believers versus those who wouldn't agree with a conservative if he or she said that the sun will rise in the east tomorrow. Yet another reason is complexity. Any adequate history of conservatism would have to deal, simultaneously, with the ideas, the issues, the personalities, and the interactions: how the fundamental notions got generated, then what happened to them as they moved into practical and cultural politics. Of special interest would be the astonishingly complex story of how the Republican Party, at the local levels so often dominated by ideologues and zealots, learned at the national level to honor conservatives just enough to avoid taking them too seriously while giving them just enough to keep them coming back for more: a platform plank that no one really believed, a judgeship here and there, an occasional attorney general. Meanwhile, much of the rest of the country nodded, shrugged, agreed whenever convenient, and for the rest of the time, didn't think much about it at all.

Yet another reason is chaos. Will Rogers liked to quip that he belonged to no organized political party; he was a Democrat. From the fifties to the present, American conservatism has never been a coherent movement. Paleocons, neocons, Manhattan intellectuals, and Beltway policy wonks coexist (if such it can be called) with Sunbelt nouveaux riches, hard-core evangelicals, and California dreamers. The history of conservatism is also the history of constant tension, more than occasional ugliness, and the frenetic herding of cats. And then there's the perennial conflict between the need to get the money and the votes, and the desire to remain at least cosmetically true to principle. It's never easy, and rarely pristine. Trying to understand it sometimes seems like working a Rubik's Cube: all manipulation, no results.

Still, American conservatism has evolved a sanitized official history of sorts. One recent example may suffice. In November 2003, the Heritage Foundation, the Gipper's favorite think tank except maybe for Stanford's Hoover Institution, published *Heritage Lecture #811*. The presenter was Lee Edwards, PhD, the Distinguished Fellow in Conservative Thought in the Foundation's Kenneth B. Simon Center for American Studies. The lecture is evocative in that Dr. Edwards gave it in Beijing and Shanghai. Presumably, when one addresses a foreign audience, especially a Chinese audience, one chooses carefully what to leave in, what to leave out.

For Dr. Edwards, modern American conservatism began in 1953, not with *National Review* fusionism, but with the publication of Russell Kirk's *The Conservative Mind*. "The central idea," he notes, "of The Conservative Mind, upon which American conservatism is essentially based, is ordered liberty." To achieve and maintain this condition, conservatism—indeed, humanity—must adhere to Kirk's "six basic 'canons'" for organizing and running a civilization. We must believe that:

A divine intent, as well as personal conscience, rules society.

Traditional life is filled with variety and mystery, while most radical systems are characterized by a narrowing uniformity.

Civilized society requires orders and classes.

Property and freedom are inseparably connected.

Man must control his will and his appetite, knowing that he is governed more by emotion than by reason.

Society must alter slowly.

Dr. Edwards concludes: "With one book, Russell Kirk made conservatism intellectually acceptable in America. Indeed, he gave the conservative movement its name."

For the next fifty years, according to the lecture, "a succession of conservative philosophers, popularizers, philanthropists, and politicians marched across the American political stage." It was a magnificent progression, helped along by the ever-more-evident failure of the welfare state. Even the movement's greatest electoral defeat, Barry Goldwater's 1964 landslide loss to Lyndon Johnson, could be explained as 60 percent of the voters reacting against a false image of the senator, not as a victory for LBJ. According to the official spin, 60 percent of the voters certainly did not mandate, and had no intention of mandating, the extension of the failed New Deal that President Johnson promised as the Great Society.

Nineteen sixty-four notwithstanding, the Republican Party got the conservative religion, and that's the way it stayed. Richard Nixon isn't mentioned. Realignment ensued as the "New Right" discovered how the Sunnybelt of South, Southwest, and West could balance out the East, and would donate handsomely for the opportunity to do so. And then, it had to follow as the night the day, Mr. Reagan made it "Morning in America" once again. Arrivistes, rednecks, and the Winnebago crowd provided the votes. Manhattan neocons and Beltway public intellectuals looked after the ideas, while direct mail fund-raising gurus and endless other organizations tended to the nagging. Then in 1994 (George H. W. Bush isn't mentioned) conservative Republicans took over Congress, but "grossly underestimated President Clinton's political skills." (Don Devine calls it "surrender.") But now, according to the

lecture, President George W. Bush presides over the latest iter-
ation, a commitment to fight the War on Terror with a "prudential multilateralism" and with the same tenacity his
predecessors brought to the Cold War, while simultaneously
"stimulating the economy without massive federal spending
and federal regulation." Dr. Edwards continues:

> *The transforming power of modern American conservatism
> over the last 50 years has been unmistakable. . . . The one
> political constant throughout those 50 years has been the rise of
> the Right . . .*

And finally:

> *The President is fortunate in that he can call on the myriad
> resources of a mature conservative movement. . . [for] the con-
> servative movement has become a major, and often the domi-
> nant, player in the political and economic realms in America."*

The Culture War is not mentioned.
Hardly a surprising interpretation from a senior true
believer. His take, what he leaves in and what he leaves
out, is predictable, with a predictability that itself
attests to a certain degree of truth. But there's another
way of looking at conservatism's last half-century: as
betrayal and irrelevance. Betrayal of conservatism's own
best instincts, and therefore, a mounting irrelevance. A
half-century's worth of betrayal and irrelevance. Not a
total betrayal, by any means. The Gipper got it right
about the Soviet Union. Perhaps the Evil Empire would
have collapsed, no matter what we did or didn't do. But

Reagan made it happen decades earlier, and not by force of arms. He simply helped the process along by recognizing the Soviets' situation and confronting them with the logic of their ways and choices.

In all other areas, however, conservatism has failed. *For all the sound and fury, and despite the electoral successes, there is virtually nothing in America today that would be fundamentally different had conservatism never existed.* Today, any return to limited government, even slowing the rate of governmental expansion in everything from Medicare to domestic surveillance, seems no more feasible than reducing greenhouse gases by asking everybody to hold their breath. Culturally, Russell Kirk's "canons" seem little more than quaint, especially the parts about the need for "orders and classes" and "altering slowly." Regardless of what the surveys and the indicators du jour might be manipulated into suggesting, there will be no return to that pastiche of values and practices that allegedly most moral of societies, fifties America, allegedly embraced and enforced. As for the production of ideas, perhaps Michael Lind, a former conservative and Bill Buckley protégé, sums it up best:

> *The conservative movement has had half a century to stimulate a similar [to other great American intellectual movements] efflorescence; its leaders have had vast financial resources and public attention at their disposal. What is the result of the conservative intellectual renaissance of late twentieth-century America? A few position papers from think tanks subsidized by the aerospace and tobacco industries; a few public-policy potboilers slapped together by second-rate social scientists or former student journalists subsidized by probusiness foundations; a few collections of op-eds by right-wing syndicated columnists. Not one philosopher of world*

*rank, not one great political or constitutional theorist, not one
world-class novelist or poet has been enrolled in the ranks of late
twentieth-century intellectuals, or had anything more than
fleeting association with them. It is not just that the postwar conservative intelligentsia has failed to produce equivalents of
Aristotle or Petrarch or Shakespeare or Kant. It has not even
lived up to the standards of previous American intelligentsias. No
Emerson, no Hawthorne, no Melville, no Robert Penn Warren
or Allen Tate has emerged from the amply subsidized groves of the
American conservative Parnassus. . . .*

*Conservatives cannot point to economic thinkers like Milton
Friedman and Friedrich von Hayek—for all their influence on
republican economic policy, they have refused the label conservative, calling themselves, accurately enough, libertarians or
classical liberals.*

The indictment is not without its bitterness, but not for that
reason invalid. So, to ask it again, Excepting the brilliant Cold
War endgame, what has fifty years of conservatism wrought that
is either permanently successful, or worthy of other kinds of permanence? Not much. But if conservatism is a half-century's worth
of self-betrayal leading toward irrelevance, it matters to understand the nature of this self-betrayal and this irrelevance. It derives,
I have suggested, from more than the need to make the inevitable
compromises that politics and governance require, although they
certainly form part of the problem. It also comes from conservatism's determination to fight the battles it wants to fight, not the
battles it needs to fight. It comes, most of all, from conservatism's
belief that its programs and preferences constitute universal truth.
The 1960 "Sharon Statement," charter document of the Young
Americans for Freedom, calls conservative principles, including
those enshrined in the Constitution as federalism and separation

of powers, "eternal truths." * From this belief there derives another: that those in possession of eternal and universal truth belong at the center of the universe. Call it a double false consciousness. And when those who believe themselves the center of the universe find that it's no longer so, their response is often to search for ways to return to their putative rightful status. Sometimes they become prophets. Sometimes they become false prophets. And sometimes, prophecy fails.

★   ★   ★

It is untrue that conservatism sprang into existence, fully formed and (to borrow a bit of fifties deejay patois) "in living color and horrendous sound" the day Dr. Kirk published his book, or *National Review* got the fusionist bug. Much of *The Conservative Mind* was dedicated to linking modern American conservatism to European forebears such as Burke, de Maistre, and others, and to demonstrating that although "many dull and unreflecting people have lent their inertia to the cause of conservatism," some pretty nifty thinkers had signed on, too. Or at least, they could be made retroactively to contribute and approve. Some literary scholar once wrote a waggish piece on the influence of great writers on preceding generations. What he did in satire, spoofing the academic tendency to analyze forces and movements discernible only to them, Dr. Kirk did in earnest and for real. Still, pedigree mattered, if only because

---

* The "Sharon Statement" takes its name from Bill Buckley's estate in Sharon, Connecticut, where the meeting was held. YAF was founded the same year as the better known Left-wing Students for a Democratic Society. For this analysis and the Statement itself, see Rebecca E. Klatch, *A Generation Divided: The New Left, the New Right, and the 1960s* (Berkeley: University of California Press, 1999).

conservatism had so little of it. Yes, American conservatism could, with a bit of dexterous manipulation, trace itself back to the Federalists. Some even claimed Machiavelli and Plato. But the sixteen decades after Philadelphia had not generated a wealth of admirable forebears. Prior to the Civil War, much thought that would later be classed as "conservative" came from the South, and even the most sympathetic historians of ideas have found it hard to sever invocations of tradition and limited government from an atavistic, self-interested defense of that region's "peculiar institution," slavery. Later, conservatism's ancestors tended toward two mutually hostile extremes: populists and robber barons. Populist ressentiment has always been a staple of conservatism, just as it has been for the Left. But it was much less clear that nineteenth-century conservatism should cast its fate, so exuberantly and uncritically, with large-scale capitalist enterprise. So antithetical was capitalism toward cherished conservative values—tradition, community, religion, individual responsibility, and integrity—that Clinton Rossiter calls the linkage "The Great Train Robbery of American Intellectual History." In truth, it was less a robbery than a buy-in. The mighty industrial captains and families established their universities, endowed their chairs, and acculturated generations of scholars and students to the notions that ten-year-olds had the right to contract for employment as equals of Standard Oil, and that the Social Darwinism of Mr. Herbert Spencer's *Social Statics* was indeed endorsed and enshrined by the Constitution of the United States. Nor had the early-twentieth-century Progressive Era, with its emphases on direct governmental action and the superiority of disinterested expertise over mere tradition and scripture, been much fun. As for the 1933 to 1953 liberal ascendancy: By the midfifties, an entire generation had grown up that knew nothing else. Still, as Rossiter notes, after decades of depression, war, and postwar stress, "by 1950 we were ready for at least a modest dose of conservatism."

We wouldn't get it. After the Korean War began in June 1950, Truman was no longer able to provide much of anything, liberal or conservative. Ike wisely did not provide it, preferring caution to ideology. He also became the first of four presidents (Eisenhower, Nixon, both Bushes) to genuflect toward the ideas, do an occasional conservative thing, but also keep his distance. Ike did a masterful job of giving the American people what they wanted, which was not much. Few wanted much by way of domestic change. Even fewer looked forward to a future of blood-soaked foreign adventures, and it's absolutely astonishing today to realize how many wars Ike *didn't* get us into. But in some vague and troubling way, America also wanted something more than Eisenhower's not much. Conservatism saw a chance to provide it. But what they chose to offer was exactly what few Americans wanted—mostly the domestic turmoil of undoing the welfare state and the incalculable risks of seeking victory over communism abroad. And conservatives chose to offer it in a manner seemingly calculated to fail.

George Nash, in his dated but still very useful book, *The Conservative Intellectual Movement in America since 1945*, writes:

> *In 1945 no articulate, coordinated, self-consciously conservative intellectual force existed in the United States. There were, at most, scattered voices of protest, profoundly pessimistic about the future of their country. Gradually during the first postwar decade these voices multiplied, acquired an audience, and began to generate an intellectual movement.*

Nash distinguishes three distinct yet nonetheless related strands of this intellectual renaissance: classical liberals and libertarians fearful of collectivism; traditionalists fearful of modernity; and evangelical anticommunists fearful of the Kremlin Master Plan for World Domination. In all cases, *fear* was the operative word. They all peddled fear—fear sometimes masquerading as standard intellectual *Weltschmerz*, fear more often used as a goad. FDR had proclaimed, "We have nothing to fear but fear itself." But now fear, it seemed, would make us good again, restore us to our senses, compel us to undo the damage of welfare statism at home, and shed the wimpy doctrine of the containment of communism around the planet.

It was not a subtle or an effective strategy. Nor did the libertarians remain much longer within the movement, preferring to head off for their own brand of pristine antipolitics. If a conservative is a person who, when told about something going on in the world, answers, Yes, but how did it work in the past? a libertarian is someone who answers, Yes, but how would it work in theory? Libertarian theory can be charming, seductive, even compelling. The primacy of civil society over government; the primacy of the individual over civil society; and the realization that it would all work beautifully, if everybody would just become libertarians—all have their appeal. But they don't get you elected. Nor do they get your policies adopted. By the sixties, libertarianism had settled into an incubator of ideas, a very fine incubator of ideas, for other people to develop and implement. Libertarians have seemed more or less content with that good and useful function ever since.

Still, conservatism had something else to offer, something precious and powerful. But conservatism chose not to offer it. An aristocratic devotion to an excellence of inclusion and humane regard might have proven a fine antidote to fifties complacency. But as much as the fifties were about complacency, they were even more about shame. And *arete* was the proper antidote to that, too.

Shame can be a powerful emotion. At the individual level, it can redeem. Or it can paralyze. Nations, too, can be redeemed or paralyzed by shame. Most often, shame attaches to specific deeds and conditions. These we can change, or make amends or excuses for, or numb ourselves and evade. But what do you do— what does a nation do?—when the shame is vague and mixed with foreboding, when the shame deals less with what was or is than with what we might be drifting into, and there's neither clear shamefulness yet, nor any overwhelming reason to stop?

In his charmingly daft memoir of Madison Avenue, *From Those Wonderful Folks Who Gave You Pearl Harbor*, adman Jerry della Femina tells of an encounter he had with an account executive. Advertising executives were, in the popular culture of the fifties, what investment bankers were to the eighties: soul-bereft abominations and worse. In World War II, this man had been a legendary fighter pilot. Fifteen years later, he'd become a prematurely middle-aged, Miltown-popping, three-martini-expense-account-lunch-eating, nervous, craven little man. As Mr. della Femina tells the tale:

"I once asked him what happened between the time that he was shooting down planes and now, when he is a terrified account executive. He looked at me and said, 'Well, for one thing, the Nazis never tried to take away one of my accounts.'"

And thus the shame of America as the fifties wore on. Life was good, but also trivial. Millions were doing better than they'd ever dared imagine, and this mattered greatly. But they had also learned what their prices were, and how seldom they were doing work that they could respect. Yet another Madison Avenue anecdote tells of a boy who watched some idiotic television commercial, then asked his adman father, "'Dad, am I to understand that a bunch of grown men sat around and thought up that thing? And another bunch of grown men sat around and said it was a good idea? And another bunch of grown men went to all the work to make a movie of it?' What could I say?"

And there were other kinds of shame. The shame, for one, of having survived World War II to prosper, when so many others had perished or failed. The shame of permitting that war to have been, in literary scholar and combat veteran Paul Fussell's phrase, "Sanitized beyond recognition." Of all the items that fell into the fifties category of *no reason to talk about it*, World War II was the greatest. It wasn't, of course, that we ignored it. We simply converted it into entertainment. Whether the men and women who fought, and endured that agony, ever accepted Hollywood's wartime offerings as truth may be debated. I suspect that their grasp of reality was sufficiently accurate and intense that they didn't need Tinseltown to educate them, and could accept mere entertainment as mere entertainment. But America, young America especially, certainly embraced Hollywood's and television's postwar offerings as gospel. We also converted the war, in Fussell's formulation, to an unquestionable moral resource for the next four decades—the same years that an entire generation, traumatized and stressed, spent in communal evasion, while their kids grew up for the most part ignorant of both the reality of war and the torments their parents had endured.

Trauma festers into shame. Hannah Arendt, the great political philosopher, somewhere once wondered how many killers people passed on the street every day: men carrying their wartime memories within, men dimly or not so dimly cognizant of what those memories, unattended, were doing to them, their lives and loved ones, their nation.

It's hard not to wonder whether Dr. Arendt and that fighter

ace ever passed each other on some Manhattan street. And hard not to realize, as The Greatest Generation now leaves us, that they deserved so much more, spiritually, than they got.

Of course, the history texts don't quite present the fifties as an era of shame. Historians spin it differently, as a "troubled feast" or a counterpoint of "anxiety and affluence." They note the rise of an increasingly tawdry "mass culture" and the proliferation of "houses made of ticky-tacky, all in a row." They cite the great national obsession with "conformity" and the bemoaning, back then, of "planned obsolescence," meaning that more and more of what you bought was junk. The texts also concede that people back then felt that morals were declining, along with America's position in the world. The Cold War was not going well, or so it seemed to those who regarded communism as both a global menace and a personal affront. And some debts regarding race, gender, and a few other matters were starting to come due, heedless of Dr. Kirk's canon that change must come slowly. Or perhaps blacks and women, gays and other minorities, and those concerned with myriad other issues, were concluding that "slow" really meant "never."

But shame? Certainly not. And certainly not a shame so intense that America either had to deal with it directly or evade it totally.

America chose a more diffuse evasion. America did so in a complex, sometimes furtive, sometimes agonizingly apparent set of ways. And in so doing, America established a pattern for future evasions. Russell Kirk saw it coming when he predicted that, in all probability:

America's contribution to the civilization of the future . . .
shall be just this: cheapness, the cheapest music and the cheapest
comic books and the cheapest morality that can be provided. . . .

More than any other people, the Americans have come to wor-
ship the mammon of the Short Run. . . . The American
divorce-rate, the prevalence of waste, the giddy veering of the
public fancy, the new Pontiac beside the decrepit shack, the girls
on the quarter reprints . . ."

Conservatism could have addressed the shame of cheapness, and the obscenity of how much it cost to produce such tawdriness. Conservatism could have offered political and cultural alternatives beyond mere reverence for the past and the putative upholding of "standards." It could have chosen to emphasize creative excellence over both ticky-tacky and ancestor worship, gracious modesty over conspicuous consumption, prudential calculation over promiscuous foreign crusading, and an ethos of humane aristocracy which, when labeled several decades later as "compassionate conservatism," drew mostly incredulity and yawns. Why conservatism chose not to is addressed later. For now, it's necessary to look at the structure of evasion that America built to cope with the cheapness and the shame.

★   ★   ★

In his best-selling novel *Advise and Consent*, Allen Drury remarked, almost en passant, that a "dry rot" had overtaken American in the fifties, and everyone knew it. Call it dry rot, call it shame, the uneasiness was the same. But America hit on three evasions, effective because they resonated with so much of what was going on in that era. Historian Daniel Boorstin, in his still eminently relevant 1961 book *The Image*, wrote of "how we have used our wealth, our literacy, our technology, and our progress to create the thicket of unreality which stands between us and the facts of life." Boorstin was considering phenomena such as celebrity, image politics, tourism, and advertising. But the "thicket of unreality" motif also applies to aspects of the 1950s trinity of evasions: Consensus. Containment. Convenience.

As used back then, "consensus" did not denote specific agreements so much as a sense that what united us as Americans was more important than what divided us. An unexceptional notion, save for two factors. One was that "consensus" provided something of a Unity-Lite after the ferocious communal commitments of the war years. It was thus less an affirmation of deep and primary bonds than a form of national "togetherness"—a popular word of that era when applied to personal relationships, in lieu of, say, passion or commitment. So in the fifties, America contrived a "consensus school of history," dedicated to proving the point. Consensus historians such as Richard Hofstadter, Daniel Boorstin, and Arthur Schlesinger Jr. turned out several dozen books and major articles demonstrating that consensus was the American Way and the "vital center," the purest expression of American politics. America discovered additional consensus in the Judeo-Christian heritage. Once, this particular hyphenate referred to historical and theological commonalities of interest primarily to scholars. Now "Protestant, Catholic, Jew" became yet another area of comfy consensus, and television commercials exhorting us to "Worship at a church or synagogue of your choice"—denatured millennia of religious distinctiveness and strife. Religious consensus now meant that you believed in something, something Judeo-Christian, at any rate, and that what you believed mattered less than that you believed it. That venerable slogan, "The family that prays together stays together," apparently, also applied to the American family as a whole.

The other problem was that consensus elided or ignored some very real and very deep fissures that would, soon enough, crack into chasms: race, gender, sexual orientation, generational gaps, conflicts of viewpoint and of spirit—a cauldron of strife that, for decades, would make divisiveness, friction, and, in sociologist Todd Gitlin's memorable phrase, "the narcissism of small differences" seem far more the American Way than a nation in love with itself.

Consensus was cheap back then. It was a cheap substitute for a real unity that could only be forged when life and death were on the line, and forged only among people who meant what they said and said what they meant. And it was a cheap substitute for taking a hard, honest look at some of America's more grievous imperfections.

Containment, also, was cheap. After World War II, America wisely chose not to pursue a hyperaggressive policy of "rollback" against the Soviet Union. Wisely, because rollback, let alone total victory, were not to be had at any price that the American people might have been willing to pay, even in the absence of nuclear war. Like consensus, it was a halfway house. And like consensus, it had two flaws.

First, although containment was cheap in the sense that it did not ask of the American people a degree of commitment and sacrifice they were patently unwilling to endure again, it was expensive in other ways. In his 1961 Farewell Address, President Eisenhower warned famously of a "military-industrial complex" that, although necessary for national security, possessed "the potential for the disastrous rise of misplaced power." Today, the military-industrial complex (in more modern usage, the Military-Industrial-Congressional Empire, or MICE) is renowned mostly for waste, fraud, abuse, pork, cost overruns, and magnificent high-tech weaponry that may or may not be relevant to the threats at hand. But Ike's warning went beyond, far beyond, the megabucks:

> *The total influence—economic, political, even spiritual—is*
> *felt in every city, every Statehouse, every office of the Fed-*
> *eral government.*

Economic, political, even spiritual . . .

In a magnificent book that has received virtually no attention since its publication in 2002, political scientist and entrepreneur Derek Leebaert has told us just what the cost of the Cold War really was. Dr. Leebaert, a lifelong conservative, wrote *The Fifty-Year Wound* in the conviction that the Cold War was necessary, but that we paid a far higher price than we had to. Indeed, we've yet to reckon the final cost. Not just the hundreds of trillions we wasted buying junk and supporting tyrants, although that mattered greatly. Economists tell us that the true price of any purchase is its "opportunity cost," as all the alternatives are foregone. It was also about the human waste: millions of people, from assembly-line workers to "defense intellectuals," making nonproductive careers out of the Cold War. It was also about the social and cultural distortions. Universities turned into federal convenience stores, vending R&D, arcane theories, and weapons for use against both bodies and minds. America accepted background checks, security investigations, and secrecy as routine ways of life, even though millions of checks turned up practically nothing and an awesome tonnage of classified material needed no protection. A "channeling" Selective Service system manipulated millions of men into taking advanced degrees, jobs, and wives they neither needed nor wanted in order to beat the draft. And most of all, America accepted centralization and bigness as the necessary price of living in a world of constant peril and "crisis."

Crisis.

In medical terminology, "crisis" pertains to the moment

when the patient either dies or starts to recover. During the
Cold War, crisis became the normal order of things, to the
point where no president could be considered a success
unless and until he'd mastered his obligatory "crisis," and, of
course, issued his obligatory "doctrine." Those who
schmucked up their crises have not been remembered fondly.
And now, the crisis mentality extends to nearly every aspect
of American politics. No issue gets taken seriously until it's
repackaged as a crisis. And if the crisis happens to coincide
with that other staple of American public life, scandal, so
much the better.

The second problem with containment was that the permanent crisis mentality led to a progressive inability to distinguish
vital from peripheral interests, and to an absolute miasma about
the nature of America's global "leadership." It's not just that we
believe that everybody, all right-thinking people at least,
secretly want to be like us. It's that we believe that all right-
thinking people worry about the same things we do, in the
same order. To disagree, to refuse to accept our "leadership,"
bespeaks, at best, ignorance; more likely, evil.

The doctrine of containment, as originally formulated by
American diplomat George Kennan in his 1946 "Long
Telegram" from Moscow and his pseudonymous 1947 *Foreign
Affairs* article, "The Sources of Soviet Conduct," made sense.
Containment of the Soviet Union until it mellowed into a
normal authoritarian mess was to be patient, primarily nonmil-
itary, and discriminating. It mattered mostly in Europe, Japan,
and to some extent, the Western Hemisphere. Then, under
Harry Truman, containment morphed into a potential blank
check written on the blood and treasure of the United States.
The 1947 Truman Doctrine, extending aid to Greece and
Turkey, asserted that the United States must assist governments

resisting armed minorities and outside forces. Then, in 1949, after the fall of China to the communists and the first Soviet atomic bomb test, a White House document known as NSC-68, written to justify massive peacetime rearmament, codified the change:

> *The risks we face are of a new order of magnitude, commensurate with the total struggle in which we are engaged. For a free society there is never total victory, since freedom and democracy are never wholly attained, are always in the process of being attained. But defeat at the hands of the totalitarians is total defeat. . . . in the context of the present polarization of power, a defeat for free institutions* anywhere *is a defeat* everywhere. [Emphasis in the original.]

Why? Because we said it was. Perhaps the emerging class of professional Cold Warriors honestly believed that all places were now equally important, and that not a sparrow should fall to earth without the CIA determining whether it was a communist or an anticommunist bird. Lost in this promiscuous globalization of commitment was the old common-sense axiom that he who attempts to defend everywhere, defends nowhere—unless you honestly believe that all the world's a stage for you to demonstrate your resolve. Lost also was a fact that America has yet to grasp. To us, decolonization—the liberation of the "third world" from European domination—was an adjunct to the Cold War. What mattered was who was with us, who against us. To much of the rest of the world, the Cold War was an adjunct of decolonization. What mattered was getting the white skins and the round eyes out.

But when you're the leader of the free world—*now as well as then*—the needs and opinions of those whose duty it is to follow, matter less. And indeed, Kennan, for all his prudential calculation, could not resist ending his 1947 article:

> *Surely, there was never a fairer test of national quality than this. In light of these circumstances, the thoughtful observer of Russian-American relations will find no cause for complaint in the Kremlin's challenge to American society. He will rather experience a certain gratitude to a Providence which, by providing the American people with this implacable challenge, has made their entire security as a nation dependent on their pulling themselves together and accepting the responsibilities of moral and political leadership that history plainly intended them to bear.*

For Kennan, the Kremlin's challenge was to American *society*, indeed to the American soul, and both Providence and history expected America to meet it. Thank God for the Russians, ran a proverb of that era. Without them, how would we know if we were ahead or behind?

The final tally of the Cold War must be reckoned, then, in quantities of arrogance and self-delusion as well as in cash and damage done. America was willing, rightfully, to oppose communism. Up to a point. Where that point lay, no one really knew; few wanted to find out. And perhaps there lay a bit of shame in that, too.

Consensus. Containment. Convenience. It was, all things considered, convenient not to look too deeply into what might be coming at us in terms of domestic strife. Social historian Elaine Tyler May has suggested, aptly, that containment was a fixture of American domestic life as well as foreign policy—just keep the lid on. It was also convenient not to look too deeply at what we might be doing to ourselves and the world, in the name of anticommunism, that maybe didn't need to be done . . . or to realize that, to nations divesting themselves of centuries of white domination, we too were white.

And there were other conveniences, other aspects of the "thicket of unreality" by which America evaded both the facts of life and the gnawing shame. Economics, it seemed, had gone from precarious to guaranteed. As intellectuals like John Kenneth Galbraith assured the nation in books such as *The Affluent Society*, the "problem of production" had been solved. What remained was to consume the ever-increasing output of an advanced economic system that now ran, with a bit of Keynesian fine-tuning, automatically. Obsolescence applied to cars that fell apart after three years, not to the factories that produced them.

So this was the world of the fifties. It was not a stupid world. It was quite a creative and successful era in many ways, Ike's placid stewardship notwithstanding, or perhaps *because* of Ike's stewardship, and all the bad things, wars especially, that he ended or kept from happening. But it was also, sometimes openly, more often covertly, a time of a dim, vague, 3:00 A.M. sense of "Pay me now or pay me later." When feminist Betty Friedan wrote in *The Feminine Mystique* of the "problem with no name," sometimes aka "Is this all there is?" she was expressing the doubts of more, far more, than frustrated suburban housewives. But the fifties were the decade when "buy now/pay later" became a way of life, and "easy payments" a national slogan. America opted for later. Unfortunately, the payments would not be easy.

So what did the nascent conservative movement of that decade, so pessimistic about America's future, offer a country such as we were back then? It offered anathemas against Big Government, willfully oblivious to the fact that most Americans had made their peace with, or had chosen not to ponder too deeply, Big Government, in both its welfare state and national security state incarnations. It offered a stance against communism far more aggressive and hazardous than most Americans deemed prudent. It offered a libertarian defense of an "individual" who, for the most part, no longer existed. Not for nothing was "conformity" one of the more baleful indictments of the era, with "the organization man" and "the man in the gray flannel suit" its exemplars of stressed-out mediocrity. I retain a vivid if imperfect memory of a fifties television special, "Whatever Happened to the American Man?" It showed an advertising executive—always an advertising executive—droning through his life while enduring flashbacks to his war days: memories at once traumatic and ennobling.

But conservatism back then also offered, or at least could have offered, aristocracy. Not aristocracy in the hereditary sense, although a certain amount of snobbery and affectation hung about many of the era's early writers. And certainly not standardized meritocracy, where value is measured by test scores and compensation packages. Rather, the kind of aristocracy that I'd first encountered with Ayn Rand and, later, with Ortega y Gasset. In his *Revolt of the Masses*, he declares that aristocracy has nothing to do with picking the right parents or attending the right parties, but everything to do with a certain state of mind. True aristocrats know that, no matter what their positions or callings, they are responsible for a human world in need of perpetual renewal and care. "For me, then," he avows, "nobility is synonymous with a life of effort, ever set on excelling oneself, in passing beyond what is to what one sets up as a duty and an obligation."

The masses, on the other hand, believe that civilization is second nature, self-sustaining and always there. The mass man, according to Ortega, is characterized by "the free expansion of his vital desires, and therefore of his personality; and his radical ingratitude towards all that has made possible the ease of his existence."

And it was this mentality,—in so many ways, the mentality of fifties America, that posed an irreducible and ineluctable threat to those qualities that permitted creativity, and also mandated prudent resistance to communism. As Ortega wrote, "If you want to make use of the advantages of civilisation, but are not prepared to concern yourself with the upholding of civilisation—you are done."

It was in conservatism to do this: to broaden, not contract its horizons; to appeal to the best within us, not the worst or the easiest or the most comfortable. It was in conservatism to assume its place as a guardian of this civilization, and steward it through the changes that lay ahead, especially the changes regarding minorities and women. That would have been virtuous, aristocratic, and effective, a conservatism of inclusion and of aristocratic yet benign regard.

It was this sense of aristocracy, the aristocracy of creation and effort and responsibility, that first drew me to conservatism. I found its clearest expression, not in any words of its own, but in the writings of a brilliant liberal historian who, as he put it, "wishes the conservatives almost as well as he wishes the liberals." As Dr. Rossiter described the phenomenon:

> *The most important element in the Conservative temper is the aristocratic spirit. Although many modern Conservatives have abandoned the belief in a fixed aristocracy, their mood is one in which the urge to lead and serve, to set high standards, and to grade both men and values remains strong to the point of dominance. . . . The Conservative temper . . . is a subtle synthesis*

of reverence, traditionalism, distaste for materialism, high morality, moderation, peacefulness, and the aristocratic spirit.

And yet, it was this spirit, this style, this set of virtues, that conservatism jettisoned almost at the very moment that it became an active political force. Conservatism jettisoned it because, in the American politics of the sixties, as of today, appeals to aristocracy don't get you the money or the votes.

But maybe, just maybe, more was involved than a strange tandem of political tactical calculation and an unsalable program. For conservatism to have become truly a matter of *aret⁻e* it would have had to reach a probably unacceptable conclusion: that aristocracy and virtue could express themselves in many ways. Conservatives held no monopoly on either. It would not have been the first time in human history that a society faced this challenge. In his classic study of the crises of ancient Greece, *The Discovery of the Mind in Greek Philosophy and Literature*, Bruno Snell noted what happened when the ancients began to question their own ways:

> *As the interest in discovering virtue grew stronger, the objective seemed more and more difficult to realize. At the beginning of Greek thought, men had very decided notions of what was expected of them. But when human behaviour became an object of detailed investigation, many practices which had earlier been regarded as highly estimable did not withstand the pressure of the new criticism. . . .*
>
> *As more sections of society become aware of their own merit, they are less willing to conform to the ideal of the once-dominant class. It is discovered that the ways of men are diverse, and aretē may be attained in many [ways] . . .*

★   ★   ★

And this is exactly what was beginning to happen in fifties America, this discovery of excellences beyond the traditional white male Christian. Conservatism should have embraced the process, aided it, and tempered it. Conservatism instead turned its back on it, opposed it, and ultimately disgraced itself because of it.

And then there was Barry. Big Mike Goldwasser's grandson. Handsome, affluent, radiant with the certainty that there are certainties, and that he had them. Senator from Arizona, come out of that desert to lead the conservative movement to its first great victory: capturing the 1964 Republican presidential nomination.

IN YOUR HEART, YOU KNOW HE'S RIGHT. So proclaimed the campaign button I wore. The kids knew the appropriate Democratic response. In Your Guts, You Know He's Nuts. Conservatives got revenge of sorts during the 1980 campaign, when Jimmy Carter confessed to *Playboy* magazine that he'd lusted after women, and the slogan went out: In His Heart, He Knows Your Wife. But the most telling riposte I ever encountered came from an old Marine colonel. He claimed that a friend had warned him, "You vote for Barry Goldwater and in twelve months, we'll be in a land war in Asia." Said the old Marine: "He was right. I voted for Goldwater and twelve months later, we were in a land war in Asia."

In the fifties and early sixties, conservatism established itself as at least a potential national force in the typically American manner by which most political forces establish themselves. First came the thinkers and pseudothinkers, largely academic or academically oriented. Then came the popularizers and their magazines and organizations and funders. *National Review.* ISI, the Intercollegiate Society of Individualists. Young Americans for Freedom. A plethora of other groups and publications, some grassroots, some single-issue, most now mercifully for-gotten. Then came the infiltration, a move described by polit-ical scientist Mary Brennan as both "methodical" and "somewhat surreptitious," into the Republican Party.

It proved, simultaneously, a hard and an easy task. Easy in one sense: Millions of new Republicans in the Southwest and West and, somewhat later, the South, had no use for the Eastern estab-lishment. Conservatism, a kind of pick-and-choose, cafeteria conservatism at any rate, seemed more natural to them than either liberal Rockefeller Republicanism or the go-along-and-get-along attitudes of so much of the rest of the party.

But it was also hard. As Brennan notes, "Forging an alliance of ideological grassroots conservatives, intellectual right-wingers, and pragmatic right-leaning politicians was no easy task." Rather often, then and since, conservatism seemed to operate on the slogan No Friends on the Right. Intramural squabbles have always been fierce. Conservatism also carried baggage: unrepentant McCarthyites, John Birchers, Bible Belt fundamentalists given to offering definitive pronouncements on God's attitude toward everything from the Taiwan, Né Formosa crisis (now well past its fiftieth year) to farm supports. Finally, there was the dilemma faced by every ideological movement: how far to sacrifice principle in order to win power.

Still, in the months after Richard Nixon's 1960 loss to John Kennedy, it was clear that the 1964 presidential nomination was available. At least, that's how it seemed to those who started peddling GOLDWATER 64 buttons and bumper stickers in the pages of *National Review*, even before JFK had informed us of our willingness to once again "pay any price, bear any burden" . . . and years before we realized that it wasn't any longer true.

Barry Goldwater was something of an aristocrat in Ortega's

sense of the word. He cared deeply about civilization. He was also humane, one of his party's few who took issues such as civil rights, women's rights, and the environment seriously. When an LBJ aide was arrested on a morals charge in a DC men's room, Goldwater refused to make it a campaign weapon. His acceptance speech at the 1964 Republican convention is remembered almost entirely for a single couplet:

> Extremism in the defense of liberty is no vice. Moderation in the pursuit of justice is no virtue. [Emphasis in the original.]

But he also spoke of how America had "lost the brisk pace of diversity and the genius of individual creativity," and of the need for the "emancipation of creative differences" and for cherish[ing] diversity of ways." And he savaged, with a righteous, truthful contempt, the Kennedy/Johnson policies on Vietnam.

> *It has been during the* Democratic *years that we have weakly stumbled into conflict—timidly refusing to draw our own lines against aggression—deceitfully refusing to tell even our own people of our full participation—and tragically letting our finest men die on battlefields unmarked by purpose, pride, or the prospect of victory. . . .*
>
> *We are at war in Vietnam—yet the President who is the Commander in Chief of our forces refuses to say whether or not the objective is victory. His Secretary of Defense continues to mislead and misinform the American people."* [Emphasis in the original.]

Goldwater never stood a chance against LBJ. Perhaps no one

would have. Kennedy's memory was impervious, Johnson's oft-proclaimed intent to "complete the New Deal" irresistible, no matter how convinced conservatives were that nobody wanted it. So were LBJ's manipulative skills. And Goldwater was so easy to caricature. Two previous books, *The Conscience of a Conservative*, and *Why Not Victory?* had led too many to picture him as not much more than the mad bomber suggested in that infamous "Daisy" commercial. For those unacquainted—the Johnson campaign ran (apparently, only a few times, so great was the uproar) a commercial showing a little girl counting petals on a daisy, while a voiceover did a countdown of a more ominous nature. The girl disappeared into a mushroom cloud, LBJ quoted a line from a poem by Yeats—"We must love each other or we shall die"—and the announcer urged everyone to vote because "the stakes are too high to stay home."

So why was Goldwater so easy to caricature? Theodore H. White, in his magnificent *The Making of the President 1964*, calls him, not a homicidal maniac or even a deluded crusader, but a combination of outraged prophet and frustrated intellectual

come late in life to the wonder of books and ideas. Thus, ideas, for him, seemed to have a vigor and validity and virulence strange to those inoculated by learning earlier in life. His outrage was that of a man who could perceive all things with the brittle certainty of the frustrated intellectual—with mechanical precisions and fixes entirely unreal . . .

Perhaps. White, and so many others, have contended that Goldwater

profoundly undermined the worthy cause he had set out to champion, the cause of American conservatism, which was

> *deprived of the voice and the clarity it merits. In 1964 that*
> *cause was exposed as formless in ideas and hollow of program.*

Or was it? Certainly, Goldwater's domestic agenda had no chance. But that made it neither formless nor hollow. Certainly, his uncompromising anticommunism and his You're-with-us-or-you're-against-us worldview made people nervous. But had he been president, would he have done as LBJ subsequently did in Vietnam? Impossible to say. Predicting the past can be tricky. But I sometimes rather suspect that, given his respect for prudence, he might have been able to tell the American people: Look, it's just not worth it. The Vietnamese Commies may be Commies, but they're nobody's stooges. We can live with a Southeast Asian version of Tito's Yugoslavia. What we can't live with is the human and financial cost of fighting what everybody with an ounce of military sense knows would be a long and ugly war. And let's face it—you don't impress your enemies by squandering your strength.

Some years later, Americans started muttering, half in admiration, half in disgust, a new cliché: "Only Nixon could go to China." To wit: only a staunch, lifelong anticommunist could possess the political capital to recognize that regime. Perhaps it might have been the same with Barry Goldwater. But then, predicting the past can be tricky.

I wore my Goldwater button with a certain perverse pride. At least it got people speaking to me. I even volunteered at a local storefront campaign room, and was told, rather brusquely, to come back some other time. I never did, and learned only decades later that the campaign had been an organizational disaster. Utilizing volunteers appeared to have been an area of special incompetence. A while later, bored at last by the taunting, I took my button off. Either no one noticed, or saw no need to congratulate me on "finally coming to my senses."

One lunch break at school, several of the more popular girls put on an impromptu campaign rally. It consists of singing a little number adapted from a popular musical, *Bye Bye Birdie*:

We love you, Lyndon.
Oh, yes, we do.
We love you, Lyndon.
And we'll be true.
When you're not near to us,
We're blue.
Oh, Lyndon, we love you.

Followed by:
Cause he's a fine, upstanding,
Healthy, normal,
Patriotic
American President!

It would not have surprised me to learn that, a few years later, those same girls had taken up a different chant.

Hey, hey,
LBJ.
How many kids
Did you kill today?

Chapter 3

Yale

It would be many years before I realized that conservatism was content with the lowest common denominator, and that, in the end, conservatism would rather complain than create.

—Philip Gold

A CONSERVATISM OF INCLUSIVE excellence and humane regard would have welcomed and supported the black struggle for equality. It would have welcomed and supported women's rights. It would have recognized that virtue comes in many forms, and that excellence does not reside only in the past. It would have found a way to oppose the Vietnam War. It would have brought its grace and rationality to those movements, and perhaps have made those movements' subsequent excesses far less excessive. Perhaps the rights of minorities and women, and the celebration of diverse virtues, could even have become core conservative issues. In short, conservatism might have become a creative part of a rapidly changing nation.

Perhaps it was too much to expect that conservatism, or any major twentieth-century American movement, might choose to stand rationally for its greatest principles, choose not to participate in the race to the bottom that American politics and culture have become. In any event, it did not happen. Conservatism chose instead to continue its self-betrayal.

Ressentiment triumphed over *aretē*. By the seventies, conservatism had adopted its more or less permanent stance: opposing the Left for the sake of opposing the Left. That conservatism would adopt such a negative approach need not surprise. It's part of what you do when you want to get funded and/or elected. But it would be many years before I realized that it went deeper; that conservatism was content with the lowest common denominator; and that, in the end, conservatism would rather complain than create.

This was unfortunate. In 1995, historian Christopher Lasch, he who'd given us the best-selling *The Culture of Narcissism*, Jimmy Carter's handbook on malaise, came out with something new. He titled his book, *The Revolt of the Elites and the Betrayal of Democracy*, in conscious reversal of Ortega's masterpiece, and proclaimed:

> *Once it was the "revolt of the masses" that was held to threaten social order and the civilizing traditions of Western culture. In our time, however, the chief threat seems to come from those at the top of the social hierarchy, not the masses.*

Professor Lasch had in mind primarily the Left, most of all those who would become known as the blame-America-first crowd. There was much truth to his indictment. But the Right, for all its preaching and scolding, was little different. It had abandoned the hard tasks of rectification and creation for the far less strenuous agenda of complaining and resenting, self-pity and cant. In this sense, the Right as well as the Left had adopted the mass mentality, the belief that civilization was automatic and self-sustaining, and required neither constant nurture nor, from time to time, serious rethinking. Conservatism likes to believe that, for all those decades, it stood for "standards" of excellence as well as traditional values. Indeed it did. But not in the way that might have worked—the aristocratic way that takes responsibility for creation as well as conservation, and for radical change when radical change is needed. Conservatives took the easy way out. And from that first betrayal, others flowed.

★   ★   ★

I received my acceptance to Yale University while on my knees. Literally. Back then, a lot of colleges mailed their decisions to arrive on April 15, perhaps on the theory that, since everybody's parents were already overstressed by the other significance of that day, a little more wouldn't hurt. However, April 15, 1966, was on a weekend, so notification day was the following Monday. A lot of kids stayed home. I did. I saw the mailman coming up the walk to my house and knelt before the mail slot by the front door. The letter from Yale—a rather large envelope, actually— fell into my hands. I knew the answer before I opened it. Rejections come in thin little letter envelopes. Acceptances are accompanied by forms to fill out. I opened the package, confirmed my intuition, gave heartfelt thanks to a deity who'd been pissing me off nonstop for the past decade, and didn't learn until the next day that Harvard had sent everybody thick envelopes. Packets for the few, the happy few, and for the rejects, a detailed statistical analysis informing them of precisely why they hadn't been good enough. Fine young men had been turned away. Deity, no doubt, heard from them, too.

Since Yale was the only college that let me in, I decided to go. Oberlin had rejected me some weeks before, suggesting that I seek a less challenging environment elsewhere. The University of Pennsylvania had blown me off with a form letter that can only be described as nasty, brutish, and short. To this day, I still don't know why I even applied to those two. No matter. I was happy with the contents of my envelope from Yale, and mailed back my acceptance within the hour. Only one other time in my life did I answer my mail so quickly: four years later, when my draft notice came. I grabbed my finest Yale University stationery and scrawled:

> *Thank you for the draft notice, which I am returning to you. Please permit me to inform you that I have no intention of serving in the United States Army, will never serve in the United States Army, and would appreciate it if you'd stop wasting my time, your time, and the government's postage. Sincerely Yours. P.S. I recently joined the Marines.*

But that was still in the future, and there was the matter of high school to wrap up. From my point of view, it was already over. But in fact and rather surprisingly, it began anew the next day. The final weeks were not unpleasant. As people who had gone to school together, some since kindergarten, compared their destinies, a strange sort of mellowness overcame them. All the frictions, the social stratification of fraternities and sororities and clubs and cliques, the whole overdramatized who-talks-to-whom and who-goes-out-with-whom pettiness, and the rest of the adolescent apparatus of torment, suddenly seemed slightly . . . well, shameful. I was going to Yale. At least a few people saw me at least a little differently. I was spoken to more often, and once even got a ride from one of the prettiest and most genuinely popular girls in the class. A strange, tingling experience, and even though I couldn't quite figure out why she'd offered, it felt a bit like closure.

Classes no longer concerned me. I'm pretty certain that I graduated. In any case, I never looked back and never went back. But I do confess to one residual curiosity. About two-thirds of Taylor Allderdice High School was affluent Jewish. The final third, a thousand or so, were Gentiles, often the children of the mill workers. How many of the Jewish guys ever wore a uniform? How many of the Gentiles ended up with their names on The Wall? Many years later, journalist James Fallows would write an article entitled "What Did You Do in the Class War, Daddy?" He described his experiences as a Harvard senior, successfully mucking up his draft physical—confessing to nonexistent thoughts of suicide, that kind of thing. As he and his fellow antiwar students departed from the recruitment center, a busload of guys, "thick white proles" from Chelsea, arrived, and James Fallows suddenly knew who was going to die—who had been dying—in his place. Some years after that, I asked James Fallows what he would do, had he that moment to live over. He told me that he would have gone to prison instead of faking it. I believed him.

But such items mattered little to me in the summer of 1966, which I spent working in a local deli. It was an experience that left me with some ugly realizations about how some people believe that spending money gives them the right to torment and humiliate the help, and with profound and permanent empathy for all retail clerks everywhere. Still, we were far from without options for vengeance. After closing, I'd join the other young workers to scrub hams, drain rancid reefers, engage in jellybean fights (we sold the beans later), and exchange snide comments about the customers. Yes, I knew there was a war on, a pointless war as far as I could tell. But war or no war, pointless or not, I'd gotten exactly what I wanted. And knew beyond a doubt that all my problems were now solved, or would be the moment I beat feet out of Pittsburgh.

Another theory shot to hell by the facts.

★   ★   ★

Yale was indeed wonderful. I arrived the first day the place was open for freshmen, found my suite in Vanderbilt Hall on the Old Campus, picked out a bunk and a desk, and settled in to await my roomies. A moment later, I noticed a strange, soft buzzing sound outside the open window. I was about to investigate when a gent arrived from across the entryway. He introduced himself, pulled out my desk chair and sat down, leaned back, stuck his bare feet out the window into the ivy, lit up a Benson & Hedges without benefit of ashtray, and informed me in no uncertain terms that all his life, people had treated him as a genius. He was, however, sick to death of being treated as a genius, and he would appreciate it greatly if I would not treat him as a genius. I was formulating my answer when he confirmed for me something I'd already begun to suspect: There was indeed a hornet's nest in the ivy. He emitted a single loud, long shriek, drew in his feet, and I recall being quite impressed by the speed with which he was able to move from the chair to the ceiling, and also by what's known in football as his "hang time." Unfortunately, what goes up must ultimately come down. So down he came and there he lay, and fifteen minutes later, when he'd calmed down enough to resume dragging on his weed, I told him that I could probably see my way clear to not treating him as a genius. This pleased him.

My three freshman roomies, and indeed most of the men I met as a member of Yale's last all-male class of '70 were good guys. Having friends was a treat. So was discovering that people will generally take you at your own self-presentation, and that me being me wasn't nearly as bad as I'd thought.

The teachers were spectacular. Never in four years did I

encounter a teacher (titles such as professor and doctor were rarely used) who was either incompetent or didn't want to be there. Of course, there were a few mild eccentrics. One old political scientist insisted on reading his lectures, which he'd published, and were available from the co-op. Whenever he lost his place, which was often, some guy in the audience would start reading aloud from the published lectures until the old gent found an appropriate spot to take up the chant again. Another teacher, a psychologist somewhat deficient in bifocal vision, had a habit of walking into blackboards or off the podium. One year, the economics department decided to offer a survey course comparing market and planned economies. The teacher, allegedly a former CIA analyst, did a fine job, except for a certain inability to distinguish between capitalism and socialism when drawing graphs on the board. So the class learned to rely on the teaching assistant, who sat in the back shaking his head yes or no, as appropriate. More than once, the teacher turned from the blackboard to face his class, only to see nearly a hundred students rotated toward the assistant. He seemed not to mind.

Thirty years later, I heard a tale about CIA economists that falls into the category: If it isn't true, it ought to be. Apparently, the agency was wondering why its analysts had so egregiously overestimated the Soviet economy, almost until the final collapse of the USSR. Consultants were brought in. They concluded that the analysts had been so far off target because they'd relied on Soviet figures. Had they gone to Russia and stood in line for milk or shoes for a few hours, or waited five years for a phone, they might have reached other conclusions. The Soviet figures were worthless. And the Soviets knew it. So—irony can be pretty ironic—apparently the Soviets had gotten into the habit of relying on CIA estimates, which told them what fine shape they were in. Poor Gorby.

Classical Civilization (aka Classi Civ) courses held special delight. One was taught by Erich Segal, rather a fine scholar, then basking in the joy of having written the script for the Beatles' cartoon film, *Yellow Submarine*, and, soon enough, to write the best-selling novel, *Love Story*. One article that I later read on the Love Story phenomenon began with a quote to the effect of: I got halfway through when I realized how it was going to end. I cried and cried, then went back and finished it. The writer then commented: A typical reaction. Unless you happen to be the author. At any rate, Segal was so enamored of his popular work that he began using Beatles lyrics as "identify the passage" items on his tests:

> *And it really doesn't matter if I'm wrong I'm right*
> *Where I belong*
> *I'm right*
> *Where I belong.*

Clearly, wrote the students, this comes from the Agamemnon, or maybe Oedipus at Colonus, and demonstrates the dilemma of the tragic hero as he . . .

Wrong. It's from Sergeant Pepper's Lonely Hearts Club Band. Specifically, the "I'm Fixing a Hole," cut. Now, how about the passage that begins, "I used to get mad at my school/ The teachers who taught me weren't cool . . ."

But Classi Civ also drew me to epiphany. It was nearly dawn, the morning the final paper was due. Fatigue was cascading, the biphetamine had left me mildly stoned. And I found myself typing: "The literary progression from Aeschylus to Euripides exemplifies man's progression from futile nobility to noble futility."

Damn, that's good. Dunno what it means, but it sure sounds academic.

The paper came back with a 99 percent and a summons to go see Mr. Segal. He explained that he hadn't given me a hundred because a hundred meant perfection and he could not conceive of a perfect paper. But he'd loved that one line above all else, and wanted to use it, with appropriate attribution, in a scholarly paper he was doing.

Sure. All yours. No need to cite me. But if you ever figure out what it means, do let me know.

Many years later, I learned what it meant. My teacher then was also a classicist—this time a man who'd won the Medal of Honor in the Hanoi Hilton for his role as, in his words, "the lawgiver of an autonomous colony of Americans who happened to be located in a Hanoi prison."

E. A. Havelock was a different kind of classicist: old, curmudgeony, fierce, great fun. He liked neither women nor Commies. His lecture on *Medea*—"She wasn't a Greek, she was a Russian"—was always well attended. He also had a theory about the role of the chorus that to this day I find evocative, even if I'm still not sure whether he meant it.

The ancient texts were not full scripts as we understand the term. There were no divisions into act and scene; specific lines were not designated for specific characters. In fact, there was no punctuation at all. Just one long run-on. How you divide the passages and assign the roles can, as in the Bible, change meanings mightily. In Greek tragedy, the putative role of the chorus is to express the conventional wisdom of the community by commenting on the action and the players. But according to E. A. Havelock, the chorus was actually Muzak—a signal that it was time to take a break, head for the restroom or the wine bar. The conventional wisdom, in short, was what the audience ignored, and was expected to ignore.

But the most memorable teacher I ever encountered was Alvin Kernan. Shakespeare. The student course critique described the workload as "Everything by Shakespeare, everything about Shakespeare, and the rest of the library." The course was always oversubscribed and if you wanted a seat, you had to get there early. Guys were known to wander in on LSD, just to listen. He was that good.

In 1990, Kernan, by then at Princeton and semiretired, published an anguished tract entitled, *The Death of Literature*—death by deconstruction, death by pseudointellectual posturing, death by those with political agendas, death at the hands of a generation of feminist scholars determined to cleanse Western civilization of all that oppressive male chauvinist/sexist/racist crap. I read his book, then called him.

"You don't remember me. I took your Shakespeare course in 1968, and we never spoke. But you were my favorite teacher and my model when I started teaching at Georgetown. I've read *The Death of Literature* and want to do a feature on it. May I drive up and interview you?"

Replied Alvin Kernan: "Does this mean that you can take me to an expensive restaurant?"

"I'm on my way."

It was among the most fascinating interviews I'd ever done. Alvin Kernan turned out to have been a World War II Navy enlisted man, a Pearl Harbor survivor who later won the Navy Cross, a decoration second only to the Medal of Honor. After the war, he'd dedicated his life to literature, only to have the radical deconstructionist and feminist takeover of the Ivy League's English departments render him superfluous at best, and more often an odious relic. The conversation grew heated, then sad. I finally said, "Look. It was you, your generation. You hired them, promoted them, gave them tenure."

He shook his head. "I guess we were a little too willing to let them do what they wanted."

After *The Death of Literature*, Kernan wrote two more books, *Crossing the Line*, a memoir of his war experiences, and *In Plato's Cave*, an intellectual autobiography. Both are wondrous, as contact with brilliance and as history.

He was a magnificent aristocrat, a citizen-warrior-scholar who gave us much. We shall not look upon his like again.

Other activities proved more problematic. Aspiring writer that I was, I wanted to work for the literary magazine or, as the practice was traditionally known, "heel the *Lit*." I failed to impress, mostly due to my abysmal ignorance of fellow Pittsburgh expatriate Andy Warhol, and left the interview with a strange uneasiness over what seemed to me the shallowness of it all. Then I tried the Yale Political Union. The Party of the Right was filled with tidy eccentrics, and I rather liked them, even if the annual memorial service for King Charles I of England ("Charl the Martyr," as he was affectionately known) seemed a bit over-the-top, or at least off to one side. Anyway, my friends were in the Conservative Party. So I joined that, but let it slide when I realized that their chief activity seemed to be getting William F. Buckley Jr. up to speak as often as possible.

Not that Buckley wasn't intriguing. Sitting far to the left in the Law School auditorium, it was possible to look across the stage and watch him, behind the podium, unbuckle his belt, unzip his trousers, tuck in his shirt, and redo it all without ever missing a single polysyllabic syllable. It was also amusing to have him explain to the Yale Political Union president that "I entered the New York mayoral race to reify the situation. You do know what reify means, don't you?" And then to have the president announce on the stage that "I will now condescend to introduce . . ." and, turning to Buckley, say, "You do know what condescend means, don't you?"

But there was a flatness to the Conservative Party of the Yale Political Union. It was a flatness that troubled me, if only because it seemed symbolic of a greater failure: the failure to offer a serious alternative to the likes of a guy I knew who went about proclaiming, "There isn't a party far enough Left for me."

And I was troubled, also, by its failure to oppose some of the guys who slouched into the breakfast meetings at the beginning of each academic year, in the dining halls of the various residential colleges, class by class. You got your coffee and your donut. They gave you your course schedule and other relevant forms to be filled out and collected. Among them was the application for the automatic II-S student draft deferment. Few eyes met when it came time to fill out that form, but occasional mutterings could be heard.

Fucking fascists.

There was also brittle self-congratulation on once again avoiding complicity with the War Machine. And sometimes there were comments, at once menacing and ludicrous, about what "we" were going to do to about Amerika, come the Revolution.

We, again.

Yale was wonderful. I loved it then. I love it still. But a few weeks into my freshman year, I began to get a strange sensation.

There's something wrong here.

It would take decades for me to understand what that something was, and a decade or two more to understand why conservatism had proven so powerless against it. The conservatives were powerless because they chose to be, preferring neither to confront America's problems nor to assume the responsibility of creation—in politics, in culture, or in any other realm. They paid a heavy price for their failure. So did America. But a great part of the price was their failure to understand what motivated so many on the Left. For although their causes were often just, their style was not. Their style was, in point of fact, crazy. But insanity has structure. And if you wish to understand it, look toward what it's attempting to accomplish.

★   ★   ★

Irony, yes, can be pretty ironic. It is, to say the least, ironic that a generation now well into midlife, a generation once predicted to redeem the world and all therein, may still best be described by the words "baby" and "boom." Whatever happened to the baby boom?

Way back in the fifties, to borrow the title of a classic child's story, it was The Little Engine that Could.

In the sixties, it became The Little Engine that Could but said, Like, why should I?

In the seventies, it was The Little Engine that Could, but said, What's in it for me?

In the eighties, it was The Little Engine that Could, but only if it's socially responsible, environmentally benign, and both sets of kids agree.

By the end of the nineties, at least a few of us were beginning to suspect that maybe we were The Little Engine that Couldn't.

Now, however, at least if you read the lifestyle magazines—lifestyles for the no-longer-young—you learn that the baby boom is going to revolutionize retirement, just as it has revolutionized everything else that it touched, and will bring to its Golden Years all the dedication, passion, and enthusiasm that it has shown ever since . . .

Ever since when? Ever since the structure of its insanity took form. For if the history of much of the Right can be written as betrayal of its own highest principles, the history of much of the Left can be written as a peculiarly destructive self-deception—

of the quest for an unearned moral stature that served its causes wretchedly and locked America into a style of cultural politics that plagues us to this day:

The quest for an unearned moral stature is based on the premise that what really matters in this world, the final criterion of value is: *How do I feel?* Against this quest for unearned moral stature via emotion and "psychologized ethics," a conservatism mired in emotions of its own offered nothing save scorn, complaint, and the invocation: "Be like us." It was not an effective response.

Demographically, the baby boom consists of 78 million people born in this country between 1946 and 1964. Psychographically, the boom may have begun and ended a few years earlier. The boom itself breaks down into a 1946–54 bow wave of about 56 million, then a birth dearth, then a final upsurge that suggests a lot of more or less unplanned third children. Of interest here are the 56 million of the "Vietnam Generation"— those who turned eighteen, draft age, from 1965 to 1973. Of these, 26.8 million were men. According to the Presidential Clemency Board, established by Gerald Ford, 10.935 million, or over 40 percent, wore a uniform in some capacity or other. Only 3,250 went to prison for all draft-related offenses, from mere evasion to conscientious refusal to accept induction.

Not exactly numbers that accord with the popular image of massive resistance. Nor, upon closer inspection, do the numbers bear out the notion that Vietnam was a war fought primarily by the disadvantaged. The military does not keep socioeconomic data on its entering members. But a massive quantity of anecdotal and statistical research has shown that Vietnam was, broadly speaking, a middle-class war. Yet, so great is the vested interest, political and personal, of so many millions, in clinging to the interpretation of Vietnam as a lower-class war, and of the baby boom (its more privileged echelons, anyway) as an avant-garde of righteous resistance, that the myth endures.

It's time to put an end to this myth. It's time to see so much of what passed for "resistance" back then as what it was—a carnival superimposed upon a tragedy. It's time to understand what that era did to American politics and culture, for ill and for good. And it's time also to understand how conservatism, by failing to oppose it effectively, became itself one of the great evils to emerge from the sixties.

★   ★   ★

In the beginning, the baby boom was a happy thing. Nineteen forty-five and 1946 witnessed an epidemic of divorces, hardly surprising at the end of a long, traumatic war. But the early postwar years also experienced an explosion in pent-up marriage, as people suddenly found themselves at least modestly able to afford it. Procreation came about.

The initial economic impact was almost uniformly positive. New families needed housing. The advent of the relatively inexpensive suburban development, all those "Levittowns," coupled with the relatively easy availability of financing through the GI Bill, meant a construction boom in the suburbs. This in turn required cars to get around, and roads to get around on. And of course, kids have needs—stuff that they actually need, and an ever-increasing tonnage of stuff that they don't. Not that much at first, perhaps. But kids grow. Soon enough, the boomer kids needed schools to go to and school clothes to wear, and baseball gloves and summer camps and orthodontia. Then the marketeers discovered that baby boomer kids disposed of an astonishing amount of discretionary income from odd jobs and allowances, and could themselves shell out for all the appurtenances of youth culture: Elvis records, magazines, stuff for their cars, clothes beyond imagining, junk food also beyond imagining, the occasional six-pack of beer and/or condoms, when such were to be had.

It was all very fine. Still, you didn't have to be a demographer or economist or sociologist to suspect that, over time, the effects of such a large cohort passing through the system would become more baleful. It was great to build schools and colleges, for example. But what would happen to all those campuses and staffs after the cohort moved on? Could there be, would there be, enough work for all those young geniuses, let alone enough followers for all those "future leaders"? And how would their retirement be financed, and by whom?

Anyone possessed of the gift of prophecy back in those pre-Nam years might also have warned about a possible confluence of forces. The boomers were being taught and reminded and reassured, constantly, that the world was theirs to do with as they would—and that they were, almost by definition, up to the task. They were also being taught that, despite the nuclear weapons nuisance and the Kremlin Master Plan for World Domination, they had the right to expect and to have pretty much what they wanted. Who was teaching these lessons? Everyone. Parents, schools, media, and commercials, not to mention social scientists and sundry other pundits. In sum, prior to Vietnam, the baby boom received the kind of adulatory attention and encouragement hitherto reserved for princelings, princesseslings, and prodigies with actual talent.

But there was a confluence coming. America had issues. Some were matters of hard injustice. Others, from sexual mores to ecology, were emerging as complex political/cultural affairs. And then there were all those Cold War hot spots, few worth fighting over, most always seemingly ready to erupt into a test of American resolve, or worse. Great Expectations were about to collide with Great Dilemmas. How would the cohort handle this mix? As their parents had taught them? No. Their parents hadn't taught them. Of all the mysteries of the pre-Nam years, of all the things that there was no reason to talk about, the courage and endurance of their parents' generation was the greatest. Young Bill Clinton may well have loved to watch World War II movies, maybe even have hoped that he would someday get a war worthy of his talents. But did he or those like him have any idea what it actually meant, after a ten-year economic depression, to sign on for "the duration plus six months"?

The sixties were a necessary upheaval. They began the process of clearing away a lot of injustice and junk. Many have argued that the baby boom, with its allegedly superior social conscience and commitment, accelerated the process. There may be truth here. But the baby boom also did immeasurable harm, both by its size and by its style. Size could not be helped, although it can be interesting to speculate on what might have happened, say, had fewer bodies been available for the Nam-era draft, or had the full entry of women and minorities into the professional workplace been achieved by a smaller group. At the very least, we might have had a shorter war and might not have had the decades-long inflation of two-income families, with or without kids, bidding up the price of everything in sight. But the issue here is style—a style, in part, that of Ortega's Mass Man, a style of radical ingratitude and disrespect. But also a style in which the ultimate goal, indeed, the sole measure of reality, became: How does this or that make me feel . . . especially about myself?

The baby boom didn't invent psychobabble or psychologized ethics. The components had been lying around for decades. The boomers simply assembled it out of shards of their own experience and inexperience, and out of preexisting intellectual materials provided by their elders. But they made it their own, their more or less permanent leitmotif, and handed it down to their juniors—a leitmotif most recently observed in the continued and utter, willfully self-absorbed irrelevance of most of what's left of the Left, as they go about opposing America's ventures in Iraq and elsewhere.

If shame suffused the fifties, the sixties were suffused by the quest for an unearned moral stature, a stature achieved by elevating internal emotive states to the status of moral absolutes, regardless of real-world irrelevance or harm. Conservatism should have embraced the issues, made civil rights and feminism and ecology and the rest into a positive, rational program of its own. Simultaneously, conservatism should have opposed the psychologized style with every ounce of its aristocratic being—opposed it not by sneering it off, but by understanding how pernicious it really was, and offering effective alternatives. Conservatism did not oppose it. Instead, in some ways, conservatism joined it. At the very least, conservatism chose to profiteer off it. And in so doing, conservatism guaranteed its own defeat. For by the time conservatism got around to recognizing both the validity of the issues and the perils of the style, perhaps sometime in the eighties, maybe later, it was already too late for conservatism to offer itself as a viable alternative. For the nation had moved on.

Yes, beginning with Vietnam, there had to be a Culture War, just as there had to be a Cold War. But neither had to take the form it did, or cost so much. And just as it matters to understand what the Cold War cost us in spirit, so does it matter to understand what the Culture War cost, as well as to understand the opportunities both of them opened.

⭐   ⭐   ⭐

It is said that if you can remember the sixties, you weren't really there . . . and if you attended college in the sixties and can remember anything you learned, you really weren't really there. Not entirely true. I can still recite the first eighteen lines of the *Canterbury Tales* in Middle English. I also know the difference between the Battles of Borodino, Navarino, and Solferino, and the entirety of Sir John Suckling's immortal poem, "His Mistress' Leg":

> *Fain would I kiss my Julia's dainty leg*
> *Which is as white and hairless as an egg.*

I can also recall learning an awful lot of stuff that just ain't so, especially in the realms of economics and political science. My senior thesis started out on the concept of decline in Western civilization. I ended up writing on Gustav Stresemann and the Treaty of Locarno. I did drugs for a while, attended demonstrations and riots, watched friends self-destruct, and laughed along with everyone else at a comic strip in the *Yale Daily News*, drawn by a classmate and known first as "Bull Tales," then commercially as "Doonesbury." It helped us make sense of the age.

But the personal sense-making process was most enhanced by a pair of books by Yale faculty. One appeared in 1965, the other in 1970. The first, I read before I arrived, the second, after I left. The first I read because I'd seen an extract of it in the *Yale Alumni* magazine, down at the Pittsburgh Yale Club

(Harvard Yale Princeton Club, actually; they shared the same building and mortgage) while I was waiting for an alumni interview. I read the second while recovering from a training injury in the Marines, mostly because I'd known something about how the book came to be written. At the time of my initial encounter, both filled me with disgust. Decades later, they explained a great deal about how and why the so-called Movement of the sixties had taken its peculiar form, and why it had survived that decade to corrupt American life ever since.

In 1965, Yale psychologist Kenneth Keniston came out with a book entitled *The Uncommitted: Alienated Youth in American Society*. He'd done a study of that most representative of all youthful cohorts, Harvard undergraduates. No one from my high school class went to Harvard, even though all had gotten mail from the admissions office. But as I read the book, I saw the kids I'd grown up with. The type was familiar, yet their motivations were still opaque. I wanted to know more.

In Keniston's formulation, "Alienation, once seen as imposed *on* men by an unjust economic system, is increasingly chosen *by* men as their basic stance toward society." The most deeply alienated were also the most privileged. In this case, they were a new psychosocial category called "youth"—privileged with affluence, opportunity, and an extended period of young adulthood without responsibility.

Ortega's Mass Man at Harvard. Civilization, automatic and self-perpetuating, its benefits there for the taking. But according to the alienated, there wasn't a whole lot there worth taking or defending, or even bothering about. With the single exception of stuff—the cars, the stereos, the rest of the young adult package—it was all so what's-the-point?

But alienation, according to Keniston, involved far more than mere youthful irresponsibility, or even the time-honored ennui of the privileged poseur. Alienation was a way of organizing one's personality or, to borrow a word not much in use back then, one's character:

> *Central to alienation is a deep and pervasive distrust of any and all commitments, be they to other people, to groups, to American culture, even to the self. . . . they see the world, the state of the universe, as causing and justifying their own pessimism.*

But also: ". . . the scorn which the alienated feel for most of their fellows is equaled by their contempt for themselves."

Nasty business, this alienation, this being stuck in a world so unworthy of you. That there might be a connection between despising the world and despising oneself, that despising oneself might be the price one pays for despising the world, the author conceded but chose not to ponder too deeply. However, Keniston saw at least a glimmer of hope.

> *But if the alienated lack clear affirmative goals and values, they nonetheless share a common search in a similar direction . . . . Among their goals are honesty, direct confrontation with unpleasant truth, unflinching awareness of evil—implicit in their rejection of pretense, hypocrisy, self-blinding rationalizations, and self-serving defenses.*
>
> *What they want . . . has to do with awareness, passion, faithfulness to experience, with pleasure and intimacy, with "circumscribing my life as little as possible." It has to do with being an individual who stands solitary against his society, unmoved by it, retaining his freedom and autonomy whatever its pressures. And finally, for many it has to do with complexity of person, with being able to express what they feel about life with creativity.*

Unfortunately, the alienated seemed so consumed by angst and free-floating anger that they consistently undercut their own goals:

> *With no criterion for selecting* the *targets, everything becomes a potential target. . . . Among the alienated, "commitment is submission," all claims are destructive.* Freedom is a burden.

For young men and women such as these, a Movement protesting a war such as Vietnam would prove an ideal exercise in—what shall we call it? Authenticity? Commitment? The politics of feeling good about yourself? The quest for an unearned moral stature? Three years later, Keniston would be writing, in tones of shock, awe, and admiration, of the new crop of young radicals:

> *To these young men and women, then, being a radical means many things. It of course means a general commitment to the general goals and tactics of the New Left. But for all, this commitment is more personal and moral than dogmatic or formally ideological.*
> *. . . Being a radical means a commitment to others, to a Movement "in motion," and to some kind of effort to create a viable radicalism in America . . . being a radical meant being open to an indeterminate future.*

And, of course: " . . . the inseparability of the personal, especially the interpersonal, and the political is underlined . . ."

Kenneth Keniston's beatification of the New Left—the redemption of the alienated, the potential salvation of America—did not long survive the sixties, or the realization that much of it served to mask self-interest, cowardice, and worse.

He moved on to other issues at other universities. Charlie Reich wasn't that lucky.

Charlie Reich. Everybody who knew him, and everybody who didn't, called him Charlie. It fit.

Charlie Reich taught at Yale Law School, but by the latter sixties, was something of a fixture at the Morse and Ezra Stiles dining halls. Yale, by way of explanation, operates on the English residential college system. Morse and Stiles Colleges are the university's Siamese twins, sixties-modern and macabre, Eero Saarinen architecture at its least livable, joined at the dining halls by a common kitchen. Whenever students in one college got sufficiently irritated with the cuisine, they would protest by dining in the other.

At first, Reich's presence seemed normal. Younger faculty often ate with students, or shared the midmorning coffee and donut fest. Reich was not young. I recall a slender, forty-something man, awkward and lonely and self-conscious, but also happy among the undergraduates he attracted. They seemed to be giving him a kind of companionship he'd found unavailable or unattainable among his peers. Rumor was, he was writing some kind of book that would provide the anthem, the battle cry, the program of the Movement. Junior faculty often hung out to avoid going back to their manuscripts. When Charlie Reich got together with his undergraduates, it seemed that they were working on his book together.

The Greening of America appeared in the fall of 1970, just as the bottom fell out of the Movement. The collapse was neither unexpected nor unpredictable. Five years is a long time to sustain anything on a college campus. People tire, drift away, sometimes even graduate. And Nixon had done his work well. America was coming out of Vietnam. The shift to a lottery-based conscription system, in which your liability was determined at random and lasted only one year, defused a lot of protest, especially since draft calls were dropping precipitously. The Kent State massacre had also made its point. And America had finally turned against the war, having sometime before turned against the people who were against the war.

And in the spring of that year, Yale had gotten sucked into the vortex . . . almost. Black Panther Bobby Seale was on trial for murder in New Haven. By that time, most of the Panther leadership was dead, in prison, or in exile. Now the remnants were living on campus. A mass meeting at the school hockey rink led to a vote on whether to support them. The vote ended, ludicrously, in a tie. Less ludicrous was Nixon's plan to tear up the campus, should the planned May Day rally get out of control. The Guard was out, the Army on alert. Nixon meant it. The May Day rally didn't get out of control. A couple decades later, I was reminiscing with a Georgetown colleague who'd been a grad student at the time. What did we do during those demonstrations? "I was a marshal," said my colleague, a Jesuit priest. "And you?" "I was a thug."

But *The Greening of America* was not about the fading Vietnam endeavor, which Reich considered only one aspect of America's self-damnation. It wasn't even about protest, however important that might be. His concern was "Revolution by Consciousness."

"There is a revolution coming," he wrote.

> *It will not be like revolutions of the past. It will originate with the individual and with culture, and it will change the political structure only as its final act. It will not require violence to succeed, and it cannot be successfully resisted by violence. It is now spreading with amazing rapidity, and already our laws, institutions and social structure are changing in consequence.*

It promises a higher reason, a more human community, and a new and liberated individual. Its ultimate creation will be a new and enduring wholeness and beauty—a renewed relationship of man to himself, to other men, to society, to nature, and to the land.

This is the revolution of the new generation. Their protest and rebellion, their culture, clothes, music, drugs, ways of thought and liberated lifestyle are not a passing fad . . .

For Charlie Reich, everything hinged on Self.

Of all the forms of impoverishment that can be seen or felt in America, loss of self, or death in life, is surely the most devastating. It is, even more than the draft and the Vietnam War, the source of discontent and rage in the new generation.

The elders, they who had survived the Depression, won a World War, and crafted a postwar world of unparalleled affluence, might be numbed beyond resuscitation and trivial beyond redemption. But the new generation would no longer tolerate "a universal sense of powerlessness" and a malaise of "living in a society that no one created and that no one wants."

The way to change the world, he concluded, is to live differently. The route to a new and different life he called "Consciousness III." Unlike the traditional Consciousness I or the industrial/technological/bureaucratic Consciousness II, Consciousness III "starts with self." It's not for those willing to abandon real life for "the prospect of a dreary corporate job, a ranch-house life, or a miserable death in war." Rather, Consciousness III is about "liberation" from all that.

Consciousness III starts with self. . . . The first commandment is: thou shalt do no violence to thyself. . . . It is a crime to be alienated from oneself . . . Consciousness III rejects the whole

concept of excellence and comparative merit . . . III also rejects
relationships of authority and subservience . . . [and] looks with
suspicion on "obligations" . . .

In sum, Charlie Reich had taken Keniston's concept of alienation, exalted it to the level of a secular messianism, and pro-
posed that it be made a permanent, revolutionary fixture of
American life.

It didn't quite work out that way politically. But culturally,
the pose stuck, and forty years of self-indulgent absurdity got
underway: the quest for an unearned moral stature based, not
upon real-world risks and accomplishments, but upon inner
emotional states and the flaunting thereof.

In the fall of 1970, a quiet purge began at Yale. Teachers who'd
been too active in the Movement, too eager to trash the institution, were given to understand that they might start looking
elsewhere for employment. Yale President Kingman Brewster,
who'd done a magnificent job of keeping the place from
exploding but incurred major alumni wrath in the process,
offered to auction off his resignation. Yale Law School alum
Gerald Ford, in one of his first acts as president, finally got him
off campus by naming him ambassador to the Court of St. James.
At some point, Charlie Reich departed. In 1976, now living in
California, he published a second book, *The Sorcerer of Bolinas
Reef.* Still enamored of "Revolution by Consciousness," he wrote:

Because of the nature of the forces we are opposing, the only
valid form for a political movement today, I believe, is one that
integrates personal growth with the search for political change.
. . . Such a movement would rest upon a radical, revolu-
tionary epistemology which declares that our feelings are
factual truth." [Emphasis added.]

The book made no impression, and Charlie Reich disappeared until 1995, when *The Greening of America* was reissued
for its 25th anniversary, along with his new book, *Opposing the
System*. I was asked to review it for the *Washington Times*. I read
the first few pages.

"We have lost the ability to imagine a better future," he
wrote. "We are fighters who cannot find the enemy even as
we suffer its blows. . . . We are burdened with a *"false map of
reality"* and a *"lack of social self-knowledge."* [Emphasis in the
original.]

Poor Charlie. Then I reread *The Greening of America* and
decided to do a phone interview. It was not a pleasant conversation, least of all when I suggested that many of his prophecies
concerning "Revolution by Consciousness" had in fact come
true. "Nothing has changed," he snarled. When I pressed him
a bit on the "cultural politics" of later decades, he answered,
"I'm starting to get mad." Remembering that happy/sad figure
of three decades before, I decided not to press him. He'd
believed too fervently, he'd needed too much. He'd known too
much pain. Leave him alone.

★   ★   ★

It is said that if you can remember the sixties too clearly, you
may have missed the last helicopter out. And if you believe that
the sixties vanished without a trace, that it ended when all those
radicals went to law school, and corporate America discovered
(to borrow a marketing cliché of that era) how to "cash in on
the cop-out," and that nothing had changed, for better or for
worse . . .

It is said that America has no real sense of history, only nos-
talgia. We do not learn from the past; we recycle it. We reduce

it to styles, to glimpses and snippets, to nothing that could make any kind of binding claim upon us. Perhaps it's because we know that those who take it too seriously—especially the pasts that they themselves have lived—get hurt.

Poor Charlie.

Chapter 4

The Corps

Now, as then, Vietnam and its legacy matter only as part of something else.

—Philip Gold

"**R**EBELS OUT OF WEAKNESS."
Thus ran sociologist Philip Rieff's definition of neurotics. By this standard, so much of the Movement was neurotic indeed. Privileged young men and women in sustained revolt against the war, the nation, each other, themselves. The putative Best and Brightest deluding themselves into believing that if they just threw a big enough tantrum, if they just did enough drugs or had enough sex or played enough loud music, the world would yield to their wishes. So did much of the rest of America view it at the time, as a tantrum, and little more. So does much of the Right still view it today, especially those who regard the sixties as the source of all of America's current evils—another fine example of missing the last helicopter out. And even Todd Gitlin, former president of the SDS (Students for a Democratic Society), one of the decade's archetypal radicals, and now a fine and thoughtful sociologist, has given the tantrum notion a certain credibility. In his 1995 lamentation, *The Twilight of Common Dreams*, he wrote of that era, and of its most vociferous protesters:

It is important to be clear about what this [radical Left] anti-Americanism of the time was and was not. It was a sentiment more than a commitment, a loathing more than a theory, a yelp of anguish more than an ideology. It was built upon disappointment—the crashing of a liberal faith in American goodness, and, as a result, the turning of that faith upside down. . . .

A sympathetic though critical onlooker, someone possessed of a large and not punitive vision, might have discerned the rage of the rejected child pleading to be let in and loved—a plea that America be refashioned, in fact, so that an outsider might find an honorable place. But the populace who recoiled were not large of vision. Their Americanness was too narrow, too resentful, too negative of itself to permit commiseration with rebels.

Perhaps. But these were neither children nor outsiders. Nor were they rejected. They were privileged. As for them being "Let in and loved"—they already were in. The problem was, they'd deemed the love of their elders, and of their country, not worth having. And whatever else the rest of America might have been, it's hard to commiserate with people who keep telling you what garbage you are. No, these were rebels out of weakness, both the weakness of their own position as youth and the weakness of their refusal to employ the one power they did possess. And because they did not use it, and chose not to face the implications of their choice, the game they played with themselves and with America was rendered more dreary, more destructive, and more lasting than it should have been.

When teaching the sixties at Georgetown University, I sometimes gave my students an exercise in viewing the Vietnam War and the Movement as mirror-image universes, identical in their willful inability to get it right. The first part of the exercise took up a military matter, as defined in Col. Harry Summers's classic,

On Strategy: A Critical Analysis of the Vietnam War. If you're serious about winning the war, what do you do? Any competent sergeant, probably even most generals, can give you the obvious answer. At the start of the war, you seal off South Vietnam by moving the borders outward, into Laos, Cambodia, perhaps into North Vietnam. You mine and blockade Haiphong harbor to cut off the flow of Soviet supplies. You shut down the railroad running south from China. You keep it shut down. You bomb the critical North Vietnamese targets, perhaps including the Red River dikes. You attack until there's nothing left to do but to make the rubble bounce. Then, with significant but nonetheless limited American ground forces, the South Vietnamese go after the Viet Cong in a sustained but leisurely manner. And you never forget that, in the end, it's their war. We're just visiting.

Would it have worked? Hard to say. Predicting the past can be tricky. What is clear is that we adopted an utterly different and far less effective strategy of large-scale ground operations, massive firepower and endless civilian casualties in the South, and "bombing as communication" * up North. Ninety percent

---

* Early in the war, McNamara and his Whiz Kids adopted a strategy in which critical targets were ignored, and air strikes and bombing pauses used to "send messages." If we started bombing closer to Hanoi, for example, that indicated we were getting tough. If we backed off a few miles, that meant we were open to negotiation. By this theory, what you bombed mattered less than that you were demonstrating your resolve. Risking American lives to bomb unnecessary or previously flattened targets was, under this theory, acceptable. The problem was never that the North Vietnamese didn't "get the message." They got the message, then kept coming. Only at the very end of the war, through a combination of B-52 strikes and use of rudimentary precision-guided munitions, did we really go after the critical targets. After he returned from the Hanoi Hilton, Jim Stockdale did a little exercise, comparing treatment of the prisoners with the severity of American bombing. He found a direct correlation—the more aggressive and effective the bombing, the better the treatment.

of the bombs we dropped fell on the country we were defending, and perhaps there is no greater example of this strange fact than the types of aircraft used. "Strategic" aircraft, notably B-52 bombers, were used liberally on the South, but not until 1972 were they used on the North. Meanwhile, "tactical" aircraft hit Northern "strategic" targets because their greater accuracy lessened collateral damage. Ironically, with the single exception of moving the border into North Vietnam via an amphibious landing in the Vinh region, everything we should have done at the beginning, we did—temporarily and ineffectually—on the way out.

Inevitably, the military part of the exercise generated a student question. If the "school solution" was so obvious, and everything we did was so at variance with getting it right, what other factors and agendas were at work? The class then went through everything from political constraints vis-à-vis the Soviet Union and China, to the assorted delusions of Defense Secretary McNamara and his defense intellectuals, to the desired postwar structures and inventories of the services. And it turned out that things that made absolutely no sense along the banks of the Mekong could make a great deal of sense along the banks of the Potomac.

The next question pertained to the Movement, and the kids discovered that things that made absolutely no sense along the banks of the Mekong, or the Potomac down around Capitol Hill, could make a great deal of sense along the banks of the Potomac up at liberal Georgetown. If you're serious about stopping the war, what do you do? If you know that the president won't pull out, and Congress won't cut off funds, and the Supreme Court won't touch it, what do you do?

The obvious answer: You go to jail. For real. You don't just get yourself arrested at some recreational protest, then bailed out a few hours later, so you can maybe make a few bucks in the class-action lawsuit later, then spend the rest of your life bragging about it. You turn in your II-S student deferment (it was automatic for undergraduates, but nobody forced you to take it). You demand accelerated induction, a procedure available to those who wished to get it over with, but also to those with other goals. Then, at the ceremony, you refuse to take the "one step forward" that indicates your consent to serve. Legally, you cannot be drafted against your will. You remain a civilian. Then you go to civilian prison as part of a serious Movement that says to the nation:

> *This war is wrong. We are not going to let the government buy us off.* For every American, for every one of our brothers who comes back in a body bag, one of us, or five or ten, will go to prison. And we'll keep it up, we'll fill the jails and stay there, until it stops.

Would it have worked? Hard to say. Predicting the past can be tricky. What is clear is that it never happened, never had a chance of happening. To repeat: Out of 26.8 million draft-age men, only 3,250 went to prison for all draft-related offenses, including but not limited to conscientious refusal to accept induction. And it is worthy of note that 6,431 women served in Vietnam. *Nearly twice as many American women went to Vietnam as American men went to prison.* This near total failure of the Movement to act in the only sustained and effective manner available, to demonstrate sincerity and commitment by putting its members in harm's way, had two baleful consequences.

One was the need of millions of young men and their women (Girls Say Yes to Guys Who Say No) to evade the facts and implications of their choices. Whatever the war, draft-dodging is draft-dodging. And whatever else might be said of reserve and National Guard service back then, these were not evasions of military obligation. Fear is natural; cowardice is a response to fear. That's hard to face. If you don't care to face something that you know you ought to face, what do you do? Millions constructed elaborate intellectual theories, justifying their draft-dodging and cowardice, and then proclaiming their righteousness and their virtue with all the vehemence available to them. This proved a considerable quantity of vehemence. Then it all got liberally larded with intellectual and pseudo-intellectual justifications, histrionics, and cant.

But there was more. People need to feel right about themselves. Not just good, but right. But unearned moral stature can be a brittle thing. And to this day, so many millions neither question what they did nor permit others to do so. For if they did, the whole shaky cathedral of self-righteousness might crumble. And they know it.

The other sad consequence was that the sixties established a style of politics still very much with us. Charlie Reich was, in his own abysmally mistimed way, a Malachi. The changes wrought in American politics by a consciousness that "starts with self" and accepts "feelings as facts" have been enormous. The hyperbolic accusing and the hypertrophic condemnations of the Blame-America-First crowd, the tawdry, treacly Politics of Feeling Good About Yourself we have had very much with us ever since. Sociologist Peter Clecak recognized this in another fashion, in his 1983 book, *America's Quest for the Ideal Self*. Dissent, he wrote, had become a form of therapy and part of the quest for personal fulfillment. What you dissented about mattered less than that you did it. If one cause ceased to gratify, for whatever reason, there were plenty of others.

How far has this gone, this redefinition of truth as emotive state, and morality as whatever makes you feel good and right about yourself? The Culture War that began in the sixties, took complex form in the seventies, and ran on until the mid-nineties, coincided with an intellectual movement known as postmodernism. This too was a complex movement, and far from entirely negative. But it was also a movement that could not be separated from the notion that America is the source of all the world's evils. The same people partook of both. Post-modernism meant—past-tense, we're in the post-post-modern era now, or so we're told—many things. Indeed, it prided itself on its resistance to classification. But there was a leitmotif. In her 1991 study, *Post-Modernism and the Social Sciences*, Pauline Rosenau named it: the belief that "truth claims are a form of terrorism. They threaten and provoke. Truth, by its very existence, is said to silence those who disagree."

And it really doesn't matter if I'm wrong, I'm right . . .

It is human nature to wish to avoid facing hard facts, especially about yourself. To some extent, all civilizations run on lies, or at least arbitrary conventions. Sometimes these conventions are wrongly called truth. But only with the postmodernism that the baby boom did so much to spawn and tried so hard to live, could truth, indeed all truth about everything, be dismissed, denied, and damned, precisely because the category itself silenced "those who disagree."

And who were these people who made their style—and it really doesn't matter if I'm wrong, I'm right—so much a part of our politics ever since the sixties? Rosenau describes those who bought into and still buy into the postmodernist package:

The postmodern individual is characterized by an absence of strong singular identity. . . . S/he is a floating individual with no distinct reference points or parameters. . . . . S/he relinquishes all normative assumptions, any possibility that one value or moral norm can ever be demonstrated to be better than any other. . . . Postmodern individuals are comfortable with personalized politics. . . . S/he is open to participation and recruitment in diverse and contradictory causes and social movements with fleeting existences. . . .

What future awaits the postmodern individual? There are good reasons to worry about him/her.

On or about 1970, Vietnam ceased to gratify. Commitment turned out to be just one more transient experience, perhaps to be recycled, more wearily and more warily, for later wars. The disagreements go on, in accordance with the great principle of the postmodernist literary theory that drove eminent literary critic and author Alvin Kernan out of the business:

"All readings are equivalent."

Strictly speaking, we did not lose the Vietnam War. We weren't there to lose. In fact, by 1970, we'd won. All that firepower, all those search-and-destroy missions, had done their job. Crudely, cruelly, hideously, they'd done their job. The Tet Offensive of 1968 decimated the Viet Cong. The 1969 American offensives finished the job, and the North Vietnamese were thereafter reduced to desultory conventional warfare plus occasional major attacks—sending a new crop of nineteen-year-olds south every few years. The 1972 Easter Offensive demonstrated that the South Vietnamese, backed by American air power, could hold their own. When the North launched the final 1975 offensive, a sixteen-division operation that could have been planned by General Patton, the B-52s could have ended that endeavor in a day or two. Both President Ford and Secretary Kissinger, to borrow a line from a famous Herman Melville short story, "Bartleby the Scrivener," said, "I would prefer not." Congress debated an aid package until it no longer mattered; there was no country left to aid. Our attempt to use Vietnam to demonstrate our resolve ended up demonstrating the opposite. And the phenomenon of the "boat people," hundreds of thousands over the next few decades, began.

We'll never know how many boat people tried to flee, or how many died at sea. We do, however, have an idea of the number of boat people prior to the fall of South Vietnam. There is a commonly accepted statistic. Zero. Not one. In all the years of all the bombs and napalm and free fire zones and search-and-destroy, not one. Apparently, the capitalist imperialist racist genocidal war was more easily endured than the people's peace.

But it didn't matter to us, by then, whether South Vietnam survived or not. Perhaps it never had mattered. Could South Vietnam have become another South Korea? Perhaps. Could American air power in 1975 have bought a long-term remission? Probably. But we'll never know. And anyway, predicting the past can be tricky.

As a matter of policy, of prudential calculation, the Vietnam War was indefensible. This was because Vietnam was a place of no intrinsic significance to the United States. It mattered only as part of something else, however that something else be defined. As part of the Cold War. As part of American electoral politics. As part of a quest for unearned moral stature and "personal growth" via protest. It was often noted, then and now, that when people argued—and argue—about Vietnam, they rarely seem to be discussing the same thing. That's because they were not, and are not. Now as then, Vietnam and its legacy matter only as part of something else.

Vietnam was not a conservative war, no more than military service back then was a litmus test of conservative beliefs. But conservatism carries a heavy share of the responsibility for creating an environment in which liberal agendas could lead to foreign war. No, there were no conservative crowds in the streets, chanting "Nuke em til they glow!" any more than, a few decades later, there were American mobs shouting "Death to Saddam!" But conservatism's incessant yammering, the whole self-indulgent, "Stand up to the Commies" mentality (not to mention the then-still-recent memory of Joe McCarthy) created a political environment in which foreign losses, no matter how trivial, could have major domestic repercussions.

For all the blather, conservatism had scant real desire to go to war in or for Vietnam. And once the decisions were made, they had scant desire to help Lyndon Johnson, but every reason to "support" his war as he and his war and his Great Society sank into the morass. Ironically, for much of the Right, supporting the war while doing the *Why Not Victory?* shtik, could seem a dandy way both to stand up to the Commies and stand down LBJ.

Ike might have gotten us into the war. He didn't. When John Kennedy succeeded him, there were 685 American military advisers in Vietnam, the number permitted by the 1954 Geneva Accords, plus the usual unofficial coming and going. When Kennedy died, there were over 16,000, perhaps considerably more, routinely going into combat. Had he lived, Kennedy might have folded the war during his second term. He'd often talked about what he could do when he no longer had to worry about reelection, or calibrate what it took to keep the right-wing crazies quiet. Barry Goldwater might have taken a good hard look at the situation, as befits the World War II pilot and Air Force reserve general he was, and either given up or nuked Hanoi. We'll never know, but I rather suspect he'd have chosen the former.

What we do know is that Lyndon Johnson made the vital decisions, and for purposes peculiarly his own.

In 1984, an obscure cultural historian and university bureaucrat named Loren Baritz brought out a book entitled, somewhat awkwardly, *Backfire: A History of How American Culture Led Us into Vietnam and Made Us Fight the Way We Did*. Like so many brilliant books coming from unexpected quarters, it never received the attention it deserves. I found it on the remainder shelf of a Georgetown bookstore, read it with fascination, then put it away until the decision-making process he described revived, this time under George W. Bush. For Baritz, we got into Vietnam the way we did, and fought it the way we did, and left it the way we did, simply because we were us. As he summed it:

> . . . *our national myth showed us that we were good, our technology made us strong, and our bureaucracy gave us standard operating procedures. It was not a winning combination.*

Our national myth, like most myths, held its truths. We were a good and generous people, sincerely ready to protect the Vietnamese, build them a nice new, proudly anticommunist country, make them more like us. Making others more like us has always been a staple of the American way. "American nationalism in its purest form," wrote Baritz, "thinks of the world as populated by frustrated or potential Americans." We would give them the greatest gift within our power: a chance to become our little brothers and sisters, by force of arms if necessary. "American nationalism," he noted, "especially when its fist clenched, went forward not to pillage, but to instruct."

Why was it so important that we offer them this chance? Because of all the "something(s) else."

By 1956, the year the United States formally replaced the French in South Vietnam, America had long been accustomed to the notion that, in the Cold War, everything mattered. We could no longer distinguish between primary and secondary interests and objectives, and "something else" was the mental process by which we did the obfuscations. "A defeat anywhere is a defeat everywhere," Paul Nitze, author of NSC-68, had proclaimed. Ike reified that notion with the "domino theory"—if South Vietnam falls, Southeast Asia falls. If Southeast Asia falls . . .

John Kennedy also played dominos, but his were as much psychological as physical. Nineteen sixty-one had not been a good year for Camelot—the Bay of Pigs, the Berlin Wall, Khrushchev's adroit bullying of the young president at the Vienna summit. Returning from that mess, Kennedy famously told *New York Times* reporter James Reston that he had to start looking tough somewhere, and Vietnam seemed a likely place.

There began a high level decision-making process that can only be described as bizarre. We knew then, and we certainly know now, that nobody believed a war in Vietnam would be either cheap or easy. Nobody was being misled. And nobody wanted a war, least of all a Pentagon whose major interest and source of budgetary justification was Europe. Like Ike, Kennedy was determined to do the minimum necessary to keep South Vietnam viable. Unlike Ike, he had, or felt he had, a few things to prove to the world about his toughness. Ike did his minimum in classic fifties style: a mix of strident rhetoric, modest open commitment, and clandestine activity of considerable amplitude. Ike was also lucky. The insurgency in the South didn't get serious on his watch.

But by 1962, the minimum necessary to hang on to South

Vietnam, and keep the Right from howling, was far from minimal. So was the price of impressing a Soviet Union that was more than happy to be impressed by watching America squander itself among the mountains and paddies. JFK did his minimum deftly. Over and over, carefully placed leaks would allude to an imminent crisis in Vietnam. War, likely, was at hand. There would be the usual crisis photo-ops—grim-faced men getting out of their limos, striding down corridors with briefcases containing God-knows-what, sitting at conferences with the commander in chief. Then the announcement would be made: only a few thousand more advisers, only a few changes in the rules of engagement. Everyone was so relieved—war had been avoided—that few noticed just how much the "minimum" for getting through the 1964 election really was.

Then came LBJ, who needed to neutralize Vietnam as an election issue. So he had McGeorge Bundy draft up a "fill in the blanks" resolution for Congress to rubber-stamp at the appropriate moment. On August 2, 1964, an American destroyer, the *USS Maddox* on an intelligence-gathering mission in the Gulf of Tonkin, was attacked by North Vietnamese patrol boats. In all probability, the attack was a mistake. They may have thought they were attacking American-sponsored South Vietnamese special operations boats, which had been raiding the North Vietnamese coast for some time. Certainly, they had nothing to gain by such a deliberate provocation. At any rate, on August 4, the White House received word that two American destroyers operating in that area were under attack. The second attack never happened. The *Maddox* and the *Turner Joy* were probably tracking friendly commando boats and mistaking them for enemy craft. Johnson knew there had been no attack. He had been told. Jim Stockdale had flown in both incidents, and had reported that the second was a false alarm. Jim then went to bed, only to be awakened to lead the first "retaliatory" air strike on North Vietnam. LBJ announced it on television as the planes were en route. He then got Congress to adopt his fill-in-the-blanks form as the Tonkin Gulf Resolution—an act of congressional cowardice and unconstitutional abdication that probably would have met the requirements of the War Powers Act, which Congress subsequently adopted to prevent further Tonkin Gulf-style resolutions such as those that authorized both wars against Iraq.

Vietnam was neutralized as a 1964 campaign issue. LBJ had indeed stood up to the Commies. He also stood up to the Commies in early 1965 by adopting a policy of "sustained reprisal"—bombing North Vietnam would no longer be tied to particular incidents—and by landing Marines. By midyear, he faced the crisis that his predecessors had finessed for so long: whether to commit major American air and ground forces to a protracted war. It was not a propitious moment. Nineteen sixty-five was to be the year that Johnson's Great Society effloresced its way through Congress. Disaster abroad would wreck his hopes for domestic reform. So once again, Vietnam mattered only as part of something else. We went to war to buy time for all the social legislation to get through Congress. In the end, the "commit" decision was made, not out of any overwhelming military or geostrategic necessity, or even in response to any clear and present danger, but for the sake of voting rights and civil rights, day care centers, adult literacy classes, Medicare and Medicaid . . . and Lyndon Johnson's desire to go down in history as the man who finished what FDR began.

It was a Democratic decision, the work of men who, in Baritz's phrase, "did not know how to win, but could not conceive of losing." Or maybe they did know how to win, but since they were just buying time, later could sort itself out later.

Lyndon Johnson didn't want to go to war in Vietnam. It was not a decision that he or any Democratic president would have made, or could have made, without enormous conservative pressure. Not pressure to go to war, but pressure to . . . what? The Republicans, and conservatives in general, did not want war in Vietnam. But too many years of too much conservative lecturing and hectoring and *Why Not Victory?* had determined the contours of American politics and ordained one of the great political truths of that era. It's dangerous to get those folks too riled up, to hand them issues, to lose anything, anywhere. They may be crazy. They may know nothing about military matters. They may not even be able to read a map. But politically, they can hurt you.

And indeed, those folks, those conservative war hawks, hurt America by their duplicity, by their constant opposition to all things communist without a clear sense of what, in any given situation, could or could not be done. Yes, communism was evil. Yes, we were right to oppose it. But conservatism failed utterly to calibrate this opposition by the art of prudential calculation. Military action could be morally right yet also not worth the cost of doing—a calculation that did not require stars on your shoulders or a PhD on your wall. And conservatism was wrong, utterly wrong, to reduce the American worldview to "It's us against them and you're with us or you're against us," and to ignore the legitimate concerns and grievances of the rest of the planet.

And conservatism would make the same mistakes, over and over again, in the Culture War.

In the end, anticommunist conservatives must share the blame for Vietnam, not as decision makers, but as irresponsible zealots utterly lacking in one of conservatism's most prized qualities: prudence—the art of applying general principles to specific situations. And it may be suggested that a conservatism of *aretē*, or at least of clear-sighted prudential calculation, might have been a bit less prone to such self-delusion. Once the war began, conservatives fell victim to a particularly tawdry opportunism. Vietnam proved a splendid issue for them, indeed. They did not, they did not have to, "defend" the war or offer any real alternatives. All they had to do was complain about how it wasn't being waged aggressively enough. And when it became apparent that there was a resentment building across the country, a resentment directed both at the Democratic pols and at a Movement that opposed the war with such offensive self-righteousness, and that this resentment offered enormous political opportunities, conservatives were only too happy to have at it. And there began four decades of reducing domestic reality to "It's us against them and damn the issues, you're either for us or against us."

For conservatives, too, Vietnam mattered only as part of something else.

In the sixties, any conservatism worthy of the name would have opposed the Vietnam War as imprudent, unnecessary, and tragic. But by then, the old "Taft Conservatives," a cautious faction led by former Ohio Senator Robert Taft, had faded. Conservatism chose instead a response of self-serving hypocrisy, and in so doing betrayed two of its cardinal virtues, aristocracy and prudence. And it betrayed another when it signed on with Richard Nixon's exploitation of the nastier aspects of the so-called "Silent Majority" (a phrase that, back in Edmund Burke's time, referred to the dead). And how they loved it when Mr. Nixon took to muttering about "the bums who are burning the books," and his designated rhetorical hit man, Vice President Spiro Agnew, did his vaudeville impression of statesmanship by castigating the "nattering nabobs of negativism" and the "effete corps of impudent snobs" who just couldn't seem to get with the program, whatever that program might be.

A conservatism of *aretē* would not have accepted, much less gloried, in this. But the pattern was set. Henceforward, the conservative approach to cultural and social issues would emphasize, not the aristocratic aspects of tolerance and noblesse oblige, and certainly not a principled willingness to face America's manifold injustices and needs. It would pander to the resentments of the masses. It was sad.

I entered Yale in September 1966. By the end of that first semester, I sensed that something was profoundly wrong. Over time, I realized that, in fact, two things were wrong. One was the quest for unearned moral stature on the part of so many of my generation, a quest that established a pattern. The other was conservatism's unwillingness, indeed inability, to offer any serious critique or alternative, beyond pandering. By 1970, I was convinced that, in the long run, the people who were against the war would do more political and cultural harm to this country than the war itself, tragic though it was. And I was also aware that, in some vague way, conservatism was gearing up to do some harm of its own. I tried discussing it with conservative friends, teachers, almost anyone I could engage. But by 1970, everybody was tired. And I guess I wasn't making much sense. That, plus it wasn't a good year for that kind of prophecy.

Then my government made me an offer I could have refused, but chose not to.

Richard Nixon and Teddy Kennedy may not have been all that *simpatico* personally, but from time to time they got together on something. Those who love managed health care can thank them for the HMO Act of 1973. But they got it right at least once when they decided to deep-six the draft.

One of the greatest mistakes of the Vietnam era was to stay with a system of conscription designed to keep as many people out of uniform as possible. The draft established after Korea operated on the correct assumption that, for the next twenty years, there would be far more bodies available than requirements. So the Selective Service System morphed into an exercise in social engineering, offering deferments for all kinds of desirable activities: college, grad school, marriage, babies, and so on. This was known as "channeling," and should not be confused with the New Age practice of communing with the Silent Majority. A man could be drafted up to age twenty-six, with the oldest taken first. But prior to the war it was relatively easy to string together enough deferments to reach that magic birthday and then move on.

Lyndon Johnson chose to fight the war with this deferment-riddled system. He did so deliberately, as one way, along with not raising taxes and not mobilizing the reserves, of buying off the middle class. On his watch, there was some tightening, perhaps most notably the abolition of grad school deferments, but the system and its inequities remained. And soon enough, How to Beat the Draft handbooks were making great stocking stuffers. By the latter sixties, practically no white, middle-class college kid willing to invest the time need have been inconvenienced by the draft. And with a little research, you could learn how to manipulate the system; how to weasel in the right words on your application for that coveted conscientious objector exemption; how to keep the appeals process from losing its appeal. You knew where to find the dentists who would put antiwar braces on your teeth; the shrinks and priests who would certify, according to need, your insanity or/and your sincerity; even how to parley that trivial antiwar riot arrest into a crime sufficiently felonious to keep you out of the Army but not out of law school.

By 1969, however, America was increasingly fed up with the draft. So Dick and Teddy decided to substitute a lottery-based system. You went into the lottery for one year only. A random drawing of birthdays determined your chance of being drafted. In the drawing for 1970, if your birthday didn't come up in the first hundred or so, you were probably safe. A friend of mine, having received a very low number, called his mother and cursed her out for a solid fifteen minutes. It seems he'd been an on-towards-midnight cesarean delivery, and if they'd just waited a few more minutes, he would have had #355 or some such.

I drew #72, ominous for a guy whose local board covered a very affluent neighborhood, perpetually short of fodder. Still, I knew I had one option. I was IV-F, medically unfit and permanently exempt, due to a documented lifetime history of asthma, hay fever, assorted other allergies, fifteen years of shots, drug dependencies, and a sad propensity toward sneezing fits at inopportune moments.

I pondered the situation for some weeks. Then, in the spring of my senior year, I did what I always knew I would. Fortified by my beliefs that the Movement was doing serious long-term harm, and some vague sense that I had to take a stand, and having ascertained that neither the Navy nor the Air Force wanted me, I offered myself to the Marines.

The Marines were not especially impressed with the long-haired Yalie who walked through their recruiting-station door and proclaimed his lifelong intent. First thing the recruiter OSO (Officer Selection Officer) asked me was, "Why didn't you join Navy ROTC and take a Marine commission?"

"Well, sir, I'm entirely self-supporting and have to work during the year. No time."

"You know that the NRO scholarship program also pays a monthly stipend?"

"No, sir. I didn't know that. Anyway, I'm on pretty much full scholarship from the school."

"Well, why didn't you go PLC?"

"PL What?"

The OSO explained that the Marines ran a summer program called Platoon Leaders Class, with no school-year activity.

"Well, sir, I've had to make as much money as possible during the summers so I could continue my education. I was thinking that I would finish school and then go to OCS (Officer Candidate School)."

"Why didn't you come to that meeting when I was on campus a few weeks back?"

"I never heard about it."

(In truth, I had. The OSO, or somebody, had posted some notices in, on, and around the NROTC building that he would be available at 0800 on a specified morning to discuss Marine Corps opportunities with interested students; please contact him to schedule an appointment. The SDS had learned of the impending event and vowed to be there at 0730 to block the door. The OSO had instructed the interested students to be there at 0700, so when the SDS assembled for their direct action, everybody was already upstairs and waving at them from the window. Defeated and depressed, the radicals adjourned for coffee and self-criticism.)

"Well, I do have an OCS quota available. You understand, though, that you probably won't be going to Vietnam."

"Fine by me. Never saw much sense in the war, anyway."

Wrong thing to say. The OSO looked skyward, exhaled, and

began the process. Some days later, down at the local Armed Forces examining station, I found myself checking No on the medical questionnaire for all matters pertaining to asthma, hay fever, and allergies. The entrance physical was based on the premise that, if there was something wrong with you, you'd tell them. They didn't have to look. And if you carried around a large note card with VOLUNTEER written on it in Magic Marker, they hardly bothered to scan you at all.

I took my oath as Nixon invaded Cambodia. I didn't advertise it much, certainly not after the Kent State killings. But several nights later, I found myself chatting with a fellow student who was telling all kinds of lies in order to evade the draft. After listening with considerable feigned sympathy, I mentioned that I also had to lie in order to achieve my purposes. When I told him about my condition, he looked at me with an expression of absolute disgust and said, "You know, I would trade my nuts for your nose." I considered the offer for a moment, then rejected it on the grounds that, even if such a procedure were possible, one and probably both of us would be rendered rather sadly dysfunctional.

Fifteen years later, I was drinking with a Marine buddy who'd played football in college, had very bad knees, and had to get a medical waiver. He mentioned that, as the doctor signed the form, he'd muttered, "You know, there are ten thousand guys on this campus who would trade their nuts for your knees." And then we had it. A new medical specialty. Nuts, Nose, and Knees. To the best of my knowledge, I and Col. Mackubin T. Owens Jr., USMCR (Ret) remain the world's sole practitioners.

But back in 1970, it wasn't quite so funny. When word got out of what I'd done, I lost a couple friends, got into a couple trivial fistfights, drew nasty stares. I even got a phone call from Harvard offering legal help, should I change my mind. When I told them that I wouldn't be changing my mind, the guy responded, "Then fuck you," and hung up.

I didn't change my mind. Not about the inalienable right and obligation of every citizen to defend the country. And certainly not about the Movement. And one Sunday afternoon three months later, I found myself sitting in the then very small and modest lobby of the main terminal at DC's National Airport, awaiting the Marine Corps bus that would take me thirty miles down Interstate 95 to OCS at Quantico, Virginia. As instructed, I'd gotten a shortish haircut. As instructed, I was wearing a sport coat and slacks. As instructed, I had an overnight bag and my orders in a government envelope. Also as instructed, I was scared. Very, very scared.

Gradually, the lobby filled with scared, sport-jacketed young men with shortish haircuts, overnight bags, and government envelopes. There must have been well over a hundred of us. No one talked much. Then around five, a pair of Marine sergeants, two of the nastiest-looking bipeds I'd yet encountered, strode to the middle of the lobby and shouted at the top of their state-of-the-art lungs:

"GET ON THE FUCKING BUS!"

And over a hundred officer candidates and (according to legend) a young insurance salesman who later explained that he "thought this was just some new way of drafting people," got on the fucking bus. I too got on the fucking bus. And the transition from Ivy League Jewish intellectual to officer of Marines, began.

Ten years later, I was a major, doing some reserve duty at the old I MAF (First Marine Amphibious Force) headquarters at Camp Pendleton, then part of Jimmy Carter's ill-conceived, misbegotten, and utterly ludicrous Rapid Deployment Force. Our collective opinion of the RDJTF, officially the Rapid

Deployment Joint Task Force, was best expressed by a cartoon on the wall. It showing a Marine under fire in a landing zone, screaming into a radio while a squad of bunnies hopped down the ramp of a helicopter behind him, with the caption: DAMMIT, I SAID *RAPID* DEPLOYMENT FORCE!

I spent my time there as a good intelligence officer should, reading pointless documents in the air-conditioned comfort of the crypto vault and wondering whether the Pentagon had sent us the joke issue of RDJTF OPLAN 1001 to defend Iran against a Soviet invasion. One morning, while walking through the operations shop, I noticed a rather tired-looking lieutenant colonel sitting at a desk in the corner. I went up, introduced myself, and told him where and how, ten years before, our paths had crossed. His eyes got wide and he exclaimed, "You mean they commissioned you? I was just trying to fill a quota."

Semper Fi, Colonel. Semper Fi.

Chapter 5

Georgetown

In response, conservatism adopted a simple strategy. Whatever the Left was for, they were against.

—Philip Gold

THE UNITED STATES MARINE CORPS is a complex institution. There's an awful lot of stuff you can safely ignore. But a few things, best you take them very seriously.

Chief among the things you must take very seriously—the United States Marine Corps.

The service motto is, as every American ought to know, *Semper Fidelis.* Always Faithful. The meaning is singular and clear. On the other hand, "Semper Fi," the informal expression, has somewhere between eight and fifty-seven separate connotations, depending on situation, tone of voice, and general level of frustration. At the essence of *Semper Fidelis* is one very simple concept: Never surrender. Not to the enemy, whomever that might be. And not to yourself. Failure is abhorrent. Defeat is unacceptable. But quitting is the sin without forgiveness.

The lesson begins on the obstacle course. This is the wall. You will go over the wall. If you cannot go over the wall, you will go through the wall. But you will not go around the wall. The lesson continues in a thousand different ways, for as long as you're a Marine. Since, as the saying goes, "Once a Marine, always a Marine," the lesson continues until you die, at which point you become a dead Marine and the lesson goes on, presumably somewhere else.

Never surrender. Not to the enemy, whomever that might be, in war or in any other endeavor. And never surrender to yourself.

Brute Krulak, a legendary Marine general and father of one of our better commandants, liked to point out that the United States does not have a Marine Corps because we need one. In truth, the Army could take over the job. The United States has a Marine Corps because the American people want one. And they want one because of what it stands for, as well as for what it does.

In the early seventies, however, the national appreciation level was not what it had been. And the United States Marine Corps was tired, with a fatigue it had not experienced since 1945. It was not a particularly opportune time to sign on. I figured I'd just take whatever came my way, do my "three and out," then head back to school to begin the rest of my life as a mild-mannered academic, teaching oversubscribed courses, making modest contributions to the corpus of human knowledge, maybe even trying my hand at a novel.

To adapt a line from that immortal poet, Robert Burns: "There's many a slip/'twixt the zipper and the zip."

From the Marine Corps point of view I was, to say the least, a curiosity. Ivy League Jew. No athletic background or skills. Sadly deficient in the more exuberant forms of celebrating one's manhood. I still recall when my class at Basic School—that's where you go after commissioning for six months of additional harassment and instruction—began two weeks of rifle and pistol training. The Corps takes marksmanship very seriously, and there was considerable pressure to get every officer qualified. Our captain gathered us round.

"How many of you," he asked, "have never fired a rifle before?"

One hand went up. The captain didn't seem surprised. Neither did my fellow brown-bars.

"How many of you have never fired a pistol before?"

I decided to vary the drill by raising my other hand. The platoon laughed and the captain muttered something on the order of, "Oh, well. At least you haven't picked up any bad habits."

I qualified with rifle and pistol, and by the end of my tour, was shooting high expert in both. A real double-dinger, as the phrase went.

Being Ivy League was no problem. A friend nicknamed me "Preppie," a term he'd borrowed from Erich Segal's *Love Story*. Small world. The name stuck, and whenever I messed up too badly it got used, along with a selection of appropriate expletives and a concluding, Well, what did you expect from a preppie? From time to time, I'd explain to them that Yale had a long and illustrious military history, which I was carrying on while my radical draft-dodging classmates attended law school to prepare for their lucrative corporate careers. Many years later, while wandering the stacks of Georgetown's Lauinger Library, which was named to honor an alumnus killed in Vietnam, I encountered a two-volume folio entitled, *Yale in the World War*, published in the early twenties. The eight or so Yale students who took Marine commissions earned more high decorations, I'm willing to bet, than any similar group during that war. I read the biographies of these genuine Best and Brightest with reverence. But before I could read them, I had to cut the pages of both volumes. No one had opened those books in over fifty years.*

Being identifiably Jewish was more problematic, even though

---

* In early 2004, while tracking down footnotes for this book in Lauinger Library, I decided to look at *Yale in the World War* again. It had been placed in permanent storage.

Jewish Marines were so scarce that I was generally treated as a curiosity, not a minority. Occasional overt anti-Semitism was best handled by giving as good as you got. This included one incident on the Camp Pendleton rifle range. It was "qual day." We were shooting for score. A sergeant near me said, by way of indicating his readiness to excel, "I'm German. If there are any Jews around, stand by." I walked over and said, "I'm Jewish." For a few seconds, I thought he was going to shoot me. He finally composed himself, and I noticed that he subsequently did everything he could to avoid encountering me outside and having to salute. I considered this a wise move on his part.

Other incidents were less inane. Circa 1977, I was a reserve captain, attending a briefing from an Israeli general named Shlomo Inbar. In civilian clothes, General Inbar looked like a grandfatherly immigrant, a retired garment district haberdasher, except not so physically fit. He started to talk, and for over an hour, in his heavily accented English, he held us rapt. Then came the Q&A. There rose from his seat a certain colonel renowned for the knots on his shaven skull, and for the way they twitched whenever he attempted thought. They were twitching now.

"General, you Israelis always talk about security on the West Bank, but you never mention the East Bank. Why is that?"

General Inbar looked at him a bit skeptically, paused, then replied:

"Dot iss bekoz der river iss between der vest bank und der ist bank."

The colonel appeared satisfied and sat down. Later that day, however, he approached me.

"Captain . . . you Jewish?"

"Yes, sir. Why?"

The knots twitched faster.

"Was there something in the general's answer that I missed?"

"Well, sir. Let's just say, he gave you a Talmudic answer."

The twitching abated. The colonel departed. He returned a few minutes later, his head a tsunami of activity.

"Captain?"

"Yes, sir?"

"Did you give me a Talmudic answer?"

"Yes, sir. I did."

He walked off again, looking at me as though I were playing some sort of obscure, disrespectful game that he wasn't quite bright enough to figure out. Some months later, I handed him a splendid opportunity for vengeance. He let it pass, either because he couldn't figure out what to do with it, or because it was Christmas.

The Marine Corps Reserve runs a program called Toys for Tots. Nowadays, it's supposed to take only new toys, but back then people could donate used items. A few days before Christmas, several Washington, DC reserve units were frantically trying to get ready for the distribution. The troops and NCOs (noncommissioned officers) were out and about, manning barrels at local shopping malls, doing pickups, whatever. This left the officers to handle the sorting and determine which used items were still serviceable.

We assembled in a warehouse at the Washington Navy Yard. The field grade officers were assigned the toys with multiple and/or moving parts. As a captain, I was placed in command of the dolls. So I went off to my pile and was sitting on the floor, sorting and sorting and sorting, when it occurred to me that, because I'd never had any sisters, I'd never been around this stuff before. As a consequence, I had absolutely no idea what a Barbie doll looked like with her clothes off. As the evening progressed and the boredom level increased, the desire to find out intensified, then overcame me. I chose one of the more amenable-looking specimens, snuck off to a secluded corner of the warehouse, and was sitting on the floor, busily undressing the thing, when the colonel found me.

He twitched not at all. Nothing. But he looked down at me with an expression of concern and asked:

"Captain . . . what are you doing?"

Since honesty is the best policy, especially after you've been caught, I of course replied:

"I'm undressing this Barbie doll, Colonel."

"Well, yes, I can see that. But why are you undressing the Barbie doll?"

"Well, sir, I never had any sisters . . ."

That drew a twitch. Then he waved his hand as though to say, *Tell me no more.* He left. When I was promoted to major and the time came for him to congratulate me, he did so with a little twinkle in his eye that indicated that, well, I might be some sort of intellectual to everybody else, but he knew better. We left it at that.

I like Marines. They're some of the best, certainly some of the most interesting and unusual people I've ever met. I like them also because Marines generally like and respect each other. And for two groups of Marines, and for their equivalents in the other services, I've gained an abiding respect.

The first might be termed the "saving remnant"—those professionals who stay in between the wars, especially when military times are tough and civilian opportunities plentiful. Our history gives full credit to the men who endured the twenties and thirties, to become the great leaders of the Second World War: Marshall, Eisenhower, Nimitz, Arnold, Halsey, MacArthur, Patton, to name only a few. But equal credit should be given to those who endured the seventies and the nineties. They did far more than endure.

The World War II leaders did not spend their prewar years sitting around the officers' club, drinking whisky and waiting for the call. They studied, they trained, they wrote, they talked, they thought, they challenged each other to think. When the time came, they were ready to build the forces America needed, and to lead them. In equal measure, those who took upon themselves the task of redeeming the Armed Forces after Vietnam and after the Cold War, spent those years immersed in thought, in intellectual effort of a quality and rigor far superior to what was going on at so many civilian universities. Their efforts required years and decades to come to fruition. Often, they found themselves fighting institutional inertia, public indifference, and political hostility all at once. It wore them down. It cost them personally. But the fruition of their effort and sacrifice was the force that did Desert Storm in 1991, and the swift conventional conquest of Iraq twelve years later. Few outside the national security world even know their names. But without them, the military supremacy America and the world so takes for granted, would never have come about.

It is said that the military is designed by geniuses, to be run by idiots. Not so about the idiots. Certainly not in America's twenty-first-century force: Idiots can't do the job. But the part about the geniuses, and the price they paid to accomplish what they did, is certainly true. To put it into a personal conclusion, based on thirty-five years as an officer, think-tank denizen, academic, author/journalist—I've encountered more strong intellect and more brilliant thought in the Armed Forces than I ever did on the campuses of America's elite universities. And whatever the uses to which our military is put, however questionable some of the political decisions, full credit and honor are always due to those who serve honorably and well.

The second group for whom I've learned an enduring admiration are the citizen-soldiers, the reservists and National Guard members. After Vietnam, the Army's chief of staff, General Creighton Abrams, made a wise and prescient decision. He would restructure the Army so that it could not undertake major war without substantial reserve and Guard mobilization, that is, without the national popular support that would make mobilization politically feasible. Over the next few years, the other services went the same route, and the Defense Department formally adopted the Total Force Policy. In essence, this meant that the citizen-soldiery would be considered the full equivalent of the active forces, and equally available for deployment.

It worked in Desert Storm. During the Clinton years, however, the policy underwent an ugly perversion. Citizen-soldiers would be used, not just to augment the regulars in time of war, but as fillers to do jobs the active forces neither could nor wanted to handle. At first, the Guard and reserves were happy to oblige—prove the point that they could hack it, and all that. But by the latter nineties, too many mobilizations for places like the Balkans were beginning to take their toll, especially in the Army Guard, which holds an unlimited liability for state emergency duties. 9-11 increased the demand for the "weekend warriors" by orders of magnitude. Today, the citizen-soldiery bears much of the burden in Iraq and elsewhere, and approaches collapse from overuse.

A trust has been broken. The role of the reservists is to hold themselves in readiness for major war, while tending to domestic needs and a number of specialized activities. Their role is not to be sent anywhere at any time to do anything. After World War II, America made a similar mistake with conscription.

Throughout the Cold War, most Western democracies drafted. But citizen military obligation was tied to specific uses, primarily homeland defense. Only the United States assumed that draftees could be used and expended without restriction. Today, the reserves and the National Guard are treated the same. It is not a wise policy.

This much about the citizen-soldiery is common knowledge. What is not generally known is that the practice of using reserves in various "specialized" ways actually began in the seventies.

I spent a relatively uneventful three years on active duty, in training, in Eleventh Marines, an artillery regiment, and at the First Marine Division HQ. When I drove my yellow Volkswagen Beetle out the Camp Pendleton main gate in July 1973 to head for graduate school at Georgetown University, a place I'd chosen because of a profound lack of interest in any more Ivy League radical crap, I had no intention of ever donning a uniform again. But I met a Marine colonel in one of my classes, who persuaded me to give the DC reserve scene a try.

The next seven years were intense.

Washington, DC, is filled with former Marines. ("Former Marine" is an acceptable term; "ex-Marine," never.) Many of these men and women are high-powered, successful, and well connected. The reserve units of the seventies had lawyers, lobbyists, staffers, politicos, and professionals galore. Many were Vietnam veterans; many worked civilian jobs in the national security field. There were, to employ a neutral phrase, interlocks. The units themselves were unusual. One, a civil affairs group, had no active-duty equivalent. There were also two counterintelligence teams and an interrogation team, which I commanded for over two years. The seventies was the decade when revelations of military spying on Americans and assorted other malfeasances made daily headlines. Active-duty intelligence and counterintelligence units were being monitored. No one, however, paid much attention to the reserves. There were also several unpaid officers-only units that did God-knows-what, plus a special outfit that met over at CIA. People were busy.

I went into the Organized Marine Corps Reserve for several reasons. One, obviously, was money. GI benefits and grad school stipends only take you so far, especially in a cash-intensive city like DC. Another was time. I had my summers free and, once I was working on my dissertation, could usually get away for a week or two or more, if called. Yet a third was pleasure, the simple fun of being with Marines . . . and of pissing off the Georgetown faculty by occasionally showing up in uniform.

It also helped me keep my sanity. One day in particular stands out. May 28th, 1978. A Sunday. Georgetown commencement day. Also the day my fellowship, my veteran's benefits, and my girlfriend ran out. What to do? What to do? The next day, I wandered on over to Headquarters, U.S. Marine Corps.

"Captain Gold reporting for duty."

"We didn't send for you."

"That's irrelevant. Send me somewhere."

To make a long and complex story very short, 12 months later, not having notified my adviser that I was taking some time off, I found myself with the French commandos. We were aboard their ship, the *Ouragon*, where wine flowed freely, Gauloises were cheap, and nobody much cared for Americans or for Jews. "Remember, *mon capitain*," my Marine interpreter, a sergeant who'd served in the French Foreign Legion, had warned me, "On this ship, Dreyfus is still guilty." We were somewhere off the coast of Sardinia, preparing for a night raid. We went down to the ship's well deck to launch our Zodiac boats. This you do by flooding the well deck and floating away. If it's not practical to flood the well deck, you can pick up the rubber boats, carry them down the ramp, and just before you walk off into the water, put them down, get aboard, and shove off .

Unfortunately, my sergeant took one step too many. Unfortunately, I followed him. With fifty pounds on your back, you don't float all that well. I was going down for the third time when the little voice inside said, *I will not die without my PhD.* Somehow I got back to the surface. We did the raid. Several weeks later I walked, unannounced and unexpected, into the office of my adviser.

"Philip, where have you been?"

"Dorothy, you don't want to know."

"OK. Welcome back."

I finished grad school with only one more major interruption. In 1980, Fidel Castro announced that anyone wanting to leave Cuba could do so by taking themselves to the port of Mariel and hopping a boat to America. The Florida Cuban community graciously provided the flotilla. Fidel also emptied his prisons, hospitals, and insane asylums, and sent those folks to Mariel. A Cuban boat would arrive to pick up, say, a half-dozen family members and friends. Fidel's on-site cruise directors would tell them to take two, plus four of the undesirables, and come back later for the rest. In this way, over a hundred thousand Cubans, ranging from political prisoners and dissident intellectuals to the dregs of society, plus more than a few spies, came to America. Soon, several bases were overflowing with refugees. There were major riots at Fort Chaffee and disturbances elsewhere. So the Army did what it always does when it gets into trouble. It calls for Marines.

A detachment of my unit, the Fourth Civil Affairs Group, headed for the National Guard post at Fort Indiantown Gap, Pennsylvania, conveniently close to the Three Mile Island nuclear facility, which had experienced some recent hiccups.

Initially, we were told that we would handle one cantonment. But upon our arrival, they split us up, making four of our five officers area commanders. The subtext was clear. When this place blows, you'll be the ones to get burnt. I was given 2,500 of what were euphemistically known as "unaccompanied males."

For over a week, I and two other Marines, a couple of fine young Army paratroopers, and a modest assortment of other people (including some Army civil affairs colonels who seemed quite content to sit around, drink coffee, and let me command), wore the refugees down. Then, late one night, I was out inspecting my domain when a refugee came at me with a bunk adapter, a heavy metal post that goes between lower and upper bunks, and makes a dandy club. Jimmy Carter had decreed that, since there were no bad boys, none of us needed to be armed. Not overly impressed with his reasoning, I carried a little .25 automatic in one pocket. The Marielito raised his club. I drew my pistol. We stared at each other a few seconds. I explained to him that he was in America now, where everyone was safe all the time. He really didn't need that. I took the club from him, let him wander off. Then, standing there in the dark, I decided that ten years was enough. It was necessary work. It had been rewarding and fun. But it wasn't my life.

Time to get back to school.

★   ★   ★

From 1970 to 1973, I paid very little attention to conservatism, or to politics in general. I did a bit of organizing during the 1972 campaign, trying to get my platoon to register to vote. I came up one short, a young Ozark corporal who refused on the grounds that he couldn't stand McGovern, but wouldn't vote for that goddam Mormon, Nixon.

"Nixon isn't a Mormon," I tried to explain. "He's a Quaker."
"Same goddam thing," my corporal scoffed.

OK, maybe not everybody needs to vote.

Nor did I pay much attention from 1973 to 1979 or so. So much was so ugly, so pointless. "America's long national nightmare," as Gerry Ford aptly described it, trended down toward Nixon's inevitable departure in disgrace. The night before his resignation, I walked past the White House. A small crowd milled around, expecting nothing in particular. Then a large Allied moving van came down Pennsylvania Avenue. The crowd applauded and cheered. When the truck failed to turn into the White House, people booed. I wonder what the driver thought. Personally, I was happy to be there. Nixon's home away from DC was San Clemente, California, a charming little town just north of Camp Pendleton, where I'd been stationed. Every time he went out there as president, we put a battalion of infantry and a battery of howitzers on alert. Infantry I could understand. But except for ceremonial salutes, I never really knew what we were supposed to do with the artillery. Level the tubes and fire beehive at the tourists, maybe. Anyway, Nixon officially ceased being president while aloft on that final flight. When Air Force One touched down at Marine Corps Air Station El Toro, he was met by a small retinue and a Marine Corps staff car. That was the moment, at least according to legend, when it truly sunk in that he was no longer president.

When you realize where he might have taken the country, had at least a few of his high crimes and misdemeanors not been discovered and publicized, it makes you cringe. Eternal vigilance is indeed the price of liberty.

Grad school was busy. Time to make up for, plus the happy discovery that I was a pretty good teaching assistant, then a very good instructor. I liked the students. For the most part,

they liked me. I also discovered a hunger in them. Tell me
something, anything, that we haven't heard a thousand times
already. Just get our brains going. I found that I could. That
mattered. I also learned to work their butts off and make them
enjoy it. First day of class, I'd explain that I loved to give As.
Every time I gave an A, it meant that I'd done my job and somebody else had done theirs. The excellence of inclusion. I also
asked them to help me realize a private fantasy—giving everybody As and saying to myself as I signed the grade sheet,
"Philip, you're a hell of a man." The students agreed, then got
a look at the course requirements.

"I just can't hate you the way I should," a student told me
once. I took that as a wonderful compliment.

I drifted back into conservatism about midway through
Jimmy Carter's reign of error. One reason was disgust with
what he had done to the country. Another was his attempt to
get the country to feel sorry for itself—all that piss-drivel about
"limits" and "malaise." But the most important reason was that,
through my studies and dissertation research, I'd discovered
something that I thought conservatism needed to know. Desperately. I wanted to tell the DC conservative community especially, what I'd found. I wanted to tell them with all the ardor of
an early Old Testament prophet. But the conservatism I
returned to was, sad to relate, a conservatism that had only
degenerated since Nam, even as it rose to ever-greater national
visibility.

Throughout the sixties, conservatism had been a relatively
modest, low-budget affair. The "New Right" expansion and the
creation of a large professional conservative intelligentsia took
enormous effort, organization, and above all else, cash. The
cash was suddenly to be had, via direct mail fund-raising and via
the advent of a dozen or so major conservative philanthropic

foundations: Scaife, Olin, Smith Richardson, Coors, Bradley, to
name only a few. In time, a complex apparatus of publications,
think tanks, advocacy organizations, and media stars arose, in
tandem with the more politicized segments of the Christian
fundamentalist movement, most notably the Jerry Falwell/Pat
Robertson branch. Within the Republican Party, this led to a
lot of grassroots activism and a lot of pressure on the national
structure. It also led to a lot of books and magazines. By the
latter seventies, the New Right partisan political/paid intelligentsia of the think tanks and media tandem was firmly established. It was a tandem far more attuned to pandering than to
the aristocratic virtues. In *The Emerging Republican Majority*,
analyst Kevin Phillips had correctly predicted a future of
Republican strongholds throughout the South, Southwest, and
West. But much of the action took place outside the party
proper. Richard Viguerie had demonstrated the potential of
direct mail fund-raising for all kinds of organizations. All it took
was a four-page letter, printed to look like it had been typed,
addressing you by your usually misspelled first name, and
warning that the Republic would founder, the planet drop out
of its orbit, and the universe implode unless YOU sent a "suggested contribution" of . . .

A return of 2 or 3 percent meant big bucks.

Dozens of other new leaders, many of them veterans of the
Goldwater campaign and organizations such as the Young
Americans for Freedom, began careers of influence that have
lasted to this day: Paul Weyrich, Ed Feulner, Phyllis Schlafly,
Morton Blackwell, to name only a few. Many drew their
funding from both the grass roots and the foundations. Almost
overnight, it seemed, the conservative establishment had
arrived.

But aside from a generational change in leadership and a

quantum expansion of conservative resources, was the New Right really new? In *To the Right: The Transformation of American Conservatism*, Jerome Himmelstein argues, yes and no.

> *[T]he basic ideology of the new Right did not change substantively: it combined a militant anticommunism with a libertarian defense of pristine capitalism and a traditionalist concern with moral and social order. . . . The emphasis of New Right Leaders in the seventies on social issues as a way of winning over blue-collar, Catholic, and evangelical constituencies certainly was new, but it largely reflected historical opportunities: the seventies gave conservatives a cornucopia of social issues on which to build. . . the New Right's emphasis on social issues did not introduce a new concern into conservative ideology and certainly not one that was incompatible with established themes.*

Quite so. But something *was* new: horrifically, tragically new. This establishment, so well organized and well funded, proved pitifully inadequate against the Left. Beginning in the seventies, the Left bombarded America with a bewildering array of issues, from abortion and the Equal Rights Amendment to sexual harassment, the environment, gay rights, antinuclear activity— dozens and hundreds of agenda items. In response, conservatism adopted a simple strategy. Whatever the Left was for, they were against. No thought was necessary, no attempt to understand the realities of any problem, scant attempt to offer constructive and practical alternatives. What creative thought there was came far more from libertarians and self-styled "classical liberals" than from card-carrying New Rightists. And the Right evolved a new tactic: offering counterproposals that had little relation to reality, but at least had the virtue of being counterproposals. "See, we've got ideas, too." To fight the environmentalists, for example, conservatism spent scores of millions on think tanks and publications "proving" that the environmentalists were wrong, there were no problems, and anyway the problems could best be solved by private enterprise. Anything you can do, we can do better. But we're not going to do anything. Yes, the Left has indulged in an unconscionable amount of "junk science." But it took the Right to come up with junk refutation.

And it took the New Right to conclude that the key to success was merely to oppose the people you love to hate.

It worked. The money and, from time to time, the votes rolled in. But conservatism also abdicated its responsibility to share in the serious discourse and governance of America. And its intransigent refusal to acknowledge that America had real and serious problems produced two utterly baleful results.

One was that, more and more, the Left sought political victory, not through the legislative or electoral systems, but in the courts. In the words of legal scholar Mary Anne Glendon, "[T]he high road to a better life would be paved with court decisions." In fact, this process had begun in the fifties with the landmark desegregation decision, *Brown v. Board of Education.* That had to happen; it was clear that neither the federal nor the state governments were going to get serious about civil rights until pressed by the law of the land. But the process begun by *Brown* (in truth, it had begun some years earlier dealing with First Amendment issues) was never meant to become and never should have become a permanent fixture of American life. Unfortunately, too many activist judges proved only too happy to undertake the direction of our lives. Much of what they've done was necessary, but should have been accomplished through the normal political process.

Another baleful result was that, as meaningful political discourse atrophied in America, it was replaced more and more by what became known at the popular level as "psychobabble" and, more academically, as "the triumph of the therapeutic." Consciousness III had become the preferred style of much of American discourse. Of itself, this was not entirely bad. But as the doctors remind us, the toxicity of anything is determined by the dosage. From the sixties through the nineties, we got a toxic dose, indeed.

About the judicial usurpations, I could do nothing. But about the dangers of surrendering discourse and ethics to the purveyors of psychologized gibberish, I tried to warn both the New Rightists and the more traditional conservatives. They laughed. Nobody, they told me, could take this garbage seriously. Let the fruitcake Left babble on all it wanted. It didn't matter. Traditional values would always triumph in the end.

They were right. It didn't matter. At least, it didn't matter until it got into the courts, the schools, the churches, the law, the bedrooms, the boardrooms, the military, the entire fabric of this civilization. Belatedly, they tried to mount a counteroffensive. First, they ostentatiously ignored it. Then, they tried to sneer it off. Then they hurled their self-evident truths. Then they stood back and waited for the miracles that never happened. And now that this civilization is groping toward a way out of the cultural mess of the last few decades, a virtuous and honorable way out, and finding it in some very unexpected places . . . they don't like that much, either. For in the "neoclassical revival" currently underway—in truth a movement that has yet to find its proper name—there lies a threat to "traditional values" far more serious than any ever posed by psychobabble.

And that's all to the good.

Chapter 6

Culture War

It's time to tell the people who tell us what our choices are,
we need not be confined to the either/or of so-called
traditional values or psychologized gunk.

—Philip Gold

NO REASON TO TALK ABOUT IT.
That one phrase, perhaps more than any other, encapsulates the conservative attitude toward the Culture War. No reason to talk about all the old injustices and inequities, all the new problems, all the inevitable changes. We've got our traditional values, our self-evident truths. And we know with absolute certainty—if the liberals are for it, we're against it.

There is anger here, and bitterness, and the realization that things I once offered as gifts, I now use as weapons. Things I once offered in love, I now offer in . . . hate? No, not exactly. Hate the faith, love the faithful. Most conservatives I've known are good people. But of all conservatism's betrayals of self and of America, its conduct during the thirty years of the Culture War seems to me the most pernicious. For conservatism has willfully refused to understand how much about America had to change, and has to change, and has changed for the better. Conservatism has willfully refused to offer itself as an effective agent of that change.

You don't set out in life to become a Cassandra. Or a Malachi. Most fourteen-year-olds, when pondering their futures, would probably not say, I want to spend thirty years trying to talk to people who either won't listen, or who will sneer me off. The day I made my little list I certainly didn't plan on the prophet-without-honor lifestyle. Nor could I have suspected that the experience might result in something of value, something worth offering.

This chapter and the next describe a personal journey that, beyond the personal, has scant intrinsic significance. It matters only to the extent that it speaks to the concerns of others; to the extent that it resonates; to the extent that it suggests some ideas relevant to our present condition and perils. It's a tale of progressive disillusionment, but also of a growing sense that, to borrow from a popular television show: "The truth is out there." It is. And contrary to postmodern notions of the tyranny of truth, it does indeed set you free. Provided you keep in mind that all truth is provisional. We can always know more, and that which we do know stands in need of constant revalidation.

My uneasiness with conservatism came early, while I was still in college. But my break came slowly, over decades, one item at a time, not least of all because I believed the people who told me what my choices were. The "them or us" mentality runs deep.

The first part to go was belief that conservatism was serious about rolling back Big Government, or even limiting its growth. You don't have to live many years in Washington, DC, to understand that it regards the rest of the country as its property. America is the medium by which and through which the Beltway works its will and its whims. Liberal or conservative—in this matter, no difference. Nor do you have to know much about practical politics to understand that people don't get elected or stay elected by dismantling, or even taking serious whacks at the structure of subsidy and favor. Republican or Democrat—in this matter, no difference. When in the 2000 presidential campaign, George W. Bush spoke of "growing the government responsibly," and only a few of the more antediluvian conservatives took umbrage, it was obvious that they'd jettisoned that notion long ago, even if they still hadn't gotten around to admitting it openly. I certainly had, if only after watching the Reagan administration's feeble, futile, farcical attempts to rein in the government. Discretionary nondefense spending may indeed have been cut as a percentage of GDP, as Don Devine suggests. But you don't cut government by "rationing the poverty." You cut by abolishing organizations and functions.

This is unfortunate. Long-term, we're headed for disaster. Pay me now or pay me later. Politicians always choose later.

My second break came with culture. The array of institutions and forces known as "cultural conservatism" have proven far more durable, although not noticeably more effective, than the anti-Big-Government movement. Conservatism blew the Culture War. Conservatives blew it because they abandoned humane virtue for the politics of mass resentment.

The Left consistently outflanked, outmaneuvered, and out-bombarded the Right. The process is sometimes called "The Long March through the Institutions." But it was far more sophisticated than a mere slog. It was a brilliant assault. Throughout the thirty years of the Culture War, the Left hit the Right with so many issues, worked the tandem of lawsuits and psychobabble so adroitly, that conservatives got absolutely punchy. All they knew was, "If the Left is for it, we're against it." It was an astute fund-raising approach. Benefactors don't often write checks paying you to see the other person's point of view. But by failing to address, or even take seriously, many and troubling problems, the Right ceded the moral and practical initiative to people who often didn't deserve it. It proved a costly, nasty failure of prudence, and of humanity. And it demonstrated that in one way, cultural conservatism differed little from corporate America. Win or lose, the people at the top got big bucks. Bill Bennett comes to mind.

For me, the almost-final break with cultural conservatism came circa 1997, when I showed something I'd written to my boss at Discovery. Bruce Chapman, a smart man and a genuine Christian gentleman of the old school, informed me in no uncertain terms and with considerable vehemence, "Philip, this is crap." Five years or so later, I ran a *Washington Times* column, suggesting one last time that conservatives could use some new Culture War tactics. On April 1, 2002, Bill Lind, director of the Center for Cultural Conservatism at the DC-based Free Congress Foundation, posted on its Web site: "New strategy for culture war already in place: A reply to Philip Gold." Mr. Lind wrote that I undervalued their work on "Cultural Independence," their attempt to create a conservative counterculture. He concluded that Philip Gold did not "see its importance or potential power, because he is in Washington. Washington does not believe anything of importance can happen elsewhere, least of all in 'fly-over land' where most of Middle America lives."

I read it. For a moment, I considered letting Bill know that, for the past six years, I'd lived in Seattle. Then I decided, what's the point? Bill Lind lives in Washington, DC. He has since the seventies. Time, at last, to move on.

The final break with conservatism came in the spring of 2002, when I reached the conclusion that the Bush/neocon agenda of invading Iraq and "cauldronizing the Middle East," and the very notions of "Hard Wilsonianism" and "The Democracy Domino Theory" were wrong in so many practical and prudential ways that they constituted a moral failure. Yes, Saddam was evil. No, America was not. And I had absolutely no hiccups with President Bush's September 2002 policy paper, *The National Security Strategy of the United States of America*, that proclaimed:

> *As a matter of common sense and self-defense, America will act against such emerging threats before they are fully formed . . . . While the United States will constantly strive to enlist the support of the international community, we will not hesitate to act alone, if necessary, to exercise our right of self-defense by acting preemptively against such terrorists . . . We must be prepared to stop rogue states and their terrorist clients before they are able to threaten or use weapons of mass destruction . . .*

Fine by me. If you have to do something, as they used to say in the Nike ads, Just Do It. But was it really necessary to conquer and occupy Iraq, in the hope that an Iraqi democracy, assuming such was even possible, would automatically spread? Were there not other matters, such as the Israeli/Palestinian mess, that required more urgent attention? Then I did the math. An easy exercise. Divisions and brigades, troop rotations and retentions, budgets and other needs. We simply did not have the forces to do this. The Clinton administration had both overused and neglected a military that was now at the beginning of a fundamental process of defense "transformation" to meet twenty-first-century needs. The people, the stuff, and the money just weren't there. We would wear out what we had and leave ourselves vulnerable around the globe. And as for the matter of mortgaging our future to our ability to turn the Islamic world into a bunch of good little middle-class, civic-minded American knockoffs, to turn Fallujah into the equivalent of Cleveland . . .

A story is told of a young psychoanalyst, new to his trade and ardent about its possibilities, who sought out the master for advice. According to the tale, Dr. Freud listened politely, then answered: "Don't try to save people. They don't want to be saved."

Wise counsel. Then and now.

In sum, then, this is a tale of thirty years of frustration, leading to my public break—a break significant only insofar as it addresses the concerns of others. But it is also a tale of groping toward a new understanding of what it means to hold a "working reverence" for the past, especially that of antiquity, and how to apply that past to our present dilemmas in some strange and unexpected ways. Maybe, just maybe, it might do some good.

★   ★   ★

It was February 1980. The Iranian hostage crisis had become a fixture of our national life. Give us this day our daily news that nothing has changed, our daily reminder of how many days it had been going on. Jimmy Carter was busily and officiously lecturing the Republic on "malaise." Between the two, I was feeling pretty malaisical. I was also staggering through the final chapters of my dissertation, supporting myself by active-duty gigs whenever the Marine Corps called. These had been taking up over half my time for the preceding several years, which kept me from wrapping up my degree, which in turn kept me dependent on active duty to pay my bills so I could wrap up my degree, which wasn't getting done because I was gone half the time. Fortunately, I'd cadged my way into a no-heavy-lifting gradership in the MSFS (Master's of Science in Foreign Service) program. I never did understand why an international relations curriculum led to an MS, as opposed to MA, degree. Even less did I understand the professor, Earl Ravenal, a former Defense Department official, devout left-libertarian, and charmingly erudite fellow.

One day when I happened to be in town, I was sitting in class, growing more and more irate over his take on current events and a few other matters. Not wishing to contradict the prof in front of the students, I started scribbling furiously. That evening, for some reason that now eludes me, I worked my notes into a column. The next morning, for no rational reason, I sent it to the *New York Times*. For no reason, rational or otherwise, that I've ever been able to fathom, they ran it. Then two things happened.

First, the world failed to change. No calls from the administration seeking my counsel. No death threats. No groupies. No job offers. I could walk down the street without expecting men to weep and strong women to step aside. In fact, the only response I drew came that afternoon in class from Professor Ravenal. He congratulated me on my publication and remarked that he was glad to see that I was making some of the same points that he was.

Alexander Haig, upon being asked by somebody why he talked the way he did, is alleged to have replied, "Sometimes it's better to be not understood than to be misunderstood." He may have been on to something.

A few days later, however, an envelope arrived. For the *New York Times* column, I'd tagged myself as a teaching assistant in the Georgetown History Department. A group calling itself the Committee for the Free World (CFW) had tracked me down. Inside was a letter from the director, Midge Decter, congratulating me on my coup and inviting me to join her organization, which even then was working furiously to rid the Republic of the Carter administration. Since they offered me membership at the reduced student rate, and since at the time I was dating a low-level White House staffer and knew how desperately we needed that good riddance, I joined. A couple weeks later, I learned that CFW ran an op-ed placement service of sorts, and I volunteered to churn out some more. They hooked me up with the old *Washington Star*; I did a couple pieces for them before they folded. I then invited myself to meet with Midge Decter. It seemed a good idea to see what else might be available for a soon-to-graduate history PhD, a wary conservative with absolutely no tenure-track job prospects—a condition due less to my own magnificent capabilities, I told myself often, than to the collapse of the academic job market and the rise of various PC litmus tests for applicants.

If Irving Kristol has been the godfather of the neoconservative movement, Midge Decter has been its godmother. Or perhaps the operative term should be queen mother. She's formidable. She's wise. She's also very well connected. I'd been admiring her work for ages, especially a collection of essays published as *Liberal Parents, Radical Children*. We chatted a bit about what I wanted to do with my unfashionable beliefs and unmarketable degree. She then arranged a meeting for me with Irving Kristol on my next trip to New York, referred me to a literary agent, and was in general wonderful.

Nothing came of it immediately. But a couple months later, upon staggering home from a Marine expedition, I received another envelope. This one had a street return address, but no indication of the identity of the sender. I was going to toss it, but the stationery seemed too fancy for mere junk mail. So I opened it, and found an invitation from the Smith Richardson Foundation to apply for a grant. Midge and Irving had come through after all.

I went to New York to sell them my proposal—a dissection and indictment of "psychologized ethics" that would knock the psycho-socks off the entire Left and provide the Right with several arsenals worth of high-velocity, liberal-piercing intellectual ammunition. The man across the desk seemed unimpressed. Actually, he told me, the foundation was thinking more along the lines of a book on why we need the draft back.

And that's how I met Mac Owens: Marine Corps hero of Vietnam, political philosopher, journalist, and raconteur, currently a professor at the Naval War College, writing the definitive history of civil-military relations in America. And also, back then, a man who knew how to party hearty. At first, I noticed only that he was large, very large, with the absolute largeness of a college football player who also dabbled in rugby. I learned later that he'd won the Silver Star and two Purple Hearts in Vietnam, the second for getting shot in the head—an event to which he attributed his subsequent decision to get a PhD. He told me not to worry, he'd help me with the draft book. Since a $50,000 grant and subsequent book contract looked more appealing than unemployment, I went along.* And there began a strange twenty years, working primarily on defense issues with always one eye toward the cultural issues that were the real contribution I wanted to make.

Mac did indeed help out, introducing me to realms of philosophy that I'd never considered before: the ancients, the Machiavelli of the *Discourses*, and the Radical Whigs who meant so much to the Founders. I repaid the favor several years later, when he quit his job at the foundation to go to work in DC as legislative assistant to Sen. Bob Kasten. Mac called to tell me

---

* It turned out to be my first book, *Evasions: The American Way of Military Service* (New York: Paragon, 1985).

his decision, and wondered if he could share my bachelor pad while he sold his house on Long Island and found a new home for his family. Of course, I said yes, come on down.

It proved an adventure. The memories are somewhat vague now, and those that remain may have improved with the telling. But I do recall one particularly nasty Friday afternoon blizzard. An airplane had just crashed into the Potomac, shutting down the Fourteenth Street Bridge. The government released its workers in a manner timed to cause maximum additional gridlock, per its usual practice. Mac got to my office just as the Metro stopped running, due to its first fatal accident. We spent the next several hours working our way up Connecticut Avenue, one bar at a time. Approaching my apartment in the fashionably multicultural Adams-Morgan area, Mac learned why it's a bad idea to start snowball fights with gangs of lesbians. We made it through my door barely alive, took a good look at each other, then went out again. We got back long after dark. Mac's wife called to find out if he was still planning to take the train up to New York for the weekend.

"I don't think so, ma'am," I said.

His wife must have sensed the obvious.

"Can I speak to Mac, please?"

"No, ma'am."

"Why not?"

"He can't come to the phone right now."

"Has he been drinking?"

"Yes, ma'am."

"Do you think that's a good idea?"

"Compared to what he wanted to do, sure."

It was not a statement that assuaged her. But as a Marine wife, she knew that her husband was in the good hands of a fellow Marine. That, or she'd learned long ago not to worry.

Mac, I learned long ago, is a man worth listening to. Now a contributing editor to the *National Review Online*, he writes columns that are among the most rational and thoughtful coming out of the Right. Indeed, several years ago, I found myself in a somewhat heated Internet exchange, defending his work against the depredations of a radical feminist with a reputation for take-no-prisoners ferocity. Erin and I are still arguing about him today.

Thanks, Mac, for bringing us together. You did good. And Semper Fi, Marine. Semper Fi.

★　　★　　★

I'd wanted to write my first book on the psychological aspects of what would shortly become known as the Culture War. I was also qualified to do so.

My academic specialty was modern U.S. cultural history. I'd done my doctoral dissertation on advertising, more specifically on the relationships between trendy psychopathologies and commercial appeals, and how the whole mess got into politics. I'd chosen that subject for three reasons. First, I wanted nothing to do with military history. I liked it, but had no desire to teach it or write it. Too specialized, too confining. Second, I'd always been fascinated by cultural "transmission belts"—how ideas get out of the ivory tower or lab or sect or whatever and permeate the larger society. And finally, I'd spent part of one summer at the New York University Graduate School of Business Administration, in something called the "Careers in Business" program. This was a venture with the Rockefeller Foundation to determine if otherwise useless liberal arts grad students could be sufficiently rehabilitated in six weeks to find work in the private sector. I applied.

I was accepted. I went. A couple dozen of us wannabe retreads lived in a dorm, worked fourteen-hour days, and learned whatever it was that we learned about management, accounting, business law, and the rest. The only subject I liked or could master was marketing. It was highly technical, but it was also highly sneaky, and advertising was the sneakiest part of the whole endeavor. So when I decided not to abandon academe for real work, I was reasonably well equipped to launch my dissertation.*

Historically, the relationships between psychology and advertising were clear enough. The use of appeals based on stimulus/response and behavioral psychology was over a century old. The fifties witnessed the application of so-called "depth psychology," invoking Freudian and other insights and pseudoinsights. As popularized by Vance Packard in his deliciously silly best-seller *The Hidden Persuaders*, convertibles are mistresses, sedans are wives. Put ragtops in the showroom but stock sedans. Fountain pens are phallic symbols. Men will pay more for a good one. Cake-baking can be a pregnancy substitute, provided the woman is allowed to express her creativity, so let her throw in the eggs. But the more subtle approaches proved, to me at least, the most intriguing.

Each era has its fashionable maladies. When neurosis was popular, advertising pandered to neurosis. When people started having identity crises, advertising sold identity. When, much due to the popularity of Christopher Lasch's *The Culture of Narcissism*, narcissism became trendy, the commercials quickly filled with narcissists. When anger became cool, commercials got pissed. And today, if it's sometimes hard to figure out exactly

---

* This later became my second book, *Advertising, Politics and American Culture: From Salesmanship to Therapy*, (New York: Paragon, 1987).

what a commercial is trying to sell you, that reflects America's psychological profile, too.

Politics always keys on the standard emotions, of course: hate, fear, ambition, resentment, need. But Jimmy Carter and Ronald Reagan both offered themselves as "therapeutic" presidents, leaders you can feel good about. And then of course there was Bill Clinton, the president who feels your pain, not to mention the whole "compassionate conservatism" routine. (By 1999, I was taking considerable delight in feeling Clinton's pain. As for "compassionate conservatism," I was relieved to see it segue into President Bush's "Faith-Based Initiative" [FBI] and then slowly molder.) But what fascinated me was not so much the history of advertising as the cultural history of psychology and psychotherapy. An entire branch of academics, populated almost entirely by liberals and Left radicals, was charting a century's worth of manipulation—the uses of psychological and therapeutic insights and techniques by business, government, the military, education, and the media, as well as the "triumph of the therapeutic" as cultural and moral discourse. Prior to the early nineties, few conservatives seemed even remotely aware of these works, or the intensity of the therapeutic hold on America. Nor were they interested. True, lawyer Mary Ann Glendon could avow that the "strident language of rights," the national tendency to formulate all issues as matters of individual rights, was "converging with the language of psychotherapy." And popular writer Charles Sykes got it rather right when he noted in his 1992 book, *A Nation of Victims*:

> *Political correctness turns out to be a subunit of the larger transformation of society reflected in the ascendancy of psychological over political terminology. What began as an attempt to politicize psychology and psychologized politics has led to the*

swallowing of each by the other and the emergence of synthesis:
therapeutic politics.

For the most part, however, the cultural Right either missed
the significance of this influence or dismissed it as beneath their
consideration. In part, they missed it because, like those super-
clusters of galaxies that astronomers kept overlooking, it was
simply too big for them to see. They also dismissed it because
it wasn't *their* vocabulary or orientation. Trendy morons might
babble on, but no right-minded person could or should deign
to consider it. Still, it occurred to me that this hold must
inevitably determine more and more of our politics and culture
. . . at least until its inevitable burnout. It also occurred to me
that so many individuals and groups with genuine grievances
used this vocabulary because they had no other, and that this
was wrong. Finally, it occurred that, given the equation
between dissent and personal growth, and the quest for
unearned moral stature via feeling good about yourself, a lot of
important issues were going to get terribly distorted.

By the early eighties, I was writing on this for anyone who
would publish, and talking to anyone who would listen. The
inevitable, predictable conservative response—a combination of,
You don't really expect us to take this seriously, do you?, and an
oft-proclaimed certainty that, sooner or later, people would shuck
the psychobabble and return to traditional values. That they
might someday shuck the psychobabble but not return to traditional values, or find other traditions for their return, seemed to
the culture warriors of the Right, impossible. And when I tried to
point out to them what an alternative tradition might look like,
and that one was indeed aborning, Bill Lind told me that it would
never happen. Too complicated. People needed simple ideas in
order to be controlled. And then there was: "Philip, this is crap."

Before moving on to the nature of the alternative that conservatives dismissed so vehemently, a bit on how the triumph of the therapeutic played out across the decades of the Culture War. First, it's necessary to understand one of the stranger aspects of this triumph: how something so utterly silly and unworkable could have come to dominate this civilization for so long, and what price we paid for submitting to it. For no "triumph of the therapeutic" would have been possible had the therapists not suffered from a few delusions of their own. Two, in particular. Everyone needed them. And their expertise was applicable everywhere.

★ ★ ★

Strictly speaking, there is no such thing as psychology, certainly not in the sense of a unified discipline, in agreement on its basics. Imagine chemistry having fifty different definitions of a molecule. In psychology, there are literally hundreds of specialties and subspecialties, from hard scientific endeavors such as physiological and cognitive psychology, to movements and schisms of a more transcendental and speculative nature. Some last longer than others, or get repackaged or recycled. Few, it seems, ever really go away.

Strictly speaking, there is no such thing as psychotherapy, and for the same reason—lack of agreement on fundamentals. There is a branch of medicine called psychiatry, of course. There are drugs. And there are endless schools and forms of "talking therapy" that counsel everything from life adjustment to revolutionary activism, from primal screams to Just Deal with It. Perhaps the most common approach is known as "eclectic." A little of this, a little of that, no real consistency because consistency is neither desired nor possible. Few approaches, few movements, ever seem to really go away. Nor do Dr. Laura and Dr. Phil.

And to a surprising extent, there is no such thing as mental illness. Conditions with physical and chemical etiologies—schizophrenia and depression, for example—are real enough. So are conditions such as posttraumatic stress disorder. So is the pain. But according to one interpretation, dominant in this country, mental illness is by and large a matter of dysfunction and behavior. To the extent that you stay legal, perform effectively, and cope adequately, you're OK. But other prominent schools of psychology and psychotherapy reject this orientation, holding that our civilization is so pathologically destructive that adjustment and effectiveness are themselves crazy. To these practitioners, our very notion of self—of separate, bounded entities for whom the world matters only as a source of frustration or gratification—constitutes insanity.

So take your choice. You're either crazy because you're maladjusted or daft because you fit in. And don't forget the corollary axiom. If you're sick and know it, you're sick. If you're sick and deny it, you're sicker. And if you're sick and don't know it, you're sickest of all.

Indeed, since Freud, normality has been an unattainable ideal, not a norm, much less *the* norm. To be human is, by definition, to be sick. The most we can hope for, as Freud suggested, is to exchange some of our inner garbage for the ordinary unhappinesses and tragedies of life. Of course, Freud never abandoned his insistence that life had purpose and that the measure of health was one's ability *lieben und arbeiten*, "to love and to work." And whatever his views on civilization's shortcomings, "culture must be preserved." Since Freud, not everyone has taken so sane a view of things, certainly not an American profession determined to minister, one way or another, to everybody.

But if psychology exhibits all the scientific coherence of a two-year-old banging keys on a computer keyboard, and if surgeons had the same cure rate as psychotherapists, there would be no surgery because they'd all be in jail for malpractice . . . that hasn't kept the therapeutic from permeating our civilization. Its concepts, its products, its vocabularies are, quite literally, everywhere. Organized professions. Academic departments. Popular entertainment. The courts. The churches. The schools. The military. There's even an official catalogue of dysfunction, the *Diagnostic and Statistical Manual* (DSM), published by the American Psychiatric Association. Once entered in the DSM, a malady achieves both official recognition and cachet. The DSM determines which conditions insurance companies will pay to treat; which excuses and accusations are acceptable in court; which maladies can get you out of the Army; which can bestow upon you that most coveted of all American conditions—the status of Victim.

How did this happen?

The history of psychological and therapeutic endeavors in this country properly begins a century or so ago, during the so-called Progressive Era. One of the great beliefs of those infuriatingly earnest years was the superiority of disinterested expertise over more traditional sources of guidance and techniques of problem solving. "Disinterested" meant that the purveyor of the expertise had no personal stake in the outcome, and the more scientific-sounding it was, the better. As historian Arthur Link well summed it, reform-minded progressives believed in social justice via social control. To them

> *justice in an industrial society depended on systematic inter-*
> *ventions in the lives of people by both private associations and*
> *governments. . . . Briefly, justice meant to them giving all*

elements of society the benefit of their expertise; control meant
authorizing them to take whatever steps they thought necessary
to achieve that justice.

The psychological and therapeutic professions may or may not have been scientific back then. They certainly did their best to be scientific-sounding. But they were far from disinterested. Psychology was a rudimentary discipline, at best. Psychiatry dealt primarily with the inmates of mental hospitals, usually society's cast-offs; and secondarily with middle-class females given to the vapors, various forms of hysteria, and other symptoms of lives—as straitened as Victorian corsets—that sometimes drove women to madness. Both psychologists and psychiatrists wanted *respect*, not to mention endowed professorships, consulting fees, and power. These they achieved by, simultaneously, expanding the purview of their studies and overpromising, by orders of magnitude, what they could do for the crazy, for the merely dysfunctional and/or unhappy, and for the world. Thus began psychology's and psychotherapy's Long March through the Institutions, until today it is utterly impossible to spend more than a few waking moments without encountering its influence.

How far has this gone, this process of declaring us all ever-more-desperately in need of these services? The Census of 1840 was the first to count America's crazies. It recognized two categories: alcoholism and dementia. *DSM IV* offers nearly four hundred separate ways to go bonkers, with more in the works, as endless groups and factions campaign to have their conditions of interest included or excluded.

In short, for over a century, the psychological and therapeutic professions have undergirded just about everything. It is arguable that this civilization could not exist without the techniques of manipulation and control they provide. But the same forces, the same insights that have worked for social stability have also contributed to its progressive breakdown. In short, whether people have wanted to adjust or to rebel, to defend or to critique, for over a century, their vocabulary and their categories of thought have been provided by the psychological and therapeutic professions.

The history books tell us that the ethos and vocabulary of psychology and psychotherapy attained their dominance and omnipresence both by aggressive self-promotion and by default. Culturally, they filled the gaps left by the decline of older forms of guidance: religion, tradition, the wisdom of cherished elders, the insights of philosophers who took on the Big Questions. But psychobabble, and the reduction of reality, with all its complexities and nuances, to emotional states, also represents the final burnout of one of the strangest experiments in world history: modernism.

Prior to the Enlightenment, the bourgeois ascendancy, and the Industrial Revolution, Western culture came in two general forms: a "high" culture reserved for the elites, and a folk culture for everyone else. Nor was there an "adversary" culture, in the sense of self-consciously criticizing, opposing, and insulting the political and economic arrangements. Nor was there any prior belief that, in order to be a "real" artiste or thinker, you had to adopt an adversarial stance. Nor could anyone conceive that, someday, it might be possible to make endless amounts of money doing just that . . . or that, the less coherent your critique, the louder your music, and the more odious your behavior, the more you'd be laughing all the way to the ATM.

Why the most successful civilization in history would adopt, as its de facto official culture, one that mocked and scorned it at every turn, remains a matter for speculation. That the psychologized aspects of this scorn, and the concomitant obsession with self as the measure of all things, became the ethos of this movement, is clear.

I would suggest here that the latter stages of the Culture War marked the beginning of the end of this ethos. We all got utterly sick of it. But it did not signal any great return to traditional values or vocabularies. The end began because the tandem of modernist contempt for society, and psychobabble's inherent shallowness and dreary self-obsessed destructiveness, had grown too obvious and too ugly to ignore any longer. What remains of it remains because it has not yet been replaced.

It's time to replace it. It's time to tell the people who tell us what our choices are, we need not be confined to the either/or of so-called traditional values or psychologized gunk. There's an alternative vocabulary, one well known to the ancients and to our Founders. It hasn't been used much of late. When it has been, its words have been corrupted to make them seem an affirmation of traditional values. They're not. They're far more complex, and far more powerful.

So what was this Culture War about? And why might it be possible to believe, as a conservative, that America is much the better for having endured its insanities, inanities, and harm?

It seems uncertain how or why the term "Culture War" or its interchangeable plural variant, "Culture Wars," came into common usage. Etymologically, the English phrase may derive from the German *Kulturkampf*, or "culture struggle," referring to Chancellor Otto von Bismarck's contentions with the Catholic influence in 1870s Germany. The American version may have been coined by, and was certainly popularized by University of Virginia sociologist James Davison Hunter, in his 1991 and 1994 books, *Culture Wars: The Struggle to Define America* and *Before the Shooting Begins*.

To Hunter, the Culture War was serious business:

"At stake," he wrote, *"is how we as Americans will order our lives together." [Emphasis in the original.]* He also held that this was total war, leading inevitably to "the domination of one cultural and moral ethos over all others."

For Professor Hunter, the dominant struggle, the one that included all the others, was between the Orthodox and the Progressive mentalities, between the Orthodox *"commitment on the part of adherents to an external, definable, and transcendental authority"* and the Progressive *"tendency to resymbolize historic faiths according to the prevailing assumptions of contemporary life. [Emphasis in the original.]*

Professor Hunter, of course, did not view it as merely the interaction of two pristine ontologies. He deplored the fact that, on both sides *"positions on complex issues are reduced to caricatures . . . public debate now rarely seems to get beyond these caricatures."*

The problem was also that, without a common *"base of knowledge about the law, without traditions of moral understanding to draw upon, and without cohesive moral communities. . . all we have left are our emotions. Public debate becomes an exercise in emoting toward one another."*

And all have fallen short. Everything is reduced to "sentiment." As for much of what passes for Orthodoxy:

> *The moral traditions from which the languages of conviction derive have by no means disappeared. Americans will invoke them as personally meaningful, but at the same time they do not view them as publicly binding. . . . principles of right and wrong are themselves articulated as feelings rather than, say, obligations.*

For Professor Hunter, Americans were no longer able to

speak to each other in words of reason, or settle their differences without the constant intervention of the state.

Reading this in 1994, all I could think of was a weary, *So you finally figured it out.*

Professor Hunter got it half right. The Culture War was indeed a clash of visions. And for most of its thirty years, it was little more than a counterpoint of emoting and power-grabbing: emoting about our feelings while simultaneously dragging anything and everything into the legislatures and through the courts. But it was also about more. Much more. And it segued into something potentially wondrous.

The Culture War may conveniently be dated from the mid-sixties to the midnineties, or perhaps from Bill Clinton's draft-dodging discovery that he loathed the military to his post-Monica realization that America did not loathe him nearly as much as it should. The Culture War had no clear ending. Perhaps it simply faded out when America, exhausted from all the screaming, began to mutter, A plague—or if you prefer, a dys-function—on both your houses. By the conventional Left/Right tally, it appeared an almost total victory for the Left. Nowadays, some indicators seem to be pointing toward more "traditional" values. Marriage, for example: More people are getting married and staying married. But this reflects more people making that decision, choosing it from among several options, not more people returning to a rigid set of norms enforced by law and social censure.

The Culture War did not come about because everything in America was copasetic. Nor was it simply a movement to deny white male Christian conservative Americans their rightful place at the center of the universe. There were real issues to be settled, new matters to be addressed. And as Professor Hunter and so many other students of the phenomenon have pointed out, the rhetoric on both sides was often far more strident and far more polarized than the majority of the American people. Put differently:

There was probably a far greater willingness on the part of the American people to deal with these issues, from women's rights and gay rights to the environment and foreign affairs, than the Left wanted to admit—for to admit it would have required engaging the citizenry in rational, extended discourse. It was easier, far easier, for the Left to keep its backers mobilized and agitated by playing to psychologized ethics—what matters is how I feel—and the quest for unearned moral stature, while simultaneously winning victory after victory in the legislatures and the courts, than it was to take the hard road of persuading middle America of the justice of its causes. And the Right, for reasons of its own, was only too happy to go along with the game, only too happy to derive its funding and support by the stance of pure negativism. If they're for it, we're against it.

The Culture War was a failure of discourse, of what Jefferson somewhere once described as the pleasure of "persuading and being persuaded." Instead, there was endless public group therapy, endless confrontation for the sake of confrontation, and the endless flaunting of the two cardinal emotions of the Culture War Left: anger for the sake of anger, and anger's ugly twin, self-pity.

Consider, briefly, a few issues, all serious, all desperately in need of national attention, and how psychologized ethics and strategies affected them.

Feminism. If any cause other than race relations ever held a claim upon the American conscience, it was and is the equality of women, their right to full participation in every aspect of this civilization, and their corresponding responsibility for it. Yet the feminism of the Culture War abandoned its moral high ground for self-obsessed emoting that alienated potential male supporters by the millions. Susan Faludi notwithstanding, there was no "backlash." There was only a great turning away in weariness. Getting yelled at and insulted ultimately becomes like hearing airplanes going overhead; you're aware, but you don't really notice. And when feminism abandoned its moral high ground of demanding equal responsibility in favor of the gimme-gimme-gimme/rights-rights-rights approach, it alienated millions more. For example, might the integration of women into the military, a necessary and long-overdue matter, have proceeded more effectively if the professional feminists had not regarded the Armed Forces as the last bastion of machismo, to be brought down, rather than as a necessary and honorable part of this civilization?

Throughout the Culture War, women presented themselves as angry victims, demanding that the world accord with their wishes and whims, not as rational citizens making rightful claims for the purpose of taking their rightful places. In *Who Stole Feminism?* Christina Hoff Sommers presented one particularly luscious self-caricature, a 1992 conference of academic feminists:

> *Throughout the day, speakers recited tales of outrage and warned of impending male backlash. Sarah Ruddick, a New School for Social Research feminist known for "valorizing" women as the gentle nurturers of our species, paid tribute to Heilbrun's "politicized anger.": "Our anger, as Carolyn puts it so well, arouses the patriarchy to disgust. . . ."*
>
> *Jane Marcus, of the City University of New York, called the afternoon "Anger Session" to order, introducing herself as an "expert on anger" and thanking Heilbrun for teaching her to "use my rage in my writing." She introduced the other panelists*

as angry in one way or another: Alice Jardine of Harvard University's French department was "angry and struggling." Brenda Silver of Dartmouth had "been struggling and angry since 1972." Catherine Stimpson, former provost at Rutgers and recently selected to head the distinguished MacArthur Fellows program, was introduced as "an enraged and engaged intellectual."

Gloria Steinem took the microphone and explained why she was enraged: "I have become even more angry . . . the alternative is depression."

That year, Ms. Steinem came out with a book entitled *Revolution from Within: A Book of Self-Esteem*, informing us, among other things, that despite all the successes of the movement, and all her personal accomplishments, she still wasn't happy. "I was codependent with the world," she moaned. As for me, I finally took up introducing myself, both in public appearances and private conversation, as a "Keynesian feminist," after the great economist, John Maynard Keynes. A Keynesian feminist holds, among other things, that the supply of angry women vastly exceeds the demand. Responses were not always endearing.

Gay Rights. Again, a set of historic injustices, plus a tragic epidemic, much in need of serious, sustained national attention. If Americans are to live together and share responsibility for this civilization as citizens, the issue of sexual orientation should be off the table. That means, among other things, legally recognized gay partnerships, the end of the military's homosexual exclusion rule, and a culture that, while according gay people the same right to a dignified life that it accords heterosexuals, also expects dignified behavior. What did we, the scores of millions of straight people who were prepared to listen and support, get instead?

We got ACT-UP, the AIDS Coalition to Unleash Power, and their slogan, We Demand a Cure! How big a tantrum do you have to throw in order to get your cure?

We got the interesting phenomenon of Gay Pride parades, where (I've seen this) camera crews from the Religious Right would goad marchers into all kinds of poses and acts. The videos would be used for subsequent fund-raising; the marchers were only too happy to oblige. And we got the rest of the panoply of, I'm Here, I'm Queer, What Are You Going to Do about It? How about, we withdraw the support we might have offered?

Animal Rights is an absurdly malmonikered movement that didn't get far beyond its public persona of enraged yuppies tossing red paint on rich old ladies in their fur coats. That, plus lawsuits, lawsuits, lawsuits and a terrorist fringe that occasionally "liberates" a medical lab or mink farm or two. But at its heart is a fundamental question: Is more than the human morally considerable? If you believe the answer is no, that the universe and all therein is meant for human enjoyment and exploitation, morality becomes at best a matter of "wise stewardship." But if other species, especially the higher forms of life, do not exist for human convenience, to what conclusions might that ultimately lead? The animal rights—now sometimes known as the "animal awareness"—movement, had the potential to force us to a serious rethinking of the questions. It opted for tantrums.

Treatment of animals forms merely one subset of the larger issue of the human impact on, and relationship to, the natural world of which we are a part. Indeed, there may be no issue more important than ecology to ultimate human survival. But no other issue attracted so much absolute nonsense, so much histrionics. Its very magnitude seemed to generate an Emotions-Are-the-

Payoff approach, to the point where sociologist and True Believer Theodore Roszak, in *The Voice of the Earth*, suggested that "we may have reached the point at which the environmental movement must take the time to draw up a psychological-impact statement." When a Theodore Roszak, a man who suggested in 1969 that "truth must have a biographical, not merely an ideological [How about a factual?] content," begins to sense that maybe things have gotten out of hand, they have.

In one sense, it no longer matters. We died by the millions of starvation back in the nineties—at least, if you believe the Club of Rome/Paul Ehrlich seventies prophecies. (The global food supply is indeed imperiled, but it's hard to take the issue seriously after so much nonsense.) Still, while waiting to starve, I did enjoy following the "Grief and Empowerment Work" of Joanna Rogers Macy, teaching people to learn to mourn for the planet, then to become sufficiently enraged to act. Ms. Macy took her basic text as herself, her own struggle to deal with her feelings about the possible demise of the planet, and the great issue of what to do with such feelings: emote, repress, or empower. She wrote that "I carried these questions inside me like a bomb in my chest," until she realized that everybody else had the same problem, whether they admitted it or not. Then she took it on the road:

> . . . *there is immeasurable pain in our society—a pain carried at some level by each and every individual . . . As their [participants in her sessions] grief and fear of the world is allowed to be expressed without apology or argument, and validated as a wholesome, life-preserving response, people break through their avoidance mechanisms, break through their sense of futility and isolation. And generally what they break into is a larger sense of identity.*

Of course, Ms. Macy wasn't the only person on the road back then, informing us that if we just got in touch with our feelings, if we just felt it strongly enough, the world would somehow change. For some years, a psychologist named Chellis Glendinning made her living helping people learn (to reverse the old "Dr. Strangelove" quip) how to start worrying and not love the Bomb. As she wrote in *Waking Up in the Nuclear Age: The Book of Nuclear Therapy:*

> *I used to be a psychotherapist in private practice helping people explore attitudes and face feelings about more personal matters, but in 1979 the Three Mile Island nuclear power plant accident happened, and my world turned upside down. To me it was not just another segment of news happening somewhere else. Although I live 2,000 miles from Harrisburg, I found myself racked with terror. . . . Each night I lay half asleep, half awake feeling myself hanging from the most slender of threads, dangling in space with no support. With core bubbles bursting and radiation spewing across the countryside, there would be no help, no ambulance, no Mommy, no Daddy.*

This led her to the realization that:

> *Before I wove the nuclear threat into my personal story, I had no concept of the effect of nuclear weapons on my life. As I explored the question, I realized two points: one, as a Baby Boomer, I had never known a world without nuclear weapons; and two, I had lived my entire life incapable of planning for the future.*

So she began offering nuclear therapy sessions, at one of which:

*By the end of the two-hour session, 150 people were pounding
their fists together, sobbing, and holding one another. Whereas
before we had stood in denial or felt alone and guarded, now
we felt angry, scared, and sad. And as we realized how connected we are by the awful fate that hangs over us, a fourth
circle spontaneously formed: one of kinship and community
unlike any we had known before. The ritual completed itself
when a woman placed her nine-month-old child in the center
of the circle, and everyone held hands and sang songs of commitment and hope.*

One might speculate, not unkindly, that if this was the
most intense experience of kinship and community they'd
every known, the fault was less theirs than America's. Indeed,
building "communities of protest" via all kinds of theatrics
and ritual was one of the overt goals of nearly every movement. If it's true that experience is what you get when you
don't get what you wanted, then perhaps community—and
mailing lists—are what you get when your protest changes
nothing.

(Some years later, I did a phone interview with Dr. Glendinning. I expected a ditz. She turned out to be a wise and interesting woman who'd written movingly on how she came to
terms with a childhood of horrific sexual abuse. We spoke of
that. She hadn't merely exchanged one form of fashionable Victimhood for another. Chellis Glendinning proved another
example of Erik Erikson's dictum that sometimes people solve
their personal problems in ways that speak to others. Would
that all those who've undergone such ordeals could speak with
equivalent grace.)

But one kind of "community of protest" seemed, to me at
least, both trivial and obscene. This was the community of

Victimhood, and has nothing to do with the communal activities of those who've suffered genuine victimization and trauma. It has to do with defining everybody as a victim. Kai Erikson, sociologist son of psychologist Erik, and others argued that to live in society was by definition to be traumatized, and therefore a victim, no matter what one's experiences. It all depends on how you react. If you feel yourself traumatized, then you are. Robert Jay Lifton, one of the most prominent antinuclear psychiatrists of the age, and one of America's most perceptive thinkers on other issues, raised this notion to the level of pure psychological and ethical democracy when he wrote that "we are survivors not only of holocausts which have already occurred but of those we imagine or anticipate as well."

So now you can derive the status of victim when you don't even have to experience anything real. Just imagine it.

And so it went until, by the nineties, all the Left's pouting, posing, and posturing had become a weary, dreary, very unfunny joke. Perhaps art critic Robert Hughes summed it best: "Did any minimally radical movement ever supply its foes with such a delicious array of targets for cheap shots?"

Mr. Hughes wrote this epitaph in a book entitled *The Culture of Complaint*. But in the end, it was the Right that proved the real Culture of Complaint. Rather than doing the hard work of prudential reasoning, of recognizing both the legitimacy of the Left's issues and the significance of the forces that had corrupted the Left, they chose to create a star system of complainers: well-paid public figures whose job was, simply, to keep up the sneering and the complaining. Some, such as Bill Bennett, became household names. Lesser stars, but favored nonetheless, ensconced themselves in the think tanks and the journals and the television slots, churning out book after book, lecture after lecture. They drowned out and took funding from their more thoughtful peers. Not all their work was trivial or mean-spirited. But very little of it has aged well.

And the process is still going on, this tormenting of serious issues, on the Right and on the Left. Each side delights in excoriating the idiocies of the other. It's a great way to avoid having to think. I recall an experience I had in 1999, when the WTO (World Trade Organization) and President Clinton came to Seattle, that brought this home to me in an exceptionally poignant way.

Globalization has serious issues, not least among them the export of American jobs, the wrecking of local economies, and the environmental aspects. But, as usual, the whole carnival-superimposed-on-a-tragedy motif took over, as well as the quest for unearned moral stature via emotional payoffs.

I wanted to see if anything had really changed, protest-wise, so I went quasi-underground to write about it for the *Washington Times*. I attended the riots as "Schlep Barocha," a Yiddish neologism perhaps best translated, "mixed blessing." For credibility purposes, I introduced myself as an elder of the Towhomit Tribe, as in "To Whom It May Concern." Our tribal motto: Of Course We're Concerned. We're Towhomit!

The "festival of resistance" was fun. So was observing preparations for the inevitable class-action lawsuits that would occur after the police were provoked into enforcing the law. Even before the gas had cleared, radical lawyers set up street-corner tables with sign-up sheets. Were you brutalized by the police? Do you think you might have been brutalized by the police? Do you wish you'd been brutalized by the police? Do you plan on being brutalized by the police?

But the oddest moment came about when a young woman, distraught, approached me.

"What's the problem?" I asked.

"I've become separated from my affinity group and I'm missing our direct action."

Man, we sure didn't talk like that in the sixties.

"Which is?"

"We're painting wall murals."

"I know a wall that could use a good mural."

"Oh, tell me where, sir. Please tell me where!"

I sent her off in the general direction of a wall, and subsequently tried to get a few conservatives to take the globalization issue seriously. They chose instead the old mantra: How can you expect us to take the issue seriously when you got all those clowns and thugs protesting? It was easier, it was always easier, to mock the cheap targets offered by the protesters, and their more than occasional incoherence, than to understand the issues. Anyway, whatever they were against, we favored. And there was, truth to tell, a lot of money out there for just that purpose. All you had to do to tap into it was to know the right people at the right foundations, write the grant applications properly, and produce as expected.

So what was the Culture War about? Many things. When did it end? Sometime in the nineties, when much of America came to regard Left and Right as two hokey wrestlers, so intent on staging their match that they didn't notice the audience leaving.

So who won? By all conventional measures, the Left. Is there a Culture War II aborning? Some on the Right would wish it so. After all, there's a lot of money at stake here, and careers to be advanced, and the "use the war to take back the culture" motif is still very much with us.

Perhaps we may be heading into Culture War II. But I would offer an alternative interpretation.

The Culture War cleared away a lot of junk. But to an ever-increasing percentage of America, it's history, someone else's war. Concepts of equality, diversity, the right of all to dignity, environmental awareness, and the rest, are now too firmly ensconced to be negated. And a lot of the excesses are being forgotten as those who fought the war, fade away.

But something else is happening. This cannot be proven, but it may be true nonetheless:

The Culture War has segued into an historically unprecedented experiment. It is now the attempt to create an "acentric" civilization, in which no race, gender, group, creed, or way of life provides the norm against which all else is measured, judged, or even tolerated. We are now moving toward a civilization in which, beyond the necessary commonalities of law and language (no small commonalities), there is no center, only choices and packages of choices.

Can it be done? More important, can it be done in time of war and terror, perhaps in time of approaching ecological danger? The vast majority of conservatives would answer, Hell no. But perhaps at least a few conservatives might conclude that it's an experiment worth trying, and that maybe conservatism might have something to say to an acentric civilization. Indeed, conservatism, a new conservatism, might make a vital contribution to this experiment. But first, it must surrender its claim to inhabit the center of the universe. And it must shed a mentality I encountered in an unusually pristine form via Bill Lind. He'd written a "futuristic" novel entitled *Victoria*. No one would publish it. So it appeared on the Free Congress Foundation Website. *Victoria* began:

The triumph of the Recovery was marked most clearly by the burning of the Episcopal Bishop of Maine.

She was not a particularly bad bishop. She was, in fact, quite typical of Episcopal bishops of the first quarter of the 21st century: agnostic, compulsively political, and radical and given to placing a small idol of Isis on the altar when she said the Communion service. By 2037, when she was tried for heresy, convicted and burned, she had outlived her era. By that time, only a handful of Episcopalians still recognized female clergy, and it would have been easy enough to let the old fool rant out her final years in obscurity. But we are a people who do our duty.

Chapter 7

Think Tanks, etc.

Think tanks are about power.
—Philip Gold

L EO TOLSTOY ONCE WROTE THAT, while every
happy family was alike, each unhappy family was unhappy
in its own way.

Leo Tolstoy never visited a think tank, where everybody is
unhappy in the same way. Endless egos to dodge, confront, or
assuage. An atmosphere redolent of arrogance and disdain for
those who dare hold other views, especially within the walls of
ideologically homogeneous enterprises where the Big Issues are
settled and the fine points become matters of ferocious strife.
And above all else, the need to keep real and potential donors
happy about the projects they're funding, the projects they
think they're funding, the projects they're thinking about
funding, and the projects that are none of their business, but
always seem to require their guidance.

A think tank, Left or Right, is a mind-numbing affair. Pity
the poor presidents and VPs/development, always out hustling
for bucks, never knowing when some senior fellow or research

associate might say or write something that blows the big bequest or gums up the gargantuan grant or fouls the federal forage. Pity the poor fellows and assistants who never know what the presidents and VPs/development are out hustling for. And pity anyone who doesn't understand that, Left or Right, the Prime Directive: Here's your money; here are your conclusions; now go do the study—is always in force.

In a sense, a think tank is a lot like an ad agency. The account people and the creative groups communicate poorly, rarely getting their music in a row and playing off the same sheet of ducks. Think tanks and ad agencies both deal in creations and campaigns on behalf of clients who have agendas of their own, and who don't like wasting money. An old adage, often attributed to department store magnate John Wanamaker, stated: I know that half the money I spend on advertising is wasted. Problem is, I don't know which half. Ditto, oft enough, for think-tank funding. It might be noted that, according to the IRS, less than 15 percent of all philanthropic funding goes toward tax-exempt policy research, so the competition for money is always ferocious. It might also be noted that, as a general rule, funders give more freely when their parties and movements are out of power or favor, so think tanks often find themselves more prosperous when they're engaged in "taking back" than when they're engaged in "taking over."

Think-tank products can be strange, ephemeral, and occasionally brilliant. Most often, they tend toward the banal, the repetitious, and the safe. Always better to produce a mediocrity that the funders or the clients can understand and explain to their boards, than to take a chance.

Thought without courage, sad to relate, is what the buyers too often want, and what the sellers are often only too happy to provide.

In certain ways, between the products of the advertising business and those of the think-tank trade, there's not that much of a difference. Both are intended to sell you something. Both do so less by angling for an immediate decision than by bringing ideas into the realm of the known, hence of the potentially acceptable, and by determining the structure of debate, the range of choices on any given issue. Those who control the terms of debate control a great deal. To the extent that America lets them format the choices, that's power.

Think tanks are about power.

The modern think tank is generally presumed to be the post-World War II progeny of Herman Kahn, founder of the RAND Corporation, originally an Air Force affair. RAND was supposed to be the prototype. Creative problem solving. Fast turnaround solutions. A bunch of brilliant guys, thinking immeasurably deep thoughts even while wandering the halls with their coffee cups. Today, RAND has both Army and Air Force projects, each dedicated to touting the strategic, geopolitical, budgetary, and moral supremacy of its service over the other.

RAND notwithstanding, the concept of the think tank, or the public policy research institute, actually goes back to the Progressive Era, when so many of America's more infuriating habits were acquired. Progressives believed above all else in the power of disinterested expertise to find the right policies, that is, those leading to justice via control. But there was a problem, dating back several decades to initial attempts to regulate the railroads. To regulate effectively, you need people who understand the business. But how do you get yourself a railroad expert who hasn't spent years and years working on the railroad and acquiring outlooks and loyalties at variance with your disinterested, justice-seeking, control-freak agenda? Expertise from outside the industry, untainted by practical experience and responsibility, was clearly needed. One way to manufacture such expertise was, basically, to pay people to acquire it by outside study, then get them into government, or at least use them as influential advisers. Research institutes would be one way to prepare these people. And since it was obvious to progressives that the new social sciences and the new discipline of psychiatry could offer disinterested solutions to just about any problem, research institutes could be useful in these areas, too.

But these early research institutes were intended to do more than speak expertise to power. The Progressive Era established a format for political and social debate that remains with us to this day. As historian Arthur Link describes it:

> *The Progressives went about methodically to achieve justice through control. They usually began by organizing a voluntary association. Next they investigated a problem, gathered mountains of data about it, and, finally, analyzed the problem according to the precepts of one of the new social sciences. From such an analysis, a proposed solution would emerge, be popularized through campaigns of education and moral suasion, and—as often or not, if it seemed to work—be taken over at some level of government as a permanent public function.*

And so it has gone, albeit at exponentially greater levels of sophistication, ever since. And think tanks long ago expanded their purview from solving problems to selling solutions via the media. The product, whether policy or idea, for or against, must be publicized. This usually happens by a two-step process of reaching "opinion leaders"—journalists, celebrities, and such—then letting them spread the word to the advertising-addled masses. So the real power of think tanks, Left and Right, lies as much in their ability to influence people as to influence government. Toward this end, there has arisen, Left and Right, an exceedingly complex latticework of think tanks, universities, media, and entertainment. Let some unexpected crisis hit and, almost immediately, think tank PR flacks are churning out their announcements that so-and-so is "available for comment." Let a crisis last more than forty-eight hours and watch the media retainers get offered. And let a crisis get solved, and watch how eagerly all those on-call experts-turned-pundits explain what else lies ahead, requiring their insights.

I took my share after 9/11, working as a talking head for KING5 TV, NorthWest Cable News, and KCTS television, all in Seattle. This last, an unpaid gig for the local PBS station, proved especially interesting, inasmuch as one of the assistant producers was a woman I'd likely thrown out of my bedroom at a Yale dorm party several decades before. We were contemporaries. She'd gone to nearby Albertus Magnus, a Catholic women's college that seemed to specialize in the production of quietly smoldering Catholic women. They scared us.

The whole experience showed me, among other things, that talking headery ain't as easy as it looks. I made every mistake in the book, then recycled a few, but emerged with Dr. Philip's Seven Golden Rules for Making It as a Talking Head.

One. Don't worry about being ugly.

Two. Remember at all times: The camera magnifies and intensifies everything about you.

Three. When answering a question, keep it to fifteen seconds or less, starting with a five-second conclusion, then ten seconds worth of explication, exegesis, and in-depth analysis.

Four. If you can't answer the question, respond to it.

Five. If the question is irredeemably idiotic or ridiculous, answer the question the interviewer should have asked.

Six. If you can't answer the question the interviewer should have asked, respond to it.

Seven. Always end the segment with a memorable and provocative insight, such as "I believe we should listen respectfully to any UN delegation whose members pay their parking tickets" or, "Why, yes, I do think the use of secret military tribunals should be expanded to cover other crimes against humanity, such as graffiti, loud car stereos, and anybody caught in possession of anything by, about, or pertaining to Britney Spears."

To which we might add: Unless you're a professional and/or very, very cute, never let your children watch you on television. Generous critics they're not.

The Progressives worshiped disinterested expertise. They were also quite religious about ignoring the fact that, once expertise moves into the public realm, it inevitably becomes partisan in one form or another, and ultimately far from disinterested. Long has the Beltway pretended to fret over the "revolving door"—people moving easily between government jobs and the private sector. Think tanks suffer from few legal restrictions in this matter, and a fine cushy office with salary to match can be a great inducement for keeping the funders happy while in office.

By the twenties, certainly by the eve of World War II, everybody had their experts. By the seventies, it was clear that some disinterested and objective experts worked for conservatives and Republicans, some for liberals and Democrats. So has it gone ever since. And best you be clear about who they are and who you are, before you ask for a job. And if you take a job, best you be clear about the fact that think tanks might sell ideas and influence, but they run on money.

So what exactly is a modern think tank? Legally, it's usually a 501c3 tax exempt research and educational institution, which is forbidden, on pain of losing its IRS status, to engage in active lobbying or politics. This stricture is generally trampled on, evaded, and ignored. Occasionally, some disgruntled administration will run up some think tank's legal bill by challenging its status and checking its books. Bill Clinton's persecution of the conservative Heritage Foundation not only cost them six, maybe seven figures, but resulted in their placing (for a time) a disclaimer on their products that they had no intention of influencing legislation or policy. Course not. We do this for fun.

Basically, then, a think tank is a mechanism for the manufacture and dissemination of ideas and proposals that somebody with money wants manufactured and disseminated. Within the Beltway, and especially on the Right, think tanks tend to be more than just ideologically homogeneous and self-selecting. They're also white-male dominated, hierarchical, compartmentalized, rigid, and crabby. They come in two basic genres: full-service and boutique. The large full-service think tanks seem to have opinions on everything, and the staff and connections to get them out. Boutiques specialize in single or related issues such as defense or environmental policy or urban affairs. Some small ones specialize in whatever they can get. Both varieties, Left and Right, are capable of solid to excellent work. But for the vast majority of products, brilliance is neither required nor desired nor rewarded. Orthodoxy counts. On the Left, this is known as PC, or Political Correctness. But there is also a conservative PC. It's "solid," as in: He's a solid thinker. Never had an original or dissenting thought in his life. He can be trusted not to embarrass you.

So who works in think tanks? An odd bestiary. Think tanks employ a lot of grim-faced young men and women, determined to bring their visions to the world. All, it seems, are former student council presidents. Some smile. They're keenly aware that they're not expected to remain more than a year or two. They're always looking, and can be easily identified at receptions and cocktail parties. They're the people trying to talk with, and be seen talking with, someone more important than themselves. When nearly everybody's more important than you are, that's not hard.

Think tanks also employ: A certain number of midlevel people who write the same studies over and over, and who are expected to die at their desks—unless they piss someone off, in which case they're expected to die elsewhere.

Fast-track younger-to-middling people preparing to go into some administration or other. They're always looking, and are often visible at cocktail parties, trying to talk with people more important than themselves. They usually end up chatting with each other.

A lot of middling-to-aging people who once held a job in some administration or other and have parlayed those years into de facto think tank tenure. Sometimes they die at their desks. More often, they expire in the halls, usually with coffee mug in hand. Some have been known to stand in the hallway, dead, for several hours before anyone notices, or cares.

Think tanks also employ some senior people, usually high-level former officials, who either don't have, or don't want to return to, their former law firm or corporation. Sometimes, they can't return. They can be observed at cocktail parties and receptions, expecting to be talked to by everyone and doing their best to avoid it. Their positions are usually described by starting with the name of whomever endowed their chair, followed by the word "Distinguished." As in, the Honorable Jack Sprat, former Deputy Assistant Under Secretary of Defense for Paper Clips and now the Margaret Hoolihan Distinguished Senior Fellow in Strategic Stapling. Also, "former" matters. For example, a person who has held several important positions may be introduced as, "Former Secretary of State, former National Security Adviser, former Harvard professor, may I introduce the former Honorable Dr. Henry Kissinger."

Think tanks also affiliate endless adjuncts. Sometimes they're paid a little, sometimes not at all. You get what you pay for. Still, they're good for making the place look larger than it is, and for guaranteeing a certain minimal attendance at conferences, colloquies, confabs, and charades.

And three times over the past few decades, a think tank welcomed me, more or less.

My first experience came with my postdoctoral grant from the Smith Richardson Foundation. As a rule, foundations do not make grants to individuals. They turn you over to some institute they're also supporting, paying them an administration fee to house, service, and monitor you. I found myself at the small Washington, DC, office of the Cambridge-based Institute for Foreign Policy Analysis, which I'd never heard of before and have rarely heard of since. IFPA was solid. Except for the folks in the DC office. There was a retired Navy rear admiral, now deceased, who came late, said little, left early, and didn't much like Jews. I never did figure out what, if anything, he did. During our sole confrontation, I controlled myself admirably. There was a young Russian emigré named David Rivkin. When I asked him how he'd gotten out of the Soviet Union, he replied, "My country traded me for wheat." David got fired, a wise career move on his part, and is now a DC attorney. And there was Jeff Record, a senior defense analyst, formerly of Brookings, formerly also of Senator Sam Nunn's staff, who took seriously the adage that, within the Beltway, a defense analyst could be either a nuisance or a whore.

Jeff was no whore. I'd never met him before, but he'd already annoyed me thoroughly by coauthoring a nuisance of a monograph on the Marine Corps while at Brookings. He turned out to be quite an education, as befits a man who dodged the draft by going to Vietnam as a civilian AID (Agency for International Development) worker. In fact, he's still quite an education, and a nuisance. In December 2003, while a visiting something-or-other at the U.S. Army War College, he turned out a study, "Bounding the Global War on Terrorism," that left the White House fuming.

The Beltway could use a few thousand more nuisances like Jeff.

Not surprisingly, we got to talking defense. Jeff also introduced me to a number of interesting and unusual people, including a sales rep/lobbyist for a German antitank missile, who took me to the most expensive restaurant I've ever entered, before or since. When he finally got around to chatting up his *Armbrust*, I chose not to observe that, for the price of the lunch, he could have provided me with a free sample. Instead, I asked him why he'd invited me at all. I assured him that, should I ever need an antitank weapon for my personal use, I'd definitely consider his. But I had no influence or authority in the matter, nor was I likely to acquire any. The gentleman sighed and gave me to understand that if he didn't spend money, his boss thought he wasn't working, and he'd already entertained everybody else.

Free lunch or not, defense was a subject I'd hoped to leave behind me that night at Fort Indiantown Gap, when I pocketed my pistol for the final time. There were other things I wanted to do more. For the moment, however, I was tasked with writing a book on conscription, not educating the Republic to the dangers of psychologized politics and ethics. Anyway, things military still interested me. Especially the Defense Reform Movement then in its maturing phase.

To this day, few Americans know or understand what happened in and to the military during the seventies and eighties. According to the popular sketch, things were a mess in the seventies. Then along came Ronald Reagan, who spent lots of money "beefing up" the force, and in 1991 we kicked butt * like nothing before.

Things were indeed a mess in the seventies. And Ronald Reagan did indeed spend money in the eighties, generating en passant some of the silliest and most overblown pseudoscandals in the history of Pentagon weapons procurement. (After the Gulf War, I ran an article on how all those "troubled" weapons systems, so plagued by cost overruns and official malfeasance, had performed so well. Nobody wanted to hear it. The weapon that gets fixed isn't news.) But the resurrection of the American military was primarily a matter of intellect and hard thought, coupled with no small quantity of courage, in the years before the Reagan "bow wave" of defense spending. Some of it took place within the think tank world. Most did not.

The Defense Reform Movement was never an organized or even a very coherent entity. Some people specialized in operational doctrine, some in force structure, some in weapons development, some in publicizing it all. Participants ranged from active-duty officers to civilian officials to congressional staffers to defense intellectuals. All were in rebellion against the

Vietnam experience and its legacies. And nearly all worshipped the unofficial leader and patron saint of the movement, an obscure retired Air Force colonel named John Boyd.

With the arguable exception of the Goldwater-Nichols Defense Reorganization Act (Barry G. was no reformer, just annoyed at how squirrelly the Pentagon had gotten), the Defense Reform Movement never got a single significant piece of legislation through Congress. There was a bipartisan reform caucus for a few years, specializing mostly in lunch. Ultimately, the movement's legacy was a style that permeated a good bit of the military, though far from all of it. Although one of its central tenets, "maneuver warfare," became Marine doctrine under General Al Gray, the Army's embrace has always been more nuanced. Many of its other ideas never got past the jawing stage. But the Defense Reform Movement shaped the thinking of thousands of young and not-so-young officers. And if it's all starting to fade away now, it was definitely the right thing at the right time.

Maneuver warfare is a complex affair, but it's based on a simple concept. War is primarily a mental activity, in which physically inferior but intellectually superior forces can often— not always and not always cheaply, but often—defeat larger opponents. Yes, size matters. And quantity has a quality all its own. But thought, thought coupled with courage, also has qualities of its own.

Boyd began to develop his concept of maneuver warfare after the Korean War, when the Air Force asked him to study why American pilots in their F-86s ran up such lopsided "kill ratios" against enemy pilots in their MiG-15s, in many ways a technically superior aircraft. Analysis of the two planes showed that, while the MiG could outperform the F-86 in individual modes, (climb faster, turn tighter, that sort of thing) the F-86 had better hydraulics, enabling the craft to transition from one maneuver to another more effectively. The bubble-top canopy also gave the pilot better visibility. Those facts, plus interviews with pilots, led Boyd over time to develop the "OODA cycle," sometimes aka "OODA loop."

Observation. Orientation. Decision. Action.

Observation: The pilot observes something.

Orientation: He places it within the total situation.

Decision: He decides what to do.

Action: He does it.

Totally obvious. But no one had ever studied it closely before. Boyd, himself a fighter pilot with Korean experience, concluded that victory most often went to the pilot who worked through the cycle faster than his opponent. This is because war is a reactive affair. Each pilot reacted to what the other was doing. However, after a couple iterations, the pilot with the faster OODA cycle found that his opponent had reached the stage of reacting to something that he was *no longer doing*. The enemy pilot noticed it too. Panic set in. The outlooped pilot either fled or threw himself into a flurry of desperate, ineffective maneuvers, hoping that he might get lucky, that something might work.

Anyone who has boxed against a much faster opponent understands this only too well. So did the late George Plimpton, who enjoyed going up against pro athletes in order to write about it later. Plimpton boxed heavyweight champion Sonny Liston. His experiences on the NFL gridiron led to his book, *Paper Lion*, and to a subsequent film. A television talk show host, Dick Cavett I believe, once asked him what he found the most frightening. Plimpton replied that it wasn't the physicality of boxing or football. He knew he was hopelessly outclassed and expected the appropriate and inevitable results. It was a profound mental failure. He was playing bridge against the world-class pro Charles Goren, getting creamed, and not having the foggiest idea why.

After Boyd retired from the Air Force he locked himself up for a year and did nothing but read. His studies convinced him that "maneuver," getting inside the adversary's OODA cycle, was the way successful armies, successful businesses, and successful countries won. And "getting inside the other guy's loop" became, to many, a talisman of victory, in its way, as much a motivational cliché as pushing the box or thinking outside the envelope.

Maneuver warfare oversold itself. Most new ideas have to. Still, it's important to remember that the maneuverists never claimed that clever thinking could substitute for hard training or proper weaponry or force structure, or always avoid costly attrition, or guarantee anything. All it promised was the potential to win by destroying the enemy's ability to fight coherently and effectively, without having to spend enormous resources or to pile up mountains of corpses. And it offered a conceptual alternative to those who sensed that old-style conventional attrition warfare was no longer either practical or necessary.

For over a century, "the American way of war" had emphasized sheer weight of resources, human and materiel, over agility and thought. Perhaps nothing expressed this attitude better than a scene from the movie, *Battle of the Bulge*, where a German Panzer colonel presents his general with a Boston cream pie, still fresh, taken from an American prisoner. The colonel asks his general if he understands what this means. The general shrugs. "It means," replies the colonel, "that the Americans have petrol to fly cake across the Atlantic Ocean."

We flew a lot of cake, and other items, into Vietnam, with not entirely satisfactory results. In the early seventies, with a sigh and a shrug and a recitation of the old, Thank God that's over with, now we can get back to soldiering, the Army bureaucracy turned back to its favorite budget-enhancing enemy, the Warsaw Pact. In Europe, America was clearly not the resource-superior power, and the question of "how to fight outnumbered and win" engaged the thinkers. For practical purposes, the issue was moot. Nobody expected a Soviet invasion of NATO Europe to stay nonnuclear. American policy was "first use" of nuclear weapons against Soviet conventional forces. And most people understood that the invasion wasn't going to happen, if only because the United States and the Soviet Union had long before reached a tacit agreement that only one side could go crazy at a time. We took our turn in Vietnam, they in Afghanistan. But it was an engaging intellectual exercise, especially when Soviet doctrine emphasized administering "crushing rebuffs" (it sounds scarier in Russian) while American doctrine spoke of attriting the enemy until we could "restore the border on favorable terms prior to negotiation."

All that thinking paid off, not in Europe, but in Desert Storm, and twelve years later in Iraqi Freedom. Most people attribute those victories to what is known to the AO (Acronym-Obsessed) as the Revolution in Military Affairs (RMA)—the application of microprocessor technologies and new materials to everything from precision targeting to communications and reconnaissance. But mere possession of gee-whiz gadgetry does not in itself guarantee anything, as the French have learned to their sorrow more than once. However, it is arguable that the technologies provided by the RMA, coupled with the intellectual agility engendered by the Defense Reform Movement and the maneuverist outlook, made this nation's military unique and, for purposes of conventional warfare, undefeatable.

Intellectually, then, the seventies and eighties were an exciting time to listen, learn, and participate, even though nobody took reviving the draft all that seriously. (By the by, the Selective Service System has been gearing up of late, and has until March 31, 2005, to report to the president that it's good to go.) It was also interesting to watch one of the Beltway's prime maneuverists in action.

Bill Lind, the man who would inform me many years later that people needed simple ideas in order to be controlled, had never worn a uniform. His military expertise came via study and service on Capitol Hill, as legislative assistant to Democratic Senator Gary Hart, one of the more avid reformers. He followed that stint with many years in residence at a very conservative Beltway think tank, the Free Congress Foundation. To describe Lind's style as brilliant but eccentric would be putting it discreetly. In his early years, while touting maneuver warfare to the Marines, his arrogance would sometimes reduce combat veterans to a searing, "Excuse me, what battalion did you say you were in?" His 1991 description of General Schwarzkopf's Desert Storm flanking movement as "too shallow" and "a typical amateur mistake" didn't win him many Army friends, either. He'd published so many articles in the *Marine Corps Gazette*, the service professional journal, some officers had taken to calling it the *Bill Lind Review*. During my year or so as the reserve rep on the magazine's editorial board, I recall a couple meetings to which headquarters sent down a brigadier to sit in silently, making sure we didn't run any more Bill Lind. Still, he was fascinating to watch and read. And I was ready to take him seriously, at least for a while, in his other great intellectual love, cultural conservatism.

Today, Lind has moved on to another concept: Fourth

Generation Warfare, or 4GW. As near as I can tell, 4GW covers nearly everybody who doesn't stand up and fight fair, that is, the way you want them to. This time, however, the nonfair fighters come equipped with a rather nasty array of weapons and options. Whether the concept may prove to be too general to be useful, if valid at all, remains to be seen. What is not debatable is the historical significance of the contribution of the defense reformers of the seventies and eighties. That, and the fact that getting inside your opponent's cycle—*works*. Especially when debating ideologues, Left or Right. So much of the so-called War of Ideas is pure attrition, wearing down the opposition. But it's also great fun to confront people with ideas and alternatives they can't respond to, yet can't ignore. Get inside their cycle, let them flounder and try to return the debate to its predictable form. Then just tell them, Sorry, I can't give you the argument you're looking for. It works. But you do need to be ready to beat feet out of there in a hurry. When conservatives don't behave as expected, liberals tend to get very, very mad.

★   ★   ★

The draft book got written. In September 1982, I got an unexpected phone call from the chair of Georgetown's history department. They'd had to add an overflow section to their EuroCiv survey course, and they needed a teacher in a hurry. Since I'd already taught it as a grad student, would I like to take the slot for one semester, renewable? I said yes, absolutely, positively, and totally yes, and I can be more explicit if you wish. I'd always planned on being a professor. If I had to go the adjunct route, so be it. I then rigged up a second appointment with the liberal studies program as a professorial lecturer, and worked on that one semester/renewable arrangement for the next fourteen years.

Both appointments had me teaching . . . defense. No matter. "War and U.S. Society: 20th Century," turned out to be one of the most popular undergraduate lectures and graduate seminars offered, which infuriated many of my more liberal colleagues. But the real fun course was "National Defense in Cultural Context," offered as a sophomore research seminar for the Foreign Service School kids, many of them ROTC. Each week, we'd dissect another issue: NATO, Star Wars, the draft, whatever. What's the military requirement? What are the political constraints? How does the culture affect both? About halfway through the semester, inevitably, a student would say to me, Things can't be this fucked up. That was my cue to announce that, next week, we'd be meeting at the Pentagon. There, I'd either get a briefing room and have several officials come in to talk about their work, or else march the students to several offices. I would also let them get a good look at the main cafeteria and then reason out for themselves why it was a bad idea to make decisions after lunch, especially if you'd had the appetizers, entrees, or desserts.

Teaching was pure delight. I was popular. Charisma by default, I guess. Most PC profs are dreadful bores.

Not all my colleagues cared for me, and the word went forth among the younger, New Left and Far Leftover teachers: avoid this guy. From time to time, students told me that teachers were commenting on me in their classes, loudly and negatively, as being "*so* conservative." The department office had a bookcase holding faculty publications. Person or persons unknown started removing my books, a practice that went on until they realized that I kept replacing them with copies I'd bought at the university bookstore and charged to the history account. It was cheery.

Also delightful was the day I learned that some of my colleagues wished to get me fired for "insensitivity." Never mess with somebody who has less to lose than you do. I put on my darkest dark glasses and my brown leather bomber jacket and walked unannounced into the office of the relevant colleague.

"I hear I'm insensitive."

The man began to tremble.

(For a number of reasons, not the least of which, that I was then working as a full-time journalist while commuting from DC to Alaska, I'd decided that I could no longer teach undergrads during the day. After six years, time to resign my history appointment. But I saw no particular reason to let these people play PC games with me.)

"Look, I've decided that this is going to be my last year teaching undergrads. I'd like to enjoy it. If that's not possible, I would welcome a well-publicized controversy. Shall we start with an op-ed in the *Wall Street Journal*?"

My colleague gave me to understand that if I was indeed resigning, there was no further need to pursue the matter, whatever that matter might have been.

"You mean . . . I'm sensitive?"

The poor guy looked like he was about to liquidate.

"Yes . . . you're sensitive . . . you're sensitive . . ."

Another sensitive Marine, Mac Owens, kept me in journalism by hooking me up with Public Research Syndicated (PRS), a small service out of the Claremont Institute that they were also supporting. PRS reached about three hundred papers, mostly small-town ones. Then, in the spring of 1982, a newspaper with an extremely unlikely owner opened for business.

"What's it like to work for a publisher who thinks he's God?" a *Washington Post* reporter asked Smith Hempstone, first editor in chief of the *Washington Times*, the new conservative paper owned by Rev. Sun Myung Moon's Unification Church. Replied Mr. Hempstone: "I've worked for a lot of publishers who thought they were God."

When the *Washington Times* first appeared, few knew what to do with it. I ran my first column that June. A few hundred more followed over the next twenty-two years, plus a couple hundred articles during the five years I worked as a full-time staff writer for *Insight*, their weekly magazine, covering national defense, advertising, and psychiatry. I'd taken the job primarily because, what with a wife and baby, income mattered. Necessity notwithstanding, it proved a wonderful experience. Star Wars one week, ecopsychology or the latest advertising enthusiasms, the next. And it confirmed again what all my teaching and previous writing has shown—the fundamental intelligence, and willingness to use that intelligence, of the American people, whenever they're afforded the chance.

But it didn't end wonderfully for me. Throughout the Reagan/Bush and Clinton years, the *Washington Times* did fine work. Today, the paper serves as little more than a cheerleader for the Bushies and the neocons. In early 2004, tired of unreturned phone calls, never-got-it e-mails, and endlessly rescheduled columns, I gave up trying to get anything placed. In a bizarre e-mail exchange with managing editor Francis Coombs, I told him that I'd been effectively ostracized for my opposition to the war. He ignored my statement, but did inform me that the paper was doing just fine under his tutelage, and was having quite an impact on the power structure. I asked him if I could quote from his e-mail for this book. He declined, but did assure me that if I asked him a question on the record, he would answer.

The Imperial Media.

★   ★   ★

In 1982, the capital of the free world was, incredibly, a one-newspaper town. No one cared to compete commercially with the *Washington Post*. No one could. So the Moonies decided to go into the publishing business and offer a heavily-subsidized conservative alternative. From the beginning, they were up front about their ownership. At one point, trying to capitalize on public aversion to the Unification Church, they ran ads of people reading the paper with bags over their heads. It wasn't all that clever or effective. But it soon became clear that this would be a serious paper. They hired serious people, especially veterans of the recently defunct *Washington Star*. Later, they brought in Arnaud de Borchgrave as editor in chief. Arnaud, a former Belgian count and newspaper legend, a man who'd covered wars by the dozen and who got his phone calls returned, insisted on serious journalism.

Arnaud was actually the first American to enter Kuwait, except for the special operations guys, during the Gulf War. A personal friend of Egyptian President Hosni Mubarak, he'd persuaded him to authorize an armored patrol that would take him a couple hundred yards across the border, then back. Arnaud always prized and encouraged initiative.

Arnaud knew that the *Times* could never get rich off advertising, the major media revenue stream. In a two-newspaper town, few major advertisers—retail, supermarkets, autos, real estate—would pay to advertise in two papers. The *Post* had that locked. But he could make the *Times* the paper that the Beltway couldn't ignore. Circulation has bounced between 80,000 and 120,000 or so for the last couple decades. But among those readers are people who matter. And of course, you can punch up the Web site without wearing a bag.

At the *Times*, I met and enjoyed working with some wonderful people. And I should like to state, for the record, that
never in over twenty years was I asked or pressured to alter a
single word because of what somebody in the business office or
the Unification Church might want. There were the usual
writer/editor dustups, of course. But there was absolutely no
pressure to change my sometimes peculiar point of view or
unorthodox conclusions . . . until the paper shut down all criticism of the war, save for one syndicated curmudgeon, Paul
Craig Roberts; an occasional libertarian broadside; and, from
time to time, Don Devine. Others may have had different experiences with the *Washington Times*. That was mine.

Insight was also an experience. Today, it's sadly shrunken and
obscure. But in its early years, before budget cuts and personnel
exodus changed it, *Insight* was one of the fastest-growing news
and feature mags in the country; circulation reached 800,000
one year. One key was style: longer stories that told people
more about a subject than *Time* or *Newsweek* might, but in an
accessible format. The other key was people. *Insight* never had
more than twenty or so staff writers and editors. But they went
on to an astonishing array of other successes, within the conservative movement and elsewhere. Consider a few:

Malcolm Gladwell, now with the *New Yorker*, author of *The
Tipping Point*.

Holman Jenkins, now columnist with the *Wall Street Journal*.

John Podhoretz, now columnist and editor with the *New
York Post*.

Tod Lindberg, now editor of *Policy Review*.

Richard Starr, now managing editor of the *Weekly Standard*.

Helle Dale, now a vice president of the Heritage Foundation.

Danielle Pletka, now a vice president of the American Enterprise Institute.

And David Brock, who made his reputation with *The Real Anita Hill*. David spent much of the nineties working for the *American Spectator*, ferreting out Bill Clinton's assorted sexual malfeasances. He got a huge contract to do an Anita-Hill-type job on Mrs. Clinton; *The Seduction of Hillary Rodham* failed miserably, commercially and as a serious attack. David then publicly apologized in an *Esquire* article, and wrote a subsequent kiss-and-tell volume, *Blinded by the Right*. I'm told it sold a hundred thousand copies. I chose not to purchase one.

Covering the Pentagon was my primary beat. I eschewed the "correspondents corridor," where the guys who specialized in rewriting press releases hung out. The real action was always elsewhere, although I do cherish a fond memory of a now-famous television anchor, wandering the hall, asking people what size a unit was. Somebody finally told him that units were like families; they came in all sizes. Some were happy, others not. Also fondly remembered: Whenever I did an on-the-record interview with a senior officer or official, some PR flack always sat in with his or her own tape recorder. One day, I asked one of them what they did with all those tapes. "We keep them until the drawer is full," he replied. "Then we throw them out."

And fondly, also:

In the summer of 1986, I attended a reporters' breakfast with Air Force General Jim Abrahamson, then director of the Strategic Defense Initiative Organization (SDIO). The Strategic Defense Initiative, aka Star Wars, was the most successful weapons system never built. Reagan had no intention of deploying anything; it was all meant to pressure the Russians into considering the costs of an arms race they couldn't afford and couldn't win. Nor did the Pentagon want it. The services had lots of other items on their shopping lists, and were more than happy to enter an alliance of convenience with the antinuclear Left, providing the Union of Concerned Scientists and the rest with an endless stream of leaks on SDI's real, alleged, and potential shortcomings. I'd recently returned from a tour of SDI labs and facilities, where it was clear that success was neither expected nor desired, and that the order of the day was the "strap-down chicken test." In defense R&D, when you need to demonstrate minimal progress in order to keep your funding, you strap down a chicken and use your weapon on it, thus proving that your weapon, at the very least, can take out chickens. SDI had gotten good at strap-down chicken tests.

At this breakfast, however, General Abrahamson was touting the commercial spin-offs of Star Wars technology, among them, a thing called Bioglass. It appeared that two scientists working on silicon gels for space-based laser mirrors had concocted a material that had uses in orthopedic and dental surgery. Arnaud de Borchgrave, feeling either bored or impish, asked if Bioglass might prove useful for female breast enhancements. General Abrahamson gave him a pained little smile and muttered something about, We're looking into it.

So, feeling bored and impish myself, I wrote in a subsequent article that Bioglass, "may, according to unsubstantiated rumor, also be useful for breast enlargements." I then forgot about the matter for several years, until I got a frantic phone call from a man who identified himself as a Dow Corning executive. He explained that their implants were getting them into all kinds of legal trouble and they were casting about for substitute materials. Could I please put him in touch with the inventors of Bioglass?

Amazing what can happen once a story gets into the system. Not willing to inform him that it had all been a dumb joke, I gave the gentleman my last contact information, then asked him to let me know what he found out. A couple weeks later, he called back. It seemed that the scientists had sold their patent and moved on to other things. Dow Corning had gotten hold of the material and run extensive tests, concluding that, for their uses, Bioglass would be "unduly firm."

Journalism can be wonderful. You travel. You meet fascinating people. And if you keep in mind Edward R. Murrow's fifties warning to his colleagues—"Just because your voice now reaches around the world, that doesn't make you any smarter than when it only reached to the end of the Press Club bar"—you maybe do some good. But during those years, there was also darkness gathering. I'd gotten divorced. My ex, an Alaskan, had moved back to Anchorage with our young son. A spectacular place, but awfully far away. After a few years, the combination of reporting and teaching, plus the Alaska commute, got a bit much. Midlife was setting in. That, and as a decade that historians may someday call the Wasted Nineties wore on, a growing sense that there was something I ought to be doing, something I ought to be saying, something that needed to be said.

And I hadn't the foggiest idea what it was.

Chapter 8

Jim

No new paradigm ever achieves full acceptance until a generation grows up that has known little else.

—Philip Gold

IN *THE STRUCTURE OF SCIENTIFIC REVOLUTIONS,* historian Thomas Kuhn suggests a model for "paradigm shift"—the process by which we change our understanding of what the world is and how it works. Scientists, and people generally, start out with what seems a reasonable understanding of things. The Earth is the center of the universe. The atom is the smallest particle of matter. The Earth is ten thousand years old. Scientific research mostly validates the paradigm. But over time, small questions, irregularities, anomalies, emerge. Over time, the little problems start to add up to a big problem. The paradigm becomes more complex as it seeks to explain that which does not fit. Finally, somebody comes along with a new paradigm that offers a simpler, better explanation. The sun is the center of the universe. The atom is a little solar system made up of electrons, protons, and neutrons. The Earth is a million years old. Then the process starts all over again.

An elegant explanation, but one that leaves out a lot. Scientists, and people generally, do not easily adopt new paradigms, even when they do a better and a simpler job of explaining things. People may have large investments, psychological, political, professional, financial, in keeping things as they are. As they say around the Pentagon, "Where you sit determines where you stand." Also, people, organizations, and societies don't make large changes in their lives, ways, or beliefs for the sake of small gains. Finally, there's inertia, whether that of simple laziness or an attitude known at the Pentagon and most everywhere else as, "I can't disprove it, I just don't like it." Indeed, it has been argued that no new paradigm ever achieves full acceptance until a generation grows up that has known little else. In human life, it's the movement by which the radical notions of one era become the received wisdom of the next, then the dreary, overworked clichés of the generation after that.

Nor is the process of paradigm shift anything that happens automatically. To get something new—an idea, a product, a style, a process—into the realm of the known, then into the realm of the acceptable, then into the realm of the accepted, requires enormous effort and, nowadays, expenditure. You have to keep at it. Indeed, the so-called War of Ideas that has allegedly raged in America these past four decades provides a splendid example of pure attrition. You bang away until your idea, whatever that might be, wears down the opposition . . . or until the opposition co-opts it and the larger society accepts it, and you find yourself an aging radical, no longer relevant by virtue of your success and the price you paid to achieve it. "Thank you for all you've done for us," I once heard a young woman say about the feminist movement. "But we don't want to end up like you. Have a nice day. If you still can."

But there is another way of waging the War of Ideas. Call it the maneuverist approach. Here the goal is not to win by defeating some idea or point of view, but to change the terms of the debate, indeed the very categories of thought. Thomas

Kuhn's *The Structure of Scientific Revolutions* describes one kind of paradigm shift. Malcolm Gladwell's *The Tipping Point* gets at another. His title invokes a medical term—the point at which a disease, something that may have stayed latent or low-grade for ages, suddenly goes epidemic. Mr. Gladwell applies the concept to social phenomena, from fads to deeper matters. The human tipping point seems to be prescient individuals and small groups whose influence resonates with something in the larger society. They're not just the official "opinion leaders" or the self-proclaimed fashionable avant-gardes. They bring something deeper out of themselves and, in one way or another, they offer it.

The essence of this book concerns crafting a twenty-first-century conservatism, if such it is to be or can be called. This cannot be done without considering two paradigm shifts. The first involves seeing the Culture War differently; the second, seeing America's role in the world differently. To take them in turn:

The Culture War of the last few decades is no longer simply a conflict of attrition: Left versus Right, humanistic versus deistic, modern versus postmodern, men versus women, whites versus people of color, straights versus gays, and so forth, ad infinitum and ad nauseam. These things go on, and will go on. Too many people are making too much money fighting each other to let the racket go too easily. But the action is moving elsewhere.

Rather, the Culture War has evolved into an unprecedented attempt to construct an acentric civilization in which no race, gender, class, creed, or way of life will provide the norm. This is not a statement that can be proven in any quantitative or even analytic sense. It's the best guess of somebody who has studied the matter for decades, and is convinced that this is probable. It's a risky experiment, no doubt. But it's underway. Ultimately, it involves recasting the entire concept of nation, perhaps even of civilization. And the question arises: Does conservatism have anything to contribute to this experiment?

It can and does. But it won't, so long as it clings to its Take Back America delusion, and the belief that this can be accomplished by opposing and mocking what's left of the Left while ranting on about traditional values. The vacuity of that long ago became apparent. The vacuity goes on. In November 2001, as the country was still reeling from 9/11, the Defense of Civilization Fund of the American Council of Trustees and Alumni, a conservative group, put out a pamphlet entitled "Defending Civilization: How Our Universities Are Failing America and What Can Be Done about It." This product consisted of a short introduction, followed by twenty pages of quotes culled from the academic membership of the out-to-lunch Left. Gems such as #81: "Many people consider the United States to be a terrorist state," or #27: "We have to learn to use courage for peace." As I read it, I found myself paying no attention to the assorted idiocies of the unnamed faculty and students. Instead, I imagined a roomful of enthusiastic young interns, mining the press and the Net for looneytoons. It wasn't hard to imagine their chortles. *Hey, we just found another one!* And I caught myself wondering: *Is this the best you can do? All of you?*

Nor will the Religious Right, in the phrase of the Christian Coalition of America, Bring Christ Back to America . . . as though such might be accomplished by lobbying, legislation, and your tax-deductible "recommended contributions." America is a religious nation, at least if you believe the surveys. Americans who make personal commitments to fundamentalist tenets are certainly free to do so. "People of faith," a groupment that might also be termed "heavy users of religion," are certainly free to offer their perspectives, on a competitive basis, in the larger society. Indeed, the fundamentalist segments of the Jewish and Christian faiths have been growing impressively over the last couple decades, and it would be both incomplete and unkind to ascribe the growth to mere inability to handle complexity. Joshua's "As for me and my house, we shall serve the Lord," can be an honorable decision—so long as people of faith recognize that America is not their house exclusively.

And there is another reason why America must place its Judeo-Christian heritage—and its growing Islamic sector—in the categories of competing ways. Godolatry: the belief that there's only one God, whose edicts concerning human conduct and governance must be enforced. America believes in freedom of religion. The state must not interfere in the free exercise thereof, or discriminate between religions, or between religion and irreligion. But there is a fundamental difference between faiths, or versions of faiths, that compel their followers to the acquisition and use of political power, and those that do not.

Imagine, if you will, that I have a tree in my backyard and that, for whatever reason, I decide to worship my tree. Nothing unprecedented there. People have worshipped trees and sacred groves for millennia; the Hebrew goddess, Ashera, sometimes appears in the Bible as a tree. So worship away.

Next, imagine that I decide my tree is so wonderful, I have to share it. I write letters to the editor and get on the Net. I stand on street corners and proclaim the good news of my tree. I go door to door. In much of America, I would probably be tolerated as a harmless, perhaps amusing, perhaps annoying curiosity. The cops might ask me to move along if I were blocking traffic; homeowners might tell me to get off their property. But that would be the extent of it.

Now imagine that I show up at a city council meeting and proclaim, *Thus saith My Tree . . .*

Nor will cultural separatism work. For decades, the Free Congress Foundation, a significant indicator of what's happening on the Right, has offered its own agenda. Bill Lind, the program's director, holds that:

> *[T]here is a necessary, unbreakable, and causal relationship between traditional Western, Judeo-Christian values, definitions of right and wrong, ways of thinking and ways of living— the parameters of Western culture—and the secular success of Western societies: their prosperity, their liberties, and the opportunities they offer their citizens to lead fulfilling, rewarding lives. If the former are abandoned, the latter will be lost.*

Once again, only we are right.

Since the eighties, Free Congress has attacked its enemies of choice, the people it loves to hate: what's left of the Left and, more recently, the Frankfurt School, a collection of emigré academics who fled Hitler and repaid us with "cultural Marxism." But in the aftermath of Bill Clinton's acquittal, and the national fury that never happened, even while Bill Bennett was writing his *Death of Outrage*, Foundation President Paul Weyrich wrote an "open letter to conservatives," proclaiming political defeat in the Culture War and advancing the only possible strategy for the right-thinking: cultural separatism. Proper conservatives, he held, should give up on politics and, to the extent possible, withdraw from the larger society, establishing their own culture and institutions, until such time as America returned to its senses and decided to join them.

Once again, the City on a Hill, showing the rest of a presumably educable world what real righteousness looks like. Since then, Free Congress has pushed its separatism—they call it Cultural Independence—with gusto. In fact, Mr. Weyrich's withdrawal from politics lasted only a short time. Since 9/11, he and Free Congress have done excellent work in defense of civil liberties and in criticism of the neocon agenda. But they remain committed to a kind of separatism that, while more than possible in an acentric society, offers far less than it could.

Should conservatives wish to withdraw into their own churches, schools, satellite TV hookups, and political parties, that is certainly a legitimate choice. It is also legitimate for them to offer themselves as a saving remnant. But the operative word should be, *offer*. And they should not be surprised if much of America yawns.

Still, a twenty-first-century conservatism might have something to offer—especially to an acentric civilization that disposes of such global power. But to see that fully will require yet another paradigm shift: from World's Sole Remaining Superpower or Global Cop or even Global Therapist to something at once more gentle and more noble. America must become, in essence, a guardian of the twenty-first century, a task that requires power and the judicious use of power, but also much more. Tragically, the neoconservative exaltation of power, and of American imperium as some sort of automatic global salvation, constitutes a national and global tragedy, as well as conservatism's fourth betrayal of its own best self.

It's time to move on, time to recognize that an acentric America, well conceived and well ordered, would make a wondrous guardian of the twenty-first century. But to recognize that requires answering one prior question.

Is there a morality appropriate to this kind of acentricity, and this kind of guardianship? Can it be shared? And can it work?

★   ★   ★

William Styron entitled his memoir of breakdown, *Darkness Visible*. By the midnineties, I knew what he meant. First to go had been the undergraduate teaching. Then I resigned from *Insight* and for a few months did nothing but read, freelance, play with a novel, wander onto campus once a week to teach a graduate seminar, and spend as much time as possible in Alaska. Arctic winters do not improve the mood, even if Alaska does have the nation's highest per capita ice cream consumption, and even if the Weather Channel was available on cable.

After a while, I got in touch with Bill Lind. We were probably the only two people in DC working simultaneously and seriously in culture and defense. Bill was always interesting, and some of what Free Congress was doing intrigued me. I prevailed upon him and Paul Weyrich to find me a grant to write a "manifesto of cultural conservatism." This they did. And I remain grateful to them, and to Heather Higgins of the Randolph Foundation, not least of all because the task helped me push aside some why-not-just-end-it-all thoughts that were getting a bit too close for comfort.

Free Congress gave me a title, senior fellow of the Center for Cultural Conservatism, and asked that I clear all writings with them prior to publication. I did, and whenever we had problems, I just used my Georgetown lectureship for an identification tag. No big deal. Free Congress didn't give me an office, which annoyed me. I was already spending far too much time alone, and the street noise outside my fashionable loft apartment made it virtually impossible to work. Buses and sirens. Sirens and buses. One day I called DC Metro. Just curious. How many buses pass my window, in both directions, during a 24-hour weekday? The lady I spoke with was also curious. She got back to me a couple days later. Five hundred and seventy-eight. And all shifting gears.

Buses and sirens notwithstanding, I settled in to write what I hoped would be my great opus. First order of business: Know Thy Enemy. Especially if your enemy offers programs and ideas that you find reasonable and necessary, but in a manner seemingly calculated to drive you and millions of other people away. The genius of this book would be that I would synthesize—Left agendas and Right values. I would no longer find myself trapped, or permit America to be trapped, between the Scylla of rocks and the Charybdis of hard places, between a Left and a Right that presumed to divide the universe between them, and between them had little left to offer save burnout.

I did a John Boyd. I locked myself in and read. For two solid months, I read. Feminist theory. Postmodern psychology. Deep ecology. Critical theory. I still don't know what critical theory is, or when the postmodern era began or ended, but I read a lot about it. Fiction of all kinds. Popular stuff. By the third month, I'd reached the conclusion that I'd been fighting for so long:

These people of the Left, most of them, had their heads so far up their butts that they were coming out their shoulders. But they were far from wrong. And the question remained: how to meld their agenda with some sort of fundamental conservative ethic? Without that, I had nothing.

The book never did get written. But I found the answer, at least the start of the answer, the night I decided that, if I was going to survive, let alone accomplish anything or have anything of value to offer, I had to "zeroize my mind." I had to blank out, at least temporarily, everything I knew and thought I knew. I had to see what might come, were I just to let it come. I found the answer, at least the start of the answer, in an unlikely place.

Hoa Lo. A prison whose name means "fiery furnace" in Vietnamese, but is better known as the Hanoi Hilton.

★   ★   ★

Everyone should have the opportunity, at least once in a lifetime, to get to know a genuinely great man or woman. By great,
I don't mean merely successful, and I certainly don't mean a
manufactured celebrity, someone who is famous for being
famous. I mean greatness as that combination of thought and
courage that enables people to do great things that matter
greatly. Plato called it "endurance of the soul." For Hemingway,
it was "grace under pressure." Our Founders certainly had it. So
does Jim Stockdale.

I first met Jim Stockdale in 1983. I was sitting at my desk at
IFPA, waiting to head out with Jeff Record for one of our
heavy-on-defense-issues two-hour lunches, idly flipping
through the day's *Wall Street Journal.* I came upon an op-ed by
retired Admiral James B. Stockdale, for over seven years a
Vietnam prisoner of war. The piece was entitled "Dignity and
Honor in Vietnam." I read it a couple times, noted that he was
currently a senior fellow at Stanford University's Hoover Institution, and picked up the phone. A few hours later, I informed
him that I'd seen his column and was flying out to California to
meet him. When could he see me?

Jim was wary, but agreed. He was also wary when I showed up
at his office door. We went out to lunch. Just me, Jim, and Jim's
lawyer, an old Iwo Jima Marine. Apparently, they found me
kosher, if somewhat odd. The lawyer departed. Jim and I went
back to his office and chatted away the afternoon. That began
an encounter—friendship would be far too strong a word, even
if I do take the liberty of using his first name here—that lasted
on and off for several years. Jim was then engaged in doing his
major writing; not all was going well. I had some ideas to offer.
I offered them in a few letters, and visits, whenever I found an

excuse to get to California. He played with those ideas, perhaps used one or two. He did a dust jacket blurb for my first
book, *Evasions*. When the made-for-TV movie version of *In
Love and War*, the book he'd coauthored with his wife, Sybil,
was ready to air, I attended a private media screening. Admiral
Stockdale was in the audience, and I found myself wondering
what it's like to watch yourself (played by James Woods) getting tortured.

At some point, we lost touch. And at some point, I mentally
filed what I'd learned from him. I gave it no more thought until
Ross Perot's unforgivable decision to name Admiral Stockdale
his "interim running mate" for the 1992 presidential campaign.
Jim, who had previously rejected getting into politics—a Senate
run from Rhode Island had been a possibility—ended up
standing with Al Gore and Dan Quayle the night of the tele-
vised vice presidential debate. It proved an awful humiliation, as
Jim revealed his utter inability to compete with two blow-dried
baby boomer pols in the factoids, barbs, and sneers department.
His hearing aid also cut out.

Gore and Quayle treated Jim with courtesy and sincere
respect. The next day, his wife appeared on several news shows,
explaining what had happened. The media, behaving decently,
just wanted to get past the whole thing. So they described him
as clearly no politician, but also clearly a wonderful old man, a
hero who'd earned the Congressional Medal of Honor for, as
one anchor put it, "helping to organize resistance among the
other prisoners."

This is what *Good Morning America* didn't tell us.

Jim Stockdale started out in life as your basic white-bread,
off-the-shelf American: midwestern, middle class, growing up
during the Depression but not all that affected by it. His father
had served in the Navy during the First World War; by 1940,

he'd decided on a naval career. He spent World War II at Annapolis. He missed the Korean War, though only after submitting so many requests for combat duty that he was threatened with reprimand should he send along any more. Nonetheless, by the early sixties, he was a fast-track pilot and test pilot, getting all the right assignments, making all the right mistakes. The decade was planned. The Navy had slotted him for squadron command at sea, then a Pentagon tour. But first, a master's degree at government expense. Jim already had one master's, in engineering, but this was for international relations. Big Picture stuff.

Jim found it boring. As he explained:

> *I came to the philosophical life as a thirty-eight-year old naval pilot in grad school at Stanford University. I had been in the navy for twenty years and scarcely ever out of a cockpit. In 1962, I began my second year of studying international relations so I could become a strategic planner in the Pentagon. But my heart wasn't in it. I had yet to be inspired at Stanford and saw myself as just processing tedious material about how nations organized and governed themselves. I was too old for that. I knew how political systems operated; I had been beating systems for years.*

One day, he struck up a conversation with a philosophy professor, Philip Rhinelander, a World War II naval officer who was surprised, or maybe not so surprised, to learn that Jim had never studied philosophy. Professor Rhinelander arranged for him to enter his "Problems of Good and Evil" course midway, and to do some private tutorials. Jim found himself enthralled, with the kind of aggressive enthusiasm typical of fighter pilots. He'd stay up all night reading, especially the ancients, especially

the Stoics, and especially Epictetus, a Greek slave philosopher
of the first century AD.

Jim's infatuation annoyed him. It was, Why am I so fascinated? I fly jets. I drink martinis. I play golf. "I just couldn't
see," he later wrote, "that what that old coot Epictetus had to
say bore any relationship to my life as a twentieth-century tech-
nocrat." This Epictetus, this "Sickness is an impediment to the
body, but not to the will. Lameness is an impediment to the leg,
but not to the will." What does this have to do with me? He got
his answer the night he arrived at the Hanoi Hilton with a
broken leg and a broken back. As he later described it in a brilliant *Atlantic Monthly* article, he had left behind the world of
technology and entered "The World of Epictetus."

Rather quickly, Jim and the other Americans discovered two
things. First, they were not prisoners in the usual sense. Normally, POWs are a nuisance. They have to be housed, fed,
guarded, handled. But the North Vietnamese considered their
captives a priceless asset. "Our pearls," they called them. If
the captives, mostly officers, many of them professionals,
could be induced to make public antiwar and other propaganda statements, American and world opinion might be pow-
erfully affected. To extract these statements and other
concessions, the North Vietnamese were ready to employ an
array of deprivations and brutalities, including the kind of torture that doesn't risk death or permanent disfigurement.

The second thing that the POWs discovered: In the torture
room, the torturer wins. This is especially true when the object
of the effort is not to extract factual information, but to con-
coct fantasies. It is also especially true when there are no
pressing time constraints. A long-term interrogation is an
exceptionally intense human relationship. The interrogator
disposes of all the power, but the source determines whether or

not the interrogator succeeds. To succeed, the interrogator must "break" the source, that is, compel that critical first submission. Once that's done, a skillful interrogator can play upon the source's guilt and shame at betraying and dishonoring himself, his comrades, his country, his code. Guilt and shame are the truly powerful tortures.

As a senior officer, Jim held an absolute responsibility to organize and maintain resistance. But how? Military discipline and law, machismo, personal honor, patriotism, religious faith, sheer hatred, the Code of Conduct: All helped. All were inadequate. In the torture room, the torturer wins. When interrogations can go on for years and the submissions start to add up and the interrogator becomes more a friend than the comrades and the cause you betrayed . . .

Then Jim remembered the fundamental edict of Stoicism. The only thing that you can truly call your own is your will or, as we might say, your spirit. The question before you is, How shall I live? And that is a matter of will, not of circumstance.

Jim and many of the other prisoners answered the question, How shall we live? in a manner that few Americans understand even today. The North Vietnamese did not want to torture their prisoners. They wanted cooperation, statements, propaganda appearances before the cameras. Those who behaved and went along were well treated. Colonel Bui Tin, a North Vietnamese combat veteran turned journalist who interviewed over two hundred POWs, estimates that about one-third did go along. But most accepted Jim's three fundamental edicts:

First, make them torture you. Never grant yesterday's tortured concession free of charge today. It is, he wrote, "the unpunished complicity, not the tortured compliance, that tears a man apart." Hang in there, as he put it, "for a good hard-won submit"—the kind that lets you submit with your honor and even your sense of humor intact. One resistance technique involved writing documents that included mistakes no American officer would make. Jim drafted one letter to the nonexistent "Political Military Division of the Navy," a phrase that had a certain Marxist cachet. "I went after that paper as if it were a bluebook in an international law exam and started cranking out the bullshit." The legal code Jim improvised got into the specifics of how much to take before making what kinds of concessions. A man who did his best, according to the code of his civilization, behaved honorably and legally.

Second, confess what you did and gave away after you submitted. Don't let the next man go in, not knowing.

The third edict: Forgive.

By and large, it worked. By and large, the men who gave away nothing free of charge returned with their sanity and their honor. Many went on to distinguished military, political, and civilian careers. Jim likes to point out that he never did his "payback" tour at the Pentagon and that "My name appears to this day in official navy records as a man whose government-paid postgraduate education was never utilized." He did, however, finish his forty years of service wearing three stars and twenty-six personal decorations, including the Medal of Honor and four Silver Stars. While serving as president of the U.S. Naval War College, he established and for a while cotaught a course entitled "Foundations of Moral Obligation." After retiring, he served briefly as president of The Citadel, a South Carolina military academy, resigning because his efforts to eliminate hazing were not well received. Several years after he returned to Stanford, he and his old mentor, Philip Rhinelander, cotaught an undergraduate course entitled "Moral Problems of War and Peace." It was so well received that the philosophy department cancelled the second offering. Their rationale: Professor Rhinelander's failure to submit his syllabus on time.

The story of Jim Stockdale, and of his wife, Sybil, founder of the League of POW/MIA Families, and a hero in her own right, recounts an existential greatness. It is for the ages. But it also coincided with the beginnings of the rediscovery of virtue ethics, in academe and elsewhere. Not virtue ethics as a treacly encomium to "goodness." Rather, virtue as the ancients and the American Founders knew it: a tough, demanding code unlike anything else that Western philosophy offers. Curiously, virtue ethics pervade the other systems, as they do much Christian thought. They pervade these other systems largely because of a slogan much beloved of the early church fathers: "Plunder the Egyptians!" Take from the pagans anything that might be of use, then use it as you will without acknowledging either source or indebtedness. Now, however, after nearly two millennia of submersion in other systems, known primarily to scholars and specialists, virtue ethics are returning on their own.

In essence, modern America offers three kinds of ethical system. Each poses its own fundamental question. Individuals are certainly free to embrace them. Millions of good people do. But each is inappropriate as an ethical organizing principle for a civilization without a one-size-fits-all normative center.

In the first system, psychologized ethics, the question is: *What do I feel? How does this or that make me feel, especially about myself?* The limitations of this approach are obvious: confusion, chaos, and a curious phenomenon known as "conscience without content." The word "conscience" derives from the Latin *con sciere*, literally to "know with" or "to know together." As Michael Walzer has suggested, without a common ethical base, conscience becomes monologue or, in James Hunter's phrase, mere "emoting." As for the practical effects on the lives of those who try to live by their feelings, look around. The wreckage now litters the landscape, and not all the *Frazier* and *Seinfeld* reruns on earth can make it funny.

A second system is the authoritative or authoritarian. Here, an external authority is accepted as legitimate, whether the source of that legitimacy be found in (to borrow from Max Weber) tradition, organizational purpose, or personal charisma. Dictates may not always be obeyed, but are nonetheless considered binding. The relevant question is: *What is the answer provided by authority? What are the rules? What does the government or the Party say? What would Jesus do? How would Patton or Elvis, A. Lincoln or B. Spears handle this situation?* Again, the problem is obvious. Whatever people's individual choices, we no longer live in a one-size-fits-all civilization.

A third system is called the consequentialist or the utilitarian, or sometimes, "situation ethics." Here the fundamental question is: *What are the consequences of my actions?* Again, an obvious problem arises. How seldom we can predict, or even know, the consequences of our actions, especially those actions that affect distant places and strangers. Deep ecology has enshrined this as the "precautionary principle." Do nothing unless you know, fully and accurately, what the consequences will be. A fine prescription for paralysis. Then there's Jeremy Bentham's "hedonistic calculus"—computing "the greatest good of the greatest number" and basing your actions on that. Movements and states that adopt this approach usually find this ample justification for trampling on, and occasionally trying to exterminate, unpleasant and unwanted individuals and minorities.

But there is a fourth system: the virtue ethics, especially of the Stoics, that worked in the Hanoi Hilton. Here, to repeat, the fundamental question is, *How shall I live?* This certainly does not preclude consulting one's emotions. The Stoics weren't against emotions, only those that you let jerk you around. It does not preclude submission to religious or secular authority. It certainly doesn't advise against prudential calculation. But the fundamental matter is always the structure and content of one's own life and, properly understood, one's place in and obligations to *cosmopolis*, literally, "the city of the world." However, virtue ethics does entail a very different and often very difficult kind of moral thought. As philosopher Julia Annas writes:

> *To us, the question, what should my life be like? may seem too particular to be a properly ethical question. Shouldn't ethics be about duty, or rights, or the good, rather than about my life? But it may also, oddly, seem too general. Couldn't a wide variety of answers be given, ranging from the life of ruthless egoism to the life of saintly self-denial; and isn't there something unfocussed about a life that allows so wide a range of answers?*

Yes, an exceedingly wide range of answers is possible. That's why virtue ethics holds that education in virtue is a necessary precondition for the successful cultivation and exercise of virtue, even and especially if, as Annas notes, "the answers themselves are not part of the theory." Virtue ethics, then, do not tell you what to do. They teach you how to think about deciding what to do, and in a way that was as common during late antiquity as it is unusual today:

> *Ancient ethics, further, is not based on the idea that morality is essentially punitive or corrective . . . Its leading notions are not those of obligation, duty and rule-following; instead of these "imperative" notions it uses "attractive" notions like those of goodness and worth. Ancient ethical*

*theories do not assume that morality is essentially
demanding, the only question being, how much does it
demand; rather, the moral point of view is seen as one that
the agent will naturally come to accept in the course of a
normal unrepressed development.*

This does not validate, or even suggest the Enlightenment
conceit that all human beings, properly educated, will reach the
same conclusions. Again, many answers, many ways are possible. But it does assume that there is among human beings sufficient commonality that the range of answers will be tolerable
to civilization, and indeed will enhance it. Virtue ethics certainly rejects any notion of individuals as isolated units, responsible only to and for themselves. Feminist scholars such as
Martha Nussbaum have noted that:

*The idea of universal respect for the dignity of humanity in each
and every person, regardless of class, gender, race, and nation—
an idea that has ever since been at the heart of all distinguished
political thought in the Western tradition—is, in origin, a
Stoic idea. . . . Furthermore, the Hellenistic focus on the inner
world does not exclude, but in fact leads directly to, a focus on
the ills of society.*

Jim Stockdale understood that. So did Marcus Aurelius, the
Roman emperor and Stoic philosopher:

*My own nature is a rational and civic one; I have a city and I
have a country; as Marcus I have Rome, and as a human being
I have the universe; and consequently, what is beneficial to
these communities is the sole good for me.*

Marcus spoke of duty. The freed slave Epictetus taught pride
well earned by dealing in virtue with whatever comes one's way.
Jim and many of the other POWs displayed in action what
Epictetus meant when he said:

> *Yet I will show you that you have resources and endowment to*
> *fit you for a noble and courageous spirit; show me, if you can,*
> *what endowments you have for complaining and reproach.*

It worked in the Hanoi Hilton. That "autonomous colony"
was never conquered. And for the past thirty years, the recovery
of virtue ethics has been quietly underway in America. Conservatives sneer it off as mere backlash and unwelcome competition. But it's happening. In the 1973 preface to *Hellenistic
Philosophy*, classicist A. A. Long wrote: "As far as I am aware, the
last book in English to cover this ground was written sixty years
ago." But in the 1985 preface to the revised edition, Long held:

> *A decade later, the fortunes of Hellenistic philosophy have*
> *changed dramatically. Through publications, seminars, and*
> *international colloquia, Stoics, Sceptics, and Epicureans have*
> *been talking to a wider and more discerning audience than at*
> *any time since antiquity.*

At the time, of course, Professor Long could not have known
that the subject of this renewed academic interest had been
tested and found valid in Hoa Lo Prison. Jim Stockdale's major
work appeared in the eighties. But by that time, a surprising
number of feminist scholars were applying virtue ethics to their
own lives: How to live, now that you are no longer told what
your choices are? The nineties witnessed a flurry of reprints of
Epictetus' *Enchiridion* and Marcus's *Meditations*. One edition of
the former advertised it as "The Manual for Living" for

women. One edition of the latter touted it as "The Book Bill Clinton Keeps by His Bedside." By decade's end, the interest had reached popular culture. In *Tuesdays with Morrie*, sports writer Mitch Albom chronicled his visits with a former professor, now teaching a seminar on how to die. Ted Koppel also covered Morrie for *Nightline*. At their first meeting:

> *Inside the office, Morrie motioned for Koppel to sit down. He crossed his hands in his lap and smiled.*
>
> *"Tell me something close to your heart," Morrie began.*
>
> *Koppel studied the old man. "All right," he said cautiously, and he spoke about his children. They were close to his heart, weren't they?*
>
> *"Good," Morrie said. "Now tell me something about your faith."*
>
> *Koppel was uncomfortable. "I usually don't talk about such things with people I've only known a few minutes."*
>
> *"Ted, I'm dying," Morrie said, peering over his glasses. "I don't have a lot of time here."*
>
> *Koppel laughed. All right. Faith. He quoted a passage from Marcus Aurelius, something he felt strongly about. Morrie nodded.*

Novelist Tom Wolfe, usually a prescient observer of trends American, wrote *A Man in Full*, a novel featuring Epictetus and the Stoic ethic in action. Wolfe wrote this while unaware of Stockdale's work. Marcus Aurelius even got a nice little role in the movie *Gladiator*.

Why the appeal of virtue ethics? They appeal, I would suggest, because they provide an enormously attractive and compelling alternative to psychobabble, rules, situation ethics, and the rest. Certainly, at the individual level, they can work. But I would also suggest that virtue ethics can provide the foundation for a twenty-first-century conservatism, and that they can make an enormous difference, not just to individuals, but in and for the world as it is.

A few liberals also know it. A small but impressive set of works on recovery of the ancient virtues has emerged, scholars looking for an alternative to anything-goes liberalism at home, and a choice between harsh realpolitik and deluded idealism abroad. At least one thinker, Sharon Krause, has defined the possibility of liberal revival as a matter of aristocracy and honor. As she writes in *Liberalism with Honor*:

> *Four features of honor as a quality of character are elaborated: its high ambition, the balance of reverence and reflexivity, partiality, and the mix of recognition and resistance. The substantive content of codes of honor may vary . . .*
>
> *To the extent that we obscure our own aristocratic capacities and liberal democracy's aristocratic elements, we deny ourselves potentially powerful sources of individual agency and withhold crucial support for individual liberties.*

A bit jargony, perhaps; Dr. Rossiter described it better a few decades ago. But one of Krause's fundamental points about how to restructure the American polity comes across loud and clear: "Those with honor above all else refuse to believe that they are the victims of their circumstances."

So, what might the ethical basis of a twenty-first-century conservatism look like? Perhaps rather like the ethical basis of a twenty-first-century liberalism. It's certainly a choice open to us all, as individuals and as citizens. But would it work for this nation in its role as one of the guardians of the twenty-first century? Would it work in the world as it is?

Chapter 9

Neocons

That which has been perverted is America. It has been perverted by Americans who claim to love America, and in the name of America's highest ideals.

—Philip Gold

IT WAS 1993 OR THEREABOUTS. I was sitting on the back deck of my apartment, looking out over a small park toward the wooded area south of the National Zoo, aware of the gunfire—"drug-related"—but too lazy to move. Those things never lasted long, and anyway, I could already hear the sirens. Also, I was on the phone with Bruce Chapman, president of Discovery Institute, né the Seattle branch of the Hudson Institute. Bruce had long nourished an ambition to start a national think tank in Seattle. While working in the Reagan White House, he'd run a little in-house think tank, and had discovered that long-range ideas could indeed have consequences, provided they were packaged to be of immediate interest and use. After leaving government service, he'd hooked up with the Hudson Institute out in Indianapolis. Once in residence, he'd somehow managed to persuade them to start a Seattle branch, with the intention of an early and amicable divorce. Hudson saw no advantage to itself in a Seattle operation, and was quite happy to cut Bruce loose when it became apparent that the branch they hadn't wanted was also a branch they couldn't control.

When I first started seeing the Discovery tag line, I was impressed. Economist and high-tech guru George Gilder was a fellow. His *Wealth and Poverty* had been one of the major conservative economic tracts of the eighties. *Ms. Magazine* had once voted him "Male Chauvinist Pig of the Year," an additional plus. His notion that a combination of twenty-first-century technology and nineteenth-century morals would redeem us, I considered a bit stiff. The "Back to School Sale" at Nordstrom was not my idea of paradise. Neither was cyberspace. But his prediction that the next renaissance would start on the Net as people found each other, made sense. Mark Helprin, conservatism's most brilliant novelist—perhaps conservatism's only brilliant novelist; perhaps conservatism's only novelist—was also a fellow at the time. So in 1992, while on the way either to or from Alaska, I invited myself to do an *Insight* story on their venture.

Bruce agreed. The story ran. A year later, fed up with the Alaska commute and irrevocably alienated from the Free Congress Foundation, I found myself asking him on the phone, totally spur of the moment, if he would like to take me on. For some utterly inexplicable reason, he said yes. So I became a senior fellow and director of defense and aerospace studies (in truth, the only person I ever directed was myself) and after a few more commutes, gave away my stuff and took Amtrak from DC to Seattle.

It was a fun three-day ride, even the unscheduled stopover in Pittsburgh. Long-distance trains constitute a separate universe, especially if you've got a sleeper. My baggage showed up a few days later. How it got from Chicago to Atlanta on its own (Amtrak doesn't make mistakes) was never clearly explained.

Seattle's a wonderful place. It took a while to get used to the courtesy, the easy informality, the smiles. But it was certainly welcome after a bizarre moment a few weeks before I moved. I was walking down Connecticut Avenue toward an area known as "Gucci Gulch," because of all the high-priced law and PR firms that have offices there. For an instant, the street scene froze into tableau, and I wondered, "In twenty-four years here, how many tens of thousands of angry faces have I passed on just this one street?"

The slower pace was also welcome. Back East, the adage goes, when you meet people, they ask you what you do. In Seattle, they ask you what you *like* to do.

Sometimes they ask in curious ways. While at Georgetown, I'd served a few years as the rugby club's faculty sponsor, a job whose duties consisted mostly of interface with the local constabulary, insurance companies, irate neighbors, and a university not given to letting us use their fields. One evening shortly after I arrived, I was walking through a somewhat mixed neighborhood, socioeconomically speaking, wearing a windbreaker that said GEORGETOWN RUGBY on the back. I noticed a very hard-not-to-notice black male coming up behind me. I walked a little faster. So did he. I picked up the pace. At the next intersection, he came alongside me and said, in a perfect Oxbridge accent: "Good evening, sir. I'm new here. I played while in England. Could you please tell me how I might find a club to join?" Happy as always to celebrate diversity, I explained that I too was new, and hadn't had time to get involved. We exchanged business cards and parted. I never did get back into it. However, one of the women at Discovery played. She explained the basics of the women's scene to me, including the annual grudge match between the Seattle Mud Hens and the Puget Sound Breakers. I attended one of her games. It scared me. They scared me. Of course, having given up weight training when I realized that the Georgetown University women's crew team could out-bench-press me, I'd already grown accustomed to intimidation. Man of the nineties and all that.

These were Seattle's glory years, before Microsoft stock options grew worthless and Boeing left town and a few hundred dot.coms discovered that, yes, in the end you really did have to make a profit. It was a strange, tense kind of glory. Seattle was no longer small, but didn't know how to be big. And they had an additional problem. They were letting in too many people like me. Not everybody was happy about it.

I first encountered this dismay when I learned a new word: "Californication," that is, what happens when too many Californians move in. Driving around with California license plates back then wasn't recommended, unless you could prove that it was either a three-day-max visit or you were headed one-way to Canada. *Schadenfreude*, literally, "joy in the sufferings of others," has been defined as a thirty-mile backup on the interstate, going in the other direction. But watching Californicators heading north to British Columbia also qualifies. And indeed, I was getting quite into the spirit of the thing when I realized that I'd let my DC driver's license expire and had to go through the whole process again.

The written test wasn't hard. You had a choice of English or Spanish. If you couldn't read either language, they waived the test and automatically gave you a taxi license. I passed in English. The road test was more of a problem. Seems that I had a burned-out turn signal. Seems the evaluator, an attractive but sternly imposing middle-aged woman, noticed. Since this was a real street test in real traffic, procedures required that I use hand signals, which I hadn't used since taking my initial test several decades before.

Soon I was flailing madly, bumping cars as I tried to parallel park, running stop signs, cutting people off. The evaluator said nothing, but with each check mark she made on her clipboard sheet, I grew more flustered. Finally, I gave up and said:

"Look, this is the way we drive back East."

"Not in my state, you don't."

"I'll be good. Promise. Can I have my license? Please?"

She glared, but passed me. I took my paperwork to the issuing counter.

"Would you like to register to vote while you're here?" the clerk asked.

"OK. Put me down as Republican."

"Registration is nonpartisan. Would you like to be an organ donor?"

"Sure. Can I leave my organs to Republicans?"

Wrong thing to say. But at least I wasn't from California. And I later discovered something important about traffic. One year, the U.S. Department of Transportation released its list of ten worst cities for congestion; Seattle outranked the DC area. Even though we had some nasty problems, I knew this couldn't be true, and wondered how they'd reached that conclusion. I learned that the study had factored in all the usual categories: cars in the area, road space available, and so on. The only thing they left out was the courtesy of the drivers. In Seattle, when people get into arguments at four-way-stop-sign intersections, it's because nobody will go first.

I enjoyed poking around the civic scene, listening to people complain about problems that most other cities would be delighted to have. David Brewster, then editor of the *Seattle Weekly*, invited me to attend his Forward, Seattle civic lunches and other illuminating events. There I met Dian Ferguson, an impressive African-American woman who operated a solo consulting

firm helping minorities shake the federal grant bush. She was
running for city council. I wrote her a small check. She lost in the
primary to architect Peter Steinbruck, son of the late architect
Victor Steinbruck, who had been instrumental in a lot of good
renewal and restoration in prior decades. There was even a little
park named for him. It turned out, though, that many of his supporters thought they were voting for the father. When Dian told
me, I couldn't resist:

"So you got whupped by a dead white male?"

She laughed. I laughed. Then I wrote her a second small
check to cover the costs of paying off a losing campaign.

The conservative scene was, shall we say, not large. For a few
years, I attended weekly meetings of the Conservative Coalition, usually at the offices of Toward Tradition, an in-your-face
conservative outfit run by Rabbi Daniel Lapin, an aristocratic
South African emigré who'd started his American life in California, and therefore didn't quite qualify as a Californicator.
There, he'd hooked up with Michael Medved, now a Seattle-
based conservative radio show host. Toward Tradition was dedicated to offering Jews an alternative to the liberal
establishment and to forging alliances with the Christian Right.
They've been more successful at the latter, even though each
side secretly (and sometimes not so secretly) considers the other
theologically ridiculous. I did several articles on his movement,
including one suggesting that Toward Tradition's board of
directors should not look like "the Sanhedrin on a bad hair
day." After 9/11, I gave up on an organization that was vigor-
ously defending fundamentalists in their diatribes against Islam,
and on a man who could talk about "the good things that will
come out of this war."

Via the Conservative Coalition, I also encountered Pastor
Hutch.

Pastor Hutch, whom God made without waiting for the environmental impact study, is a former NFL football player. He originally got into the sport because it was an acceptable way for African-American males to hurt whites. Pastor Hutch was very large then. He's still large, but after coming to Christ, he turned his energies elsewhere. He now runs the Antioch Bible Church, a mostly white and mostly affluent congregation. He's not afraid to take on touchy issues, such as whites adopting black babies. His philosophy of evangelization—"Lemme have 'em for a day." And I confess that I was impressed when he gave the invocation at the party for Rabbi Lapin's first book, *America's Real War.* He ended his words with "In Jesus' name, we pray," and every Jew in the place said, *Amen.*

That's influence.

I never got politically active, save for some desultory work for Steve Forbes before his 2000 campaign self-destructed. I'd always respected Steve Forbes. He's very much a what-you-see-is-what-you-get fellow. But since what you see is mere intelligence, competence, and integrity, he never got very far. Don Devine had recruited me. At his request, I wrote Steve a couple defense memos, with no discernible effect. All he wanted to talk about was "beefing-up" defense, and beef, I'd long ago concluded, was not what defense needed. Somewhat more effectual was a *Washington Times* column I did, an open-letter kind of thing, urging him to consider some of the nuances of the Culture War. His staff hated it, but since I was on the campaign's Washington State Board of Directors, they didn't do much about it. The campaign folded before we ever got started, and I never did get my copy of that picture of Steve and I standing together.

Local writing was fun. David Brewster had me do a number of pieces as a kind of token, but unpredictable, conservative.

One, a cover feature, "Has Judaism Lost Its Roots?" made me for a few days, David and I joked, the second most hated Jew in Seattle, second only to Daniel Lapin or maybe third, after Michael Medved. The whole thing started when I heard a local rabbi say that she sometimes wished she could go through the Torah with a bottle of Wite–Out. She refused to talk with me, even after I told her I was doing an article. I had no choice but to quote her accurately. So much hate mail poured in that David told me, "A couple more articles like this and we can raise our advertising rates." I got to cover a New Age convention/trade show, where I learned about the Three Great Links between the Physical and Spiritual Realms—Visa, MasterCard, American Express—and intrigued people by telling them that I channeled for Harry Truman. I also got to report on the creative excuses people generated to avoid paying bus fares. Personal favorite: "I just witnessed a murder and I'm too upset to pay." Also a personal favorite, the well-dressed woman who flashes a dollar bill at the driver, then gets off. See, I've got money. I'm just not giving it to you.

David Brewster retired after the paper was sold and, as often happens, his successor and I never quite connected. But in 1998, I wandered into the best writing gig of my life. And it gives me great pleasure to tell here of the finest bunch of editors I've ever worked with, and to report on their successes after years of struggle.

I'd recently finished coauthoring a book on legal reform, *Justice Matters*, with Roberta Katz, a Discovery fellow and at the time general counsel of Netscape. I'd taken it on because any and all breaks from pondering the Clinton administration's defense policies were cherished. Writing the book had been interesting. Working with lawyers, especially Roberta's attorney husband Chuck, had been a lot like . . . working with lawyers.

Nor was the experience improved when Roberta committed bibliocide. This was the high point of the Browser Wars, Netscape Navigator against Microsoft Explorer. Just as the book was due for release, the Justice Department launched its antitrust suit against Microsoft. Netscape had a great deal at stake and, as the story goes, Netscape president Jim Barksdale ordered her to do her best to make the book vanish, lest it influence the case. I found the reasoning a bit paranoid. But a great deal was involved stake and, truth to tell, in the book Roberta had come out strongly against using lawsuits as a competitive tool—exactly what Netscape was doing against Microsoft.

We finally did get the damn thing out, but it wasn't the same. Nor did I appreciate it when, at the Discovery book party/signing, I was charged $1.50 for a bottle of water. Roberta subsequently resigned when Bruce had the temerity to say something nice about Microsoft in print, and when I left Discovery there were still a couple thousand unsold copies of *Justice Matters* in the basement.

I was miffed. And it came to pass that a few weeks later, I'd dragged myself to one of David's civic lunches, and was sitting next to a woman who identified herself as editor of a new magazine called *Washington Law & Politics*. She passed her copy around. It was slick, quirky, attractive, and I had no idea what to make of it, other than that I liked it. On a whim, I asked her, "Would you consider an article on what a pain in the butt it is to write books with lawyers?" The lady allowed that she would. It ran. I did another piece. Then a few months later, I found myself sitting in a local coffee shop with the new editor, Adam Wahlberg, and a guy in from headquarters, Steve Kaplan. *L&P* has never indulged in much of an entertainment budget, and at the time, they were so poor they couldn't afford biscotti to go with the double-nonfat latte-grande. But I'm a cheap date, and would have accepted their offer of a regular column, no restrictions on topic, even without the biscotti they so graciously popped for.

Law & Politics had been founded some years before in Minneapolis by three guys whom Steve Kaplan, currently the editor in chief, calls "losers." In truth they were, but only because they'd chosen to give up successful careers to do it. Bill White, the publisher, had abandoned a law practice that he found ever more stultifying. Steve had been a successful businessman and freelance writer. Adam Wahlberg, the youngest by a couple of decades, gave up a fast-track career in public relations to sign on. He's now the senior editor.

From the start, theirs was the classic you-never-know-what-you're-going-to-find-when-you-open-the-issue approach. *Minnesota Law & Politics* went through a six-month period when lawyers kept wondering, "What the hell is this?" But they kept coming back, and took the magazine seriously.

Then they got lucky. One day, a certain Vance Opperman approached Bill White at a Federal Bar Association function and said, "So, how would you like to expand your empire?" Since Mr. Opperman had recently sold his family's business, West Publishing, for 3.2 billion dollars, Bill (as he tells it) "almost choked on my cocktail weenie." He managed to get out a *yes* and thus acquired the best of all possible magazine backers: someone with money, respect for the product, and the willingness to not interfere.

The Minnesota edition bashed on. People liked the high/low mix of serious articles, gossip, and glitz. They decided to start a second mag somewhere. Careful research told the founders that Minneapolis and Seattle were almost identical cities. Similar climates, except that Seattle is mild and rainy, Minneapolis frigid and snowy. Same goofy Scandihoovian sense of humor, except that Sven and Ollie jokes were no longer acceptable in PC Seattle. And an identical commitment to excellence—Bill Gates and Curt Cobain out of Seattle, Jesse Ventura and Walter Mondale out of Minneapolis. Not to mention two sets of professional sports teams that aspire to be less than the sum of their parts, and usually succeed.

My column proved a delightful way to test new ideas and get intelligent responses from readers who normally sold their advice for a hundred dollars an hour. I learned that inside nearly every lawyer there's a "somebody else," a frustrated poet or astronaut or archeologist, (Roberta Katz, of *Justice Matters*, had a PhD in anthropology) and if you make contact with that somebody else, it can be very worthwhile. Plus, I won awards from the Society of Professional Journalists, Western Washington chapter, in both 2002 and 2003. Since I didn't attend the banquets, I still don't know what the awards were for, except that they were second place in the columns category. Still, given that the only other award I've ever gotten came from the Propellor Club for outstanding writing on what's left of the U.S. merchant marine, I considered these new encomia significant.

And it's delightful to report that *L&P* has succeeded beyond expectation, and in an utterly unexpected way. For years, they'd done Minnesota and Washington State "Super Lawyer" issues, pointing out the best individuals and firms in various specialties. As content, it's not very sophisticated. But it can be of enormous value to people looking for lawyers or just needing to stay abreast of the local legal scene. Now they're doing "Super Lawyer" and other sections for city and state magazines around the country: Texas, Los Angeles, Northern California, Ohio, Georgia, Indiana, Massachusetts, Pennsylvania, New Jersey, with more to come. Prosperity at last. So thanks, Bill, Steve,

Adam, Shannon, and Beth. No columnist ever enjoyed a better
bunch of editors.

★   ★   ★

Discovery did not work out quite so well. Defense was not a
major priority; money was scarce. It was difficult to stay current
in Seattle. The Net began consuming my hours. Once, totally
frustrated, I decided to promote myself from director of
defense and aerospace studies to senior fellow in national security affairs.

"Bruce," I told the boss, "I've promoted myself."

"Good," said Bruce. "I believe all our fellows should engage
in self-promotion."

"No, sir. I didn't say I was engaged in self-promotion. I said
I promoted myself. I'm now senior fellow in national security
affairs."

Bruce shrugged, as befits a man who often wished there were
a "Jolly Good" foundation or corporation of some sort that he
could hit up for bucks sufficient to fund a "Jolly Good Fellow."
I ordered new business cards, then returned to my consideration of how the Clinton administration had trashed the military
by chronic overuse. It's an odd tale.

After the fall of the Soviet Union, then defense secretary
Dick Cheney and General Colin Powell, then chairman of the
Joint Chiefs of Staff, determined upon a 25 percent reduction
in forces. They planned an orderly drawdown, leading to a
force that could be "reconstituted," should the need arise. But
they also wanted, at least rhetorically, a force that could begin
the arduous process of what's known as "transformation."
Desert Storm had demonstrated only the merest hint of the
power that a high-tech conventional force could generate. In

essence, the Desert Storm force was a World-War II-style military that had appliquéd a good bit of high technology. But to exploit fully all the new gizmos and possibilities, everything from computers and satellites to robotics and nanotechnologies, it would be necessary to conceive entirely new structures and ways of doing things. The Defense Reform Movement and the Reagan spending spree had laid the foundation. Now the transformation movement, in many cases the same people, would carry on.

All very fine. Then the Clinton administration took a 25 percent cut, made it a 40 percent cut, and sent the military on over fifty overseas missions, from bombing Iraq and Kosovo to policing the Balkans and a variety of humanitarian tasks sometimes known by their IA (Inevitable Acronym) as MOOTW, or Military Operations Other Than War. In the preceding fifteen years, a much larger military had done only twenty such operations.

By the midnineties, it was clear that this was a military on its way to implosion. It was also a force that needed to start getting serious about homeland defense. And it was a force looking toward the kind of transformation that occurs only rarely in military history. How to do it?

The answer lay (and still lies) somewhere in the redistribution of "roles, missions, and functions" among the services and the combatant commands, as well as in major changes in force structure. There's a concept known around the Pentagon as the Three Martini Consensus. In essence, it holds that after that third martini or whisky or whatever, most rational officers will pretty much agree on what needs to be done. But there's that old countervailing adage: Where you sit determines where you stand. When the Pentagon deals with its favorite item, money, no senior officer, inebriated or sober, can afford to see another service's point of view or concede that somebody else could do a certain job better.

It was not always so.

Prior to the twentieth century, there was no such thing as interservice rivalry. The Army did land. The Navy did water. There were a few overlaps. The Navy might occasionally bombard a fort or shore. They might land small parties of Marines or, once every few decades, transport and supply significant quantities of soldiers. The Army, for its part, maintained coastal fortifications and artillery and, once every few decades, needed to sail somewhere. But since neither could do the other's job, neither could take the other's job.

The airplane, by blurring the absolute distinction between land and sea combat, changed all that. Shore-based aircraft could take on ships; ship-based aircraft could strike ashore. Then came an incredible mix-and-match of weapons and structures. You could put large numbers of soldiers and Marines on ships and assault heavily defended shores, or, nowadays, go around them: modern amphibious operations. You could put soldiers on airplanes and helicopters: airborne operations and air assault. You could put missiles on submarines; underwater craft could now attack deep inland. Then throw in precision-targeting, communications, satellites, computers, and the rest, and you have a situation where the services can indeed take chunks of one another's jobs.

The Roles and Missions debate raged for much of the nineties, from the old disputations of land power versus sea power and land power versus air power, to newer conundra. What should be the relationship between the services, with their responsibilities for designing, equipping, and training in their specific specialties, and the combat commands, which drew upon the services for their "force packages?"

How dependent should we become on the part-time citizen-soldiery?

And what of homeland defense? In truth, the Pentagon wanted that mission even less than it liked MOOTW. Both were expensive and exhausting, and got in the way of higher institutional priorities. Both offered endless downsides, small chance of glory. Homeland security raised legal concerns, even though the original Posse Comitatus Act, which prohibits use of the Army to enforce the laws, save when authorized, had been eviscerated during the Cold War. Finally, the "real men don't do windows" mentality was strong. MOOTW and homeland defense were considered—the phrase exaggerates, but not by much—missions unworthy of professional warriors.

I spent much of the nineties writing and speaking on these issues for both policy and general audiences. My impact on the Clinton administration was, to put it mildly, negligible. But I was always astonished at how interested so many ordinary people were, and how important it was that somebody could explain complex issues for them in plain English. It was worthwhile work. But it was frustrating. Especially as 9/11 approached and it became apparent that the Bush administration's public attitude toward Osama bin Laden was not that different from Clinton's (a fact borne out by subsequent investigations and commissions). Yeah, sure, he's the guy you love to hate. But let's not give him too much free PR by taking him too seriously.

Daniel Boorstin got it right. The "thicket of unreality." Not merely the venerable, well, maybe if we ignore him, he'll go away. This was a genuine—if we don't publicize him, then he doesn't exist.

But while the technical military debates were going on, and Osama was preparing to demonstrate his existence on television, there was another argument, this one more ethereal, playing out in the policy journals and other "opinion leader" forums. It was known back then as the America's Purpose debate. Now that the Evil Empire had landed in history's recycling bin, what grand purpose, if any, should America embrace? Many commentators, officials, and former officials said, *none*. We've spent fifty years and hundreds of trillions of dollars saving the world and running the world. Let's back off a bit, maybe pay more attention to ourselves. Not all of these men and women could be called isolationists or xenophobes. They simply believed that it was time for a break from all that.

Two other groups disagreed, and they formed a curious pair. One was the Clintonista Muscular Humanitarians, determined to use American power and influence to get the world straightened out. These were the people who favored sending American troops, including an ever-increasing number of reservists and National Guard members, wherever there was evil to be smitten and a chance to be photographed while doing good. They were also not averse to an occasional bombing campaign. Their poster child was then secretary of state Madeleine Albright, who liked to call America "the indispensable nation," and who once infuriated Colin Powell by asking, What's an Army for if you can't use it?

Allied with them—or, more aptly, sharing the same general perspective—was another group, out of power but vocal and aggressive. These were sometimes known as the conservative America's Greatness crowd. They were also called neocons.

I'd known a number of them, especially at *Insight*, and in general liked them. But by the latter nineties it was possible to sense something malign going on, a determination to use American power with an aggressiveness utterly strange to our best traditions, and also to any rational calculation of the limits of our power. Some, such as American Enterprise Institute fellow Michael Ledeen, who has become famous for his desire to "cauldronize the Middle East," could be classified as hyperactive, and treated accordingly. Others, such as Robert Kagan, now at the Carnegie Endowment for International Peace (go figger), could be thoughtful and worth considering. As for the America's Greatness poster child, Bill Kristol, son of Irving, former chief of staff to former vice president Dan Quayle, and editor of the neocon-dominated, Rupert-Murdoch-funded, 40,000-if-that circulation *Weekly Standard* . . . at one point, I found myself doing a think tank conference panel with Mr. Kristol. The audience: several hundred people. I went to the podium, expressed a few doubts, then sat back down at the speakers' table on the stage. Mr. Kristol went to the rostrum, turned to me slightly, and said something on the order of, *America must lead*—said it with such arrogance and condescension that for a moment I wanted to knock him off the stage and out of the room. Then the anger faded to chill.

I do not know Bill Kristol, and have no idea what kind of man he may be personally. But in that moment, hearing those words and that arrogance, I felt myself in the presence of evil. Evil and perversion: the perverse corruption of something that ought to be pure and worthy and good. Sad to relate, events in Iraq have borne me out.

That which has been perverted is America. It has been perverted by Americans who claim to love America, and in the name of America's highest ideals. Those who have made their careers perverting it: the current generation of neocons, mostly baby boomers, but with no shortage of younger people coming up behind them.

What are neocons? David Frum, the former White House speechwriter who coined the term Axis of Evil, and then got fired when his wife, the excellent writer Danielle Crittenden, bragged about it in a mass e-mail, claims that a neocon is now "anybody who is a hawk." Not hardly. True, neocons are hawks. Many have been called "chicken hawks," in pointed reference to their own lack of military service. But to say that all hawks, whatever that term might mean, are neocons, is spin, pure and increasingly desperate—a sad attempt to make the movement, which never was much of a movement beyond the Beltway and a few other fashionable locales, both more important and more durable than it is. I prefer a somewhat different definition: people who fall in love with their own grandiose notions concerning America's ability to redeem the world, then get mad (or start tap dancing) when reality doesn't conform. As I write these words (May 2004) the neocons, all those DC and New York "public intellectuals" so given to lecturing America on how "we"—that fucking (please pardon my yiddish) *we* again—must "stay the course" and have the "will" and the "nerve" . . . as I write these words, they're artfully starting to reposition themselves.

Some, such as David Brooks, are thoughtful about it. Brooks, formerly of the *Weekly Standard* and now with the *New York Times*, confesses that, yes, maybe they were a bit too blasé about going to war. "I never thought it would be this bad," writes this newly "humble hawk." He also condemns the "intellectual failure . . . a failure to understand the consequences of our power. There was a failure to anticipate the response our power would have on the people we sought to liberate."

If so, it was a failure that only an intellectual could make.

Others, such as Robert Kagan, blame the Bush administration for befuddlement, due mostly to insufficient aggressiveness. "All but the most blindly devoted Bush supporters can see that Bush administration officials have no clue about what to do in Iraq tomorrow, let alone a month from now." The answer is, as always, more money, more troops, and more "will." Plus that sine qua non of American self-delusion regarding democracy-building abroad: elections. Mr. Kagan, writing with Bill Kristol in the *Weekly Standard*, suggests that the administration hold Iraqi elections as soon as possible. The benefit? "Instead of focusing their anger at Americans, Iraqis would be compelled to begin focusing on the coming elections . . ."

Compelled?

Why would they be compelled? Because we say they should be. As for the great truth somewhere codified by either George Will or Garry Wills: We are not free because we have elections. We have elections because we are free—let's just stage an Iraqi election and all will be well.

Meanwhile, other neocons seem less dismayed by the present mess than fearful that it might get in the way of future ventures. In September 2002, Michael Ledeen, a former employee of and/or consultant to the Pentagon, the State Department, and the National Security Council, wrote a *Wall Street Journal* column entitled "The War on Terror Won't End in Baghdad." He complained, presciently enough, that Saddam's weapons of mass destruction were not the issue.

> *We should instead be talking about using all our political, moral, and military genius to support a vast democratic revolution to liberate all the peoples of the Middle East [including Saudi Arabia] from tyranny. . . .*
>
> *If we come to Baghdad, Damascus, and Teheran as liberators, we can expect overwhelming popular support . . .*

In January 2004, Mr. Ledeen continued:

> *In short, while Iraq is the current battlefield, the real war*

extends far beyond its borders, and we will remain under
attack in Iraq so long as the tyrannical regimes in Damascus,
Riyadh, and Tehran are left free to kill us and the embattled
Iraqis.

Under normal circumstances, I would offer a couple more
recent quotes by neocons. But after the Fallujah massacre of
American contractors, when the words *Fallujah delenda est*
started appearing, I decided that I hadn't the heart to give these
people any more publicity than they'd already received. This
Latin phrase, by the way, refers to Cato's constant admonition
to the Romans that "Carthage must be destroyed." That
Carthage was Rome's mortal enemy and Fallujah a pitiful
cesspool, seems to have escaped notice. Or perhaps the operative phrasing should have been, *Rotterdam delenda est*.

Neocons are, I believe, a transient political and intellectual
phenomenon. They have no power of their own. A few hold
high-level appointed positions at the Defense and State Departments, and on personal staffs. But none holds a genuinely
inner-circle position, and none of the present crop has ever
won, or could win, a serious election. It is not a situation
without precedent. David Halberstam's study of Vietnam decision making and other quirks, *The Best and the Brightest*, tells of
Vice President Lyndon Johnson in 1961, extolling JFK's
geniuses to his fellow Texan, House Speaker Sam Rayburn. The
old pol listened politely, then responded, "Well, Lyndon, you
may be right and they may be every bit as intelligent as you say.
But I'd feel a whole lot better about them if just one of them
had run for sheriff once."

Neocons don't run for sheriff, or anything else. They're Idea
Men. They think Geostrategic Big Thoughts. And they're ever
more hated within the conservative movement. Some find their

arrogance unendurable. Others wonder whether their commitment to Israel might not be a bit too ardent, especially since so many of them are Jewish. But probably the most unusual indictment I've encountered came from Don Devine. Writing in *Conservative Battleline*, he referred to their notion of a "grand collectivist destiny" for America. For a paleocon to describe anyone as "collectivist" indicates more than disagreement. It is a term of damnation.

★ ★ ★

I opposed this war, as did Don Devine and so many others, because we believed that it was unnecessary, imprudent, and undertaken in quest of an impossible outcome. We believed that its myriad military and political hazards added up to a moral dilemma—the wrongness of undertaking the unattainable. We also understood that the longer we stayed in Iraq, the more would go wrong. And we sensed that, for democracy to have any real chance in Iraq, we would have to stay a very long time, until a generation came to power with no memories of Saddam. But most of all, we saw in the neocons the same arrogance that led to Vietnam. Whatever we do is good because we do it. And we can do whatever we please.

How did it come to this, again? It's not that hard to understand. The neocons have always been clear about what they wanted: a world worthy of their talents as public intellectuals. Their model has always been the early years of the Cold War. Writing in the *Weekly Standard* a few weeks before Iraq got ugly, Kristol and Kagan praised National Security Adviser Condoleeza Rice's speech calling on the United States to make a "generational commitment" akin to that of the early Cold War, to saving the world from Islamic terror, and the Islamic world from itself.

"We believe the president and his top advisers understand the magnitude of the task." So now, "It is painfully obvious that there are too few troops operating in Iraq," not nearly enough troops, period, and not nearly enough money for everything we're doing, trying to do, or thinking about doing. And finally:

> *If the administration is serious about drawing an analogy with the early Cold War years [as in Dr. Rice's "generational commitment" speech], it should remember that the entire U.S. government oriented itself to the challenge. . . . Business as usual is not acceptable.*

Business as usual? As Derek Leebaert has shown so exquisitely, perpetual crisis was "business as usual" for the fifty years of the Cold War. He has delineated exactly what it meant for the entire government and nation to "orient itself to the challenge," especially when there were careers to be made out of perpetual crisis, in government, the media, academe, and commuting back and forth. And America paid for it, by creating a national security profession that attracted far too many people who had neither the courage nor the wisdom to do the job. Especially when "doing the job" meant knowing what not to do.

Neocons believe that they know what the job is, and are prepared to make their careers doing it. But will America provide them the work?

Neoconservatism did not start out that way. In the beginning, it was far more rational and far more hopeful. There was even the possibility, rarely recognized but nonetheless real, of aristocratic virtue and grace. The senior neocons, people who had grown up the hard way and struggled, had both excellence and humane regard. The junior neocons, children, who, as David Frum points out, began life neither poor nor liberal, do not. And perhaps it is not too much to suggest that, just as the present form of neoconservatism represents a betrayal of conservatism, it also represents the last great climacteric of baby boomer hubris. How delicious an irony it may be to ponder that the generational quest for unearned moral stature which started on the Left in the sixties, now expresses itself in the demented notion that America has the ability to redeem the planet by force of arms and promiscuous largesse. (That hundred billion-plus to win Iraqi hearts and minds includes fifty thousand soccer balls, plus Frisbees.) Not all neocons are boomers, of course. But how odd that the true poster child for the baby boom may turn out to be, not some SDS radical or hippie, cursing America and burning the flag. It may not even be Charlie Reich. The final exemplar may well be Bill Kristol, telling America that our ideals and our "leadership" require a few more trillions in debt; that the generation to inherit this debt should also be ready to bleed; and that, not to worry, someday the world will thank us. And we will think more highly of ourselves as we send others out to die.

Poor Charlie. Poor Bill.

Where you sit determines where you stand. Neoconservatism was originally a New York movement, where whose cocktail parties you attended also determined where you stood—not to mention what you said or didn't say about so-and-so in your book review of his or her latest. It was never an organized, or even a very coherent movement. It was more what Irving Kristol calls a "persuasion"—in this case, a gathering of kindred souls. And a strange, two-generation gathering it has been. Today, it clamors for yet more decades of perpetual crisis. But not so many years ago, it offered hope. In this case, according to Irving Kristol, it offered a chance to "convert the Republican party, and American conservatism in general, against their respective wills, into a new kind of conservative politics suitable to governing a modern democracy."

The term neoconservative first entered the public domain in the late sixties. Ten years later, it was a fixture, alien and far from welcome within national conservative politics. The elder neocons had a few things in common. Many were the children of immigrants, possessed of that special love for and tension with America that seems to be the peculiar property of kids who grow up in two worlds. Many started out poor. Many chose to direct their ambitions toward the intellectual world, as academics and in media. Many grew up and made their careers in New York or, more to the point, grew up in Brooklyn and made their careers in Manhattan. Many, though not all, were Jewish. The late Senator Daniel Patrick Moynihan, perhaps the only neocon ever to win a major election, certainly was not. Bill Bennett, ditto. And nearly all started out on the political Left, some as cafeteria socialists, some as orthodox Marxists or Trotskyites. Hence the double usage of the prefix "neo." When they became conservatives, it was new to them. And it was new to conservatism to welcome such a feisty, argumentative lot.

The breakpoint was Vietnam. By and large, they supported the war—but not, by and large, enthusiastically. Today, to the extent that they've repudiated that tragic endeavor, they call the war more an error than a crime. They had at least one thing in common with much of America. Supporting the war became a way of opposing the people who were against the war, especially the New Left, which they considered utterly nihilistic and destructive. And they had one thing in common with the New Left. Their politics were intensely personal . . . especially when confronting the parents of New Left radicals at all those cocktail parties. The memoirs of the elder neocons, especially those of former *Commentary* editor Norman Podhoretz and his wife,

Midge Decter, speak eloquently of the viciousness of those and other encounters.

Neocons became neocons because they were, in Irving Kristol's famous phrase, "mugged by reality." The comment is disingenuous. Most of the elder neocons, Depression-bred and often military veterans, had a pretty good grasp of reality. They'd known hardship, discrimination, and the standard travails of life. They were mugged by unreality: the unreality of the Marxism and collectivism they'd left behind as tyrannical and unworkable, and by the New Left's descent into psychologized politics—although like most other conservatives, they never really comprehended the intensity or complexity of that phenomenon. It was sufficient for them to bewail the crudity and unreality, often quite forcefully and elegantly, and let it go at that.

But when neocons became neocons, they did not abandon their intellectual roots and perspectives, which were often far more European and literary than American and political. This didn't always make them new friends. Paul Gottfried, a traditional conservative who once came out of a conference fuming, "The definition of an anti-Semite is not 'Someone who disagrees with Norman Podhoretz,'" also wrote:

> *Few neoconservatives ever admit to being deeply influenced by a paleoconservative. Neoconservatives are, however, rich in praise of those mentors with whom they wish to be identified.*

Neocons, for example, love emigré political philosopher Leo Strauss, but not Russell Kirk; literary critic Lionel Trilling, but not (too openly) Bill Buckley. Irving Kristol coyly agrees when he notes that, in the neocon persuasion, "conservative worthies such as Calvin Coolidge, Herbert Hoover, Dwight Eisenhower, and Barry Goldwater are politely overlooked."

By the seventies, many prominent neocons were either
drifting into the Republican Party or consorting with it as disgruntled Democrats. A hoary joke holds that one of America's
greatest lies runs, "Hi, we're from Washington, DC, and we're
here to help you." In like measure, traditional conservatives
and much of the Sunnybelt-oriented New Right did not
appreciate the, "Hi, we're from New York and we're here to
get you straightened out" approach. Neocons were arrivistes,
Jewish in an almost entirely Gentile world (Big Mike Goldwasser's grandson notwithstanding) and the paleocons would
have been other than human, had they not experienced a certain discomfort and resentment. Even worse, neocons did not
regard FDR as evil incarnate. They did regard rolling back
the welfare state as more than mildly delusional, a foible to be
tolerated with amused condescension but not taken seriously,
even as rhetoric.

Neocons, in short, displayed the innate people skills and
attractiveness of your basic high school know-it-all. Still, they
had something to offer. In his 1979 study, *The Neoconservatives*,
Peter Steinfels summed neocons as intellectual elitists who
were not averse to the welfare state, only to its excesses and
ineptitudes. Nor were they unaware of the excesses and ineptitudes of free enterprise. As Irving Kristol put it, "Two Cheers
for Capitalism." But their fundamental orientation was that of
a "crisis of legitimacy" in America that extended from foreign
policy to culture. As Steinfels wrote of their central conviction:

The current crisis is primarily a cultural crisis, a matter
of values, morals, and manners. Though this crisis has
causes and consequences on the level of socioeconomic
structures, neoconservatism, unlike the Left, tends to
think that these have performed well. The problem is

that our convictions have gone slack, our morals loose,
our manners corrupt. [Emphasis in the original.]

In short, the first generation of neocons brought to conservatism
—or could have brought—*exactly the kind of humane aristocratic
sensibility and demand for responsible excellence that conservatism
needed.* It was not welcome. Conservatism was headed in the
other direction, and had no desire to be lectured, hectored, or
improved by a bunch of Manhattan intellectuals, too many of
whom were now spending far too much time in DC. Nor did the
neocons, an often abrasive and usually tendentious crowd, help
the process of their integration into conservatism. Perhaps they
knew it couldn't happen, and therefore saw no reason even to
feign deference to the paleocons. Perhaps they didn't even want
it, preferring the quasi-outsider status in which they'd lived so
much of their lives already. Perhaps all they wanted was to continue their personal journeys, with neoconservatism as an interesting midlife chapter.

Then the neocons encountered Ronald Reagan, the man who
would simultaneously make it Morning in America again and
gird up the will to engage in some final commie-crunching.
"Will," by the way, is a favorite neocon buzzword, equivalent to
"solid" or "Politically Correct." This happened, although it had
less to do with girding wills than with squeezing the Evil
Empire with finality and finesse. The neocons did some first-
rate supporting work in their journals, and in the larger media.
Sometimes they made Ronald Reagan look absolutely moderate
by comparison: a useful service, especially since, by way of comparison, he was. A few neocons got significant jobs. But the love
affair was always more or less unrequited. Reagan had other
admirers and other concerns, and the neocons, although useful,
disposed of neither large blocs of votes nor great sums of

money. Nor did they have much of anywhere else to go, save back to a Democratic Party that had scant use for their brand of prodigality.

When the Cold War ended, it appeared that the neocon moment had, too. Irving Kristol could write, cheerfully, that its moment had passed. Some found full or part-time employment in the Culture War, but not much welcome among conservative audiences given more to fundamentalism and separatism than the graces of old-style literary criticism. True, neocons could dudgeon with the best of them over Mr. Clinton's indiscretions and the whole sixties ethos. But neocons had always been critics, not creators, critics mostly of the sixties and its real and alleged legacies. Beyond vague invocations of standards and excellence, they had no compelling alternatives to offer. Returning America to Christ was not among their options.

In a sense, the nineties America's Purpose debate saved neo-conservatism. It certainly provided the second generation of neocons, the boomers and Xers, with something to do while awaiting the next conservative administration. And indeed, it's possible to trace—opponents of the neocons have done so with zest—a nineties progression that, to some, adds up to a willful long-term plan and conspiracy.

There are even documents and milestones. According to the standard interpretation, the effort to move America toward a far more assertive global dominance began in 1992. Paul Wolfowitz, the current deputy secretary of defense, was then serving as undersecretary for policy, in which capacity he supervised preparation of an annual Pentagon document, "Defense Planning Guidance." The draft urged that:

"The number one objective of U.S. post-Cold War political and military strategy should be preventing the emergence of a rival superpower." This meant discouraging both adversaries and friends from amassing sufficient military and nonmilitary power to challenge the United States."

Nothing extraordinary there. Would any defense establishment suggest that it might be nice for a rival superpower to emerge? In any event, none was likely to. The draft document then suggested that the United States must be prepared to intervene unilaterally whenever and wherever both its interests and its leadership role are threatened or questioned.

Again, what else would you expect to find in a military document? Subsequently, Wolfowitz's boss, Defense Secretary Dick Cheney, ordered a rewrite. Again, nothing unusual. These documents go through endless agonizing iterations in order to attain the desired degree of pseudospecificity and bombastic verbiage. (It's also worth noting that every year, the secretary of defense submits an "Annual Report to Congress." Since the Cold War ended, the length of the report has been inversely proportional to the size of the force.)

Then there were the letters. Two in particular. These emanated from the Project for the New American Century (PNAC), sometimes erroneously described as a neocon think tank, in reality a small suite of offices, a few full-time staff, a Web site, and a propensity for blast-faxing the universe. The first letter, dated January 26, 1998, and addressed to the Honorable William Jefferson Clinton, noted that "The policy of 'containment' of Saddam Hussein has been steadily eroding . . ." and that the president should turn his "administration's attention to implementing a strategy for removing Saddam Hussein from power." In truth, Saddam was well contained; he'd been, in Dick Cheney's memorable phrase, "back in his box" since 1991. And if anyone was concerned about strategies for removing people from power, it was Bill Clinton, as his impeachment approached.

Three years later, on September 20, 2001, PNAC sent another letter to the president, this time George W. Bush, and this time offering specific guidance. It was not enough to bring Osama to justice, or justice to Osama. Iraq was still a problem and, the letter noted:

> *It may be that the Iraqi government provided assistance in some form to the recent attack on the United States. But even if the evidence does not link Iraq directly to the attack, any strategy aiming at the eradication of terrorism and its sponsors must include a determined effort to remove Saddam Hussein from power in Iraq. Failure to undertake such an effort will constitute an early and perhaps decisive surrender in the war on international terrorism.*

This is significant. It's one thing for a small faction of the Republican opposition to write a Democratic president a letter that everybody knows he'll never even read, much less heed. It's quite another to go on record advocating such an action when your party's in power and when your people are going into the administration. And it's significant most of all to declare failure to remove Saddam "an early and perhaps decisive surrender" without explaining why. Or was it simply one more recurrence of the great error of NSC-68, the assumption that a defeat anywhere is a defeat everywhere? And why is a defeat anywhere a defeat everywhere? Because we say it is.

Pentagon documents and open letters to presidents don't tell us all that much. But another document does, and chillingly.

Foreign Affairs, flagship journal of the Council on Foreign Relations, is a forum where elites commune with elites and potential officeholders strut their intellectual prowess or lack thereof. In July 1996, a long essay, "Toward a Neo-Reaganite Foreign Policy," coauthored by William Kristol and Robert Kagan, appeared. It holds a ring of truth—the truth of people telling you exactly what they want and intend, even though you can't quite believe it.

The essay begins by noting, correctly, that "no post-Cold War conservative view of the world and America's proper role in it" has emerged. Those not wishing to follow Pat Buchanan back to the nineteenth century have generally not given the matter much attention at all, presumably out of complacency. But complacency is dangerous, and it is time

> *once again to challenge an indifferent America and a confused American conservatism. Today's lukewarm consensus about America's reduced role in a post-Cold War world is wrong. Conservatives should not accede to it; it is bad for the country and, incidentally, bad for conservatism. Conservatives will not be able to govern America over the long term if they fail to offer a more elevated vision of America's international role.*

What should that role be? Benevolent global hegemony.

This benevolence need not be tied to anything as particular as defeating the Axis or containing the Soviet Union. Rather:

> *The ubiquitous post-Cold War question—where is the threat?—is thus misconceived. In a world in which peace and American security depend on American power and the will to use it, the main threat the United States now faces is its own weakness.*

Pure neocon. Our ultimate enemy is our own lack of will. And in the end, our own lack of will is the human race's greatest enemy:

American hegemony is the only reliable defense against a breakdown of peace and international order. The appropriate goal of American foreign policy, therefore, is to preserve that hegemony as far into the future as possible. To achieve this goal, the United States needs a neo-Reaganite foreign policy of military supremacy and moral confidence.

The article goes on to argue for peacetime defense spending in excess of anything the Cold War ever occasioned. Then the authors, invoking the heritage of NSC-68, assert that:

. . .the American people can be summoned to meet the challenges of global leadership if statesmen make the case loudly, cogently, and persistently. As troubles arise and the need to act becomes clear, those who have laid the foundation for a necessary shift in policy have a chance to lead Americans onto a new course. Finally, they reject the whole notion that America should not go abroad in search of monsters to destroy. "But why not? The alternative is to leave monsters on the loose, ravaging and pillaging to their hearts' content, as Americans stand by and watch.

One may, of course, question whether the planet's only alternatives are American hegemony or global anarchy. Certainly, much of the world does. One may even question whether American hegemony is vital to continued conservative leadership. Certainly, many conservatives have come to do so. One may not question, however, that when President Bush decided to invade Iraq, the neocons got what they wanted. Whatever their actual influence, they certainly did their best. And even today, with their influence hopefully fading, they still do their best to tell us what our choices are.

★   ★   ★

I wrote an article for the *Weekly Standard* once. In April 2001, after Boeing's surprise announcement that it was moving its headquarters from Seattle to Chicago, I got a call from managing editor Richard Starr, whom I'd known at *Insight*. Could I whip up a short piece on what was happening to Seattle, especially the Boeing departure?

Glad to oblige. I'd done several *Washington Times* pieces on "Seattle Determinism," that curious process by which whatever affects Seattle, good or ill, ultimately makes its way eastward. You know—Microsoft, grunge rock, Starbucks, antiglobalization riots, the dot.gone disaster, Alex Rodriguez, and so forth. After the WTO fracas, "The Battle in Seattle," and a nasty earthquake, "The Rattle in Seattle," people were aware of us. So I did a fun thing on our spreading malaise, which they headlined, "Seattle as Metaphor." Richard subtitled it: "The Battle, The Rattle, and Now the Skeedaddle."

A phrase that might be recycled as America ponders its experience in Iraq. We've had the battle. Ever since the insurgency began—what part of conquest don't we understand?—we've had the rattle.

Now for the skeedaddle?

Hard to say. Sometimes it's tempting to want to teach the world a lesson by proclaiming, "OK, Iraq. We're leaving. Now let's see what you do with your freedom." Of course, the world wouldn't like that much, either. Perhaps the best we can do at this moment, while awaiting events, is to ponder another lesson.

Two thousand years ago, the leader of the world's only superpower, Caesar Augustus, decided to pacify the barbarians beyond the Danube. He sent a proconsul named Quintilius Varus, who'd won a quickie victory a few years before. This time, he would finish the job.

But the barbarians had learned. Instead of meeting the Romans in open combat, they lured them into the swamps and conducted guerrilla and terror operations. The Romans panicked. Varus ended up with his head on a pike. When Augustus heard of the disaster, he suffered something akin to a nervous breakdown, wandering the halls of his palace at night, muttering, "Varus, give me back my legions."

As of May 2004, nine out of ten active Army divisions are either in Iraq or back and refitting for the next round. The Army is considering moving troops out of Korea to Iraq. The organized reserves and National Guard are exhausted. There is talk of involuntary activation of members of the Individual Ready Reserve, even of resuming conscription.

Neocons . . . give us back our legions.

Chapter 10

The World as It Is

It is impossible not to ask whether a civilization without a normative center can survive and flourish under the best of conditions, let alone in an age of violence and terror.

—Philip Gold

IN COMMON USAGE, PROPHECY refers to the foretelling of the future. Prior to the Iraq war, the administration and the neocons had prophesied with gusto on what would happen, did we not invade. Among the prophecies: Saddam would use the horrific stockpile of Weapons of Mass Destruction (WMD) that he had, or might have, or was acquiring, or might acquire. As Saddam's WMD kept getting not found, it became necessary for the administration and its apologists to spin the issue. Initial manipulations ranged from "We'll find them yet" to "Saddam had no WMD, but the ability to manufacture them quickly" to "Saddam's scientists and generals may have lied to him about how much he had, and we believed them." Then the shilling segued into what I came to think of during the nineties as the "Slick Willie Three-Step."

There is no problem. It's only a little problem. Can't we just move on?

Move on to what? In the February 14, 2004, issue of the *Weekly Standard*, neocon Max Boot, he who'd popularized the phrase "Hard Wilsonianism," offered a prophecy of his own. Mr. Boot argued that, well, first of all, the United States didn't invent preemptive/preventive attacks. There was the War of the Spanish Succession. And anyway, America has been in the preemption/prevention business for a long time. There was the Dominican Republic, there was Grenada, not to mention JFK's ponderings during the Cuban missile crisis. But look on the bright side. The Iraqi stuff wasn't there, but now our enemies have to think twice about what we might do. As for getting into the habit of conquest, occupation, and nation-building, again, not to worry. We still have lots of other preemptive/ preventive options for use elsewhere. Mr. Boot does not address the limits of American military power, but he does conclude:

> *Here's a counterintuitive possibility: The Iraq war, by showing the limits of national sovereignty, may wind up expanding preemptive interventions rather than extinguishing them. Sure, this is speculation. But . . . it's no more premature than claiming that preemption is finished. In all likelihood, it's only just begun.*

A prophecy, it is hoped, that proves false. But there are other ways of understanding prophecy. In *God: A Biography*, Jack Miles suggests an unusual interpretation of the function of prophecy. Although the Israelites had prophets almost from the beginning, it was only after the shattering of God's covenant with Israel that the real age of Hebrew prophecy began. For five hundred years, as a succession of conquerors, occupiers, and nation-builders rolled through the Hebrew homeland, God tried through prophets to answer a single question: *If this works . . .Can we begin again?* Prophecy, according to Miles, all the chaotic, cryptic, confusing, and contradictory utterances of all the prophets, was God's way of trying to repair a terribly damaged relationship, in order to make it begin again.

Much of conservatism since the fifties has been false prophecy, wrong answers to the question, *Can we—can America—begin again?* Can we begin again by junking Big Government? Can we begin again by abandoning humane aristocratic excellence for the politics of ressentiment? Can we begin again by ignoring how much of Vietnam was delusional, and how much of the delusion was of conservative manufacture and impetus? Can we begin again by retreating to "traditional values" and the "Judeo-Christian heritage" while ignoring or dismissing the grievances and agonies of so many Americans, and all the other options open to us?

Can we begin again by dominating the world and by remaking that world in our own image?

The Israelite prophets were never a consistent lot. Neither have been the conservatives. But they have been consistent in their failure. In each case, the answer has been, is, and must be, No. Each attempt has failed. Each will fail. And now, perhaps it turns out that the real contemporary Malachi is what's left of conservatism. The real Malachis are those who wish either to turn away from the world, or control it, or renew some nonexistent former Golden Era at home, or just trim the federal slice of the GDP by a percentage point or two.

Conservatism should be made of better stuff.

I no longer feel like Malachi. Rather, I feel like a prophet with something new to offer. Can we begin again? No, we cannot. America has always been obsessed with new beginnings; the word "new" seems as vital to our politics as to our advertising. But time runs one way only. Still, we can reason together.

I've suggested—consider it prophecy—that America is now engaged in an historically unique experiment: the creation of an acentric civilization in which no race, no gender, no social class, no creed, no faith, no way of life dominates, and against which all else is measured. I've also suggested that there is an ethical system, an ancient and proven system, appropriate to such a civilization. It is called virtue ethics. Its fundamental question is, How shall I live? But I have also asked, it is impossible not to ask, whether a civilization without a normative center can survive and flourish under the best of conditions, let alone in an age of violence and terror.

I believe that such a civilization can survive, flourish, and indeed give rise to a renaissance, an efflorescence such as the planet has not seen in centuries. I also believe that such a civilization, far from being vulnerable to the perils now upon us, will do a better job of confronting and defeating those perils than it is doing now. It is obvious that an acentric civilization could do a much better job of resisting encroachments on civil liberties, and the Get-with-the-Program mentality. But an acentric civilization, I believe, will also do a better job of winning the struggle for this planet. It will do so not simply because we'll be able to do a better job of understanding the rest of the world, and why, from time to time, they prefer ways other than ours. An acentric America will make a better guardian of the twenty-first century . . . provided we also understand the nature and extent of the planetary *agon*, the "struggle for the planet," now underway.

No, we cannot start again. Time flows only one way and, as Heraclitus knew, you cannot put your hand in the same river twice. But the Greeks had two words for time. One *chronos*, referred to the passing, to the flow. The other, *kairos*, has no precise translation. It can mean the right time, the critical time, the fullness of time, the time that changes both what is to come and our understanding of what has gone before. Today, we're in *kairos*.

For the Age of the Wars of Ideology is over. The Age of the
Wars of the Ways has begun. And it is, once again, America's
destiny to struggle, and duty to prevail.

But not in the way we're going about it.

The philosopher George Santayana once wrote that those
who cannot remember the past are condemned to repeat it.
Santayana was wrong. Those who remember the past do repeat
it. Those who do not remember the past are destined to be surprised when it happens.

Ever since 9/11, and certainly since the Iraq war demonstrated the truth of that venerable retail admonition, "You break
it, you bought it," the United States of America has been surprised. Surprised, occasionally dismayed, and often bewildered.
Surprised when the world turns out not to love, honor, and
obey us the way we feel it should. Dismayed when good and
evil, idealism and expedience, noble but unattainable intentions, and unintended but predictable disasters seem so con-
flated that not even a Solomon—or a George Kennan—could
sort them out. And bewildered when it seems that all we have
at our disposal to reason out this mess are dueling clichés, spin
cycles, and trash.

But perhaps the age now upon us is not so incoherent as it
seems. Perhaps what's needed is to think historically about the
history we're living and going to live: to frame it and name it,
the better to live it, and to do what needs to be done to fulfill
America's great twenty-first-century challenge:

Winning the Wars of the Ways.

The Wars of Ideology spanned three centuries, from Con-
cord Green and Independence Hall to the recycling of the
Berlin Wall and the last of the tanks in Red Square. These wars
were, like the Wars of Religion before them, about many
things, often inextricably intertwined. But the great struggles of

1775 to 1991 had as their leitmotif two collective questions. What is the proper form of political organization? and what is the proper form of economic organization?

By 1991, the verdict seemed self-evident. Some form of political democracy, coupled with some form of market economy, does more good for more people than any alternative yet devised. So self-evident did it seem, that intellectuals such as Francis Fukuyama took up proclaiming The End of History. The great crusades were over, the big issues settled. All that remained was to manage the enterprise, and to extend the benefits, gradually and peacefully, to the remaining 80 percent of the planet. And we were all, Dr. Fukuyama suggested, going to be very bored:

> *The end of history will be a very sad time. The struggle for recognition, the willingness to risk one's life for a purely abstract goal, the worldwide ideological struggle that called forth daring, courage, imagination, and idealism, will be replaced by economic calculation, the endless solving of technical problems, environmental concerns, and the satisfaction of sophisticated consumer demands. In the posthistorical period there will be neither art nor philosophy, just the perpetual caretaking of the museum of human history. I can feel in myself and see in others around me, a powerful nostalgia for the time when history existed.*

Proof once again that there are some mistakes so ridiculous, only experts can make them.

Of course, not everyone thought that way. Harvard political scientist Samuel Huntington predicted a century of violent cultural and religious wars, the "Clash of Civilizations," among and within Western, Confucian, Japanese, Islamic, Hindu,

Slavic, Latin American, and African civilizations. Robert Kaplan, a writer who knows the world because he's been there, and also because he doesn't have a PhD to confuse him, called it "The Coming Anarchy"—a condition demanding the sternest of pagan virtues and no delusions concerning the redemption of others. There will be resources to fight over, especially oil and water. Religion will also be a global casus belli, especially between Islamic minorities and Christian or other majorities in places like Russia, central Asia, and western China, and between Christian minorities and Islamic majorities from Egypt to Indonesia. In truth, all these struggles, and more, interlock.

And ever since 9/11, and certainly since the United States undertook to redeem Iraq, America has groped for a new way of understanding the world encompassing these struggles, and our role in it. Among the elites, this groping is sometimes known as the quest for the Kennan Prize—the nonexistent yet highly coveted award that will go to the politician and/or intellectual who does for the age now upon us what George Kennan did for the Cold War. Make it clear.

Despite, or perhaps because of, all those neocons, the Kennan Prize remains unclaimed. But the understanding embodied in the concept of the Wars of the Ways may hold some value.

Specifically, the struggle now upon us is not against terrorism or WMD. Terrorism can be a strategy, a tactic, a career, a way of life, a chosen death. But strategies and tactics are not enemies, no more than the purpose of World War II was to rid the earth of Panzers and kamikazes. And WMD are things, not enemies. Nor is this World War III or even World War IV—if only because it implies a structure too similar to the one that didn't happen, and the two that did.

The Wars of the Ways are far more amorphous, and far more complex. They engage and will engage those nations, regions, and groups that partake fully of the twenty-first century—its freedoms, opportunities, and advances—against those who want out: the *Jihadi* and other violent fundamentalists, the ethnic and racial separatists, the anarchists and eco-freaks, and the prophets and *Gauleiters* of creeds and movements yet to be espoused.

Our Ways, the Ways of freedom, diversity, advance, against their Ways: their Ways of bondage, intolerance, retrogression.

But the Wars of the Ways will also pit those who embrace and enjoy the twenty-first century against those who can't get in—the three and more billions of us who live in poverty and desperation, amid pandemic violence, pandemic disease, accelerating ecological havoc, and despair. These billions cannot be held down, not in this age of global communications, economics, culture, and mass emigration to the West. They will not be held down when poverty is no longer considered the inevitable lot of the masses, when *Baywatch* reruns dangle the allure wherever you can set up a satellite dish or pirate a DVD. Nor will they be held down when they come here, only to discover a new and even less tolerable kind of poverty.

But here or there, can they get into the twenty-first century? If they can't, they'll no doubt adopt as their Way that distillate of desperation: When you've got nothing, you've got nothing to lose. Increasingly, the desperate billions will ally with those who want out of the twenty-first century. Increasingly, they will dispose of and use weapons of mass destruction, mass death, and mass disruption. And increasingly, their ranks will be filled by the deadliest predator of our species: young males with no education, no skills, no hope, and no use for a world that has no use for them.

At this moment, there are between sixty and one hundred wars going on, depending on the criteria used to define a war— a fact that says nothing about what most of this planet's governments routinely do to their own people. At this moment, nearly half the human species lives on two dollars a day or less. At this moment, the United Nations hopes that, within twenty years, primary education will be available to 80 percent of the world's children.

And nearly half the desperate billions are under twenty-five.

In sum, the world now endures a set of hundreds of more-or-less interlocking conflicts. They will go on, these military and political and economic and cultural struggles between the Ways of freedom and advance, the Ways of barbarism and retrogression, and the Ways of desperation. And they may well determine the fate of our species and our planet.

Such is the age now upon us.

To survive the Wars of the Ways, let alone emerge victorious, a coherent concept of operations—I eschew the word "strategy" for reasons that will become apparent—is needed. The first task in crafting such a concept is to jettison two old and hoary, pointless and misleading false dichotomies: empire versus isolation, and unilateralist hegemony versus multilateralism.

A totally nonimperial future, sad to relate, is not an option. It never has been. There has never been a time when America was not an empire, if empire be understood as less a matter of size and conquest than of policy and rationale. Empires do more than conquer. They also bring into themselves other nations, faiths, and ethnicities, whom they may exterminate by genocide or assimilation, or offer varying degrees of local autonomy. Empires also arrogate to themselves the right to intervene in, structure, and direct the affairs of others. And most often, they come with some sort of cosmic rationale. From Alexander the

Great's Eurasian Ecumene and Rome's *Romania*, to the "White Man's Burden" and *la mission civilisatrice*, the rationales indeed tend toward the cosmic.

America knows. We began as part of an empire. We grew through the addition of chunks of French, Spanish, Mexican, and Russian empires. Manifest Destiny justified a policy of imperial genocide toward the continent's indigenous inhabitants. And from the Roosevelt Corollary and the Fourteen Points ("Soft Wilsonianism") to containment and the Bush Doctrine . . . in some ways, not that far of a journey.

We are an empire. The relevant question is: What kind of an empire shall we be? I suggest that we need to be the least violent, most tolerant, most *minimal* empire in history. For this there are two reasons. First, never has any empire amassed sufficient force to meet its self-assumed commitments. We're no different. Empires always find themselves either forced to exemplary brutality in order to deter others, or to dangerous overreliance on local surrogates, often far too unsavory to savor. We've done it before. We're paying for it still. Second, much of the necessary violence these next few decades should be precise, low-level, and conducted in twilight. This is especially true when it is against denizens of that terrorist entity known as "Jihadistan," and its denizens scattered around the world. Geographically, Jihadistan runs in an arc from North Africa and the Middle East to the Philippines and Indonesia, with a northern arc through central Asia and western China. Jihadistan also maintains outposts throughout the Western world and Latin America. Conquering countries in order to root out terrorists may prove a rather expensive approach. And many countries that would be happy to have us rid them of their *Jihadi* would prefer that we (and they) do it quietly.

Nor have we ever been isolationist, certainly not in any

xenophobic sense. Xenophobes don't let in strangers by the scores of millions, century after century. Nor have we ever been isolationist, diplomatically or economically. It was just that there were certain things, especially getting entangled in the quarrels and misfortunes of others, that we wouldn't do.

And then, century after century, we did them. And until fairly recently, we profited thereby.

Nor does the equally worn-out false dichotomy, "unilateralism versus multilateralism," much avail. We cannot go it alone. America, like all other empires, lacks the forces to meet its commitments, let alone police the world. But neither can there be any stable, U.S.-dominated multilateralism, reminiscent of NATO or the anti-Axis alliance. Too many nations dislike us too much; too many issues are involved. As for the United Nations, best it be reconceived as a service organization, not a fount of law or policy, and treated accordingly . . . and we should support its endeavors whenever desirable.

Nor should stability for stability's sake be a goal. Most of this planet's governments range from the inept and oppressive to the utterly abominable, and we'd all be better off without them. True, the number of tyrants has been diminishing of late— spectacularly in places like Iraq, more quietly in Latin America and elsewhere. But getting rid of *el jefe* solves only part of the problem. There are still all those little *jefitos* and *jefitas* running around. And more ominously, maybe half this world's countries have borders that don't make political, ethnic, cultural, economic, or ecological sense. Breaking up may be hard to do, but perhaps a few dozen divorces would be for the best.

No, the world doesn't need stability, certainly not stability for stability's sake. In any event, it won't happen. What the United States must do is find ways to manage the chaos creatively, ad hoc it for decades, sometimes going it alone, sometimes with "coalitions of the willing," sometimes with more enduring structures, sometimes with all three. We must recognize that we have no allies. We have a few, a very few friends. Beyond that, we have relationships and we have hookups of varying degrees of permanence, utility, and intensity. We must learn to distinguish. We must also learn when to let others be strong, and accept that the partner of one endeavor will be the passive bystander or active opponent of another.

In sum, America needs no "strategy." We need a concept. Bill Kristol calls it "benevolent hegemony," and there is something to recommend the phrase—provided we accept that we must also know when not to act like a hegemon, and accept the fact that our benevolence is neither automatic nor inevitable. Things are not right simply because we do them or because our declared intentions are benevolent.

So what's the concept to guide us? Perhaps the worldview enshrined in the motto of Outback Steakhouse: *No Rules. Just Right.*

But this does not mean that anything goes. Some stuff works better than other stuff. And what we must accomplish is clear. To serve as a guardian of the twenty-first century, we must do more than defeat and contain those who, to borrow from Milton, would rather reign in Hell than serve in Heaven. We must also prove them wrong—prove them wrong by bringing into the twenty-first century the billions currently left out. And more specifically: by helping them to get into the twenty-first century *as citizens.* Citizens of their towns and cities and villages. Citizens of their nations. Citizens of their regions. And citizens of the world.

It is time for much of the world to begin the generations-long process of conceiving of all human beings as sentient, participating citizens.

America cannot save anybody. We can, of course, liberate people from tyrannies: those imposed upon them and those freely chosen. We can protect them, police them, supply them with cash by the truckload, merchandise by the boatload, and all the *Baywatch* and hip-hop and harder-core porn they can handle. We can impose upon them the mechanics of democracy, from free elections and rampaging media to advanced civil and human rights. But we cannot force people to adopt the self-carriage that makes democracy more than competing demagogueries, competing ochlocracies, and taxpayer-funded shopping sprees. From Weimar Germany to postcolonial Africa (and now to Iraq?) history shows that, without a competent, empowered, and engaged citizenry, peoples and nations too often merely trade one set of evils for worse.

America cannot create citizens. America can, however, encourage the development of the preconditions for citizenship. America can work to create what civic feminist Erin Solaro calls the empowering "civic triad" that will enable men and women to become citizens—to generate that "critical mass" of citizenship without which their nations, and our species, must stagnate, fail, even fall.

For the Greeks, freedom was public. Real freedom began when the citizen left the shelter of his home and entered the public realm to participate with his equals in the business of the common world. Not for nothing does our word, idiot, derive from the Greek *idiotes*, a person obsessed with private life. To the Greeks, as to the American Founders, only the citizen fully inhabited his own life.

But the Greeks and the Founders also understood that citizenship was more than a matter of birth and of rights. Citizenship entailed responsibility well discharged. To discharge that responsibility well, the citizen required legitimate power.

The first component is the economic self-sufficiency that allows for a measure of independence and a bit of free time. This means work for men and women at wages with which they can provide for themselves and their families. This will not come from rampant "globalization," which has less to do with free enterprise than with a kind of rapine we rejected over a century ago. Lack of tariffs and barriers no more makes trade "free" than a marriage certificate guarantees eternal love. We must restructure our own economy away from dangerous dependence upon global rapine, and help others to build economies based less upon shoddy export and more upon balance. We should therefore work toward an absolute ban on child labor worldwide, and toward environmental policies that will mean you won't have to clean it up—or write it off as irreparably damaged—later.

The second component of the civic triad is education, both liberal and practical. This does more than make it possible for people to sustain themselves economically. It teaches them that actions have consequences, and why they have consequences, in both the material and the political worlds. Issues are complex. But there is no political issue whose structure the average educated citizen cannot grasp, provided he or she is willing to spend a bit of time. The devil may be in the details but, politically speaking, God is in the concepts.

Widespread literacy and access to information also mean that people are more willing to hold their governments accountable. The United States should target aid, directly and through NGOs and private enterprise, to provide for a solid primary and secondary education for all children.

The third component of the civic triad, too often forgotten, is the possession of arms and participation in genuine local self-defense militias. To the Founders, as to most of the world today, security is a continuum, with individual and communal self-defense and law enforcement at one end, and full-scale war against foreign enemies at the other. They cherished the citizen militia, available for all contingencies, but also embedded in local communities.

Much of the "third world," especially Africa, would do well to establish self-defense militias, against the day when the thugs with the machetes arrive in their villages . . . or their national armies pass through, looking for the thugs with the machetes. These militias may well become "schools of the nation" where people learn both to defend themselves and to take effective political responsibility for their communities.

To this, the United States must add firm advocacy of, and ample reward for, opening the triad to all members of a society, especially women. Houses divided against themselves have a habit of not standing, especially when the division wastes the talents of half its members.

Yes, citizenship is an alien concept to most of the world. But citizenship has one redeeming virtue. It works. And most people, given the chance, tend to like it.

Perhaps we would, too. But in order to experience the pleasures and responsibilities of citizenship, and all that those pleasures and responsibilities make possible, we must first bring meaningful citizenship back home. We must take back the right to be citizens, effective participants in the public world. This is how we must learn to live, once again. And this is what, above all else, a new conservatism must strive for:

The creation of an American citizenry that can make an acentric civilization work—no, not work, thrive—at home while winning the Wars of the Ways around the world and making this civilization an effective and a brilliant guardian of the twenty-first century. It certainly doesn't sound conservative, not as we've understood the word this last half century or so. And it certainly wouldn't be liberal, either, not as we've come to understand that word. But it's how we should live, and the example we should show to the world.

Odd, after so many years, to find myself using the word *we*. But civilization is something that we do together, and citizenship—political, economic, cultural—the best and fairest way to do it.

Let us choose to live as an aristocracy of citizens, capable of the excellence of inclusion and of humane regard, to and for each other, our nation, our species, our planet, and beyond.

It would be a start.

Afterword

THERE IS IN ECONOMICS a tool called the "index of leading indicators." It tells you where the economy may be going. There is also a tool called the "index of lagging indicators." It tells you where the economy might have been.

In tracking the conservative movement these last few decades, I've found that certain organizations provide both services simultaneously. They tell you where they think they're going. And they tell you where they think America has been.

In May 2004, the American Conservative Union turned forty. The ACU was founded in 1964, the year of conservatism's first great political triumph and first great defeat. It celebrated its fortieth—the year when, at least according to tradition, people finally realize they're grown up—with a typical Beltway bash, several hundred people at a large hotel. President Bush came as the guest of honor and told the congregation:

"The conservative movement has become the dominant intellectual force in American politics."

Several days later, ACU president David Keene (whose daughter is now a private in the U.S. Army) ran a column in *The Hill*, a DC newsletter, entitled "Bush Can Count on the Right." Four times in 791 words, he pointed out that conservatives and

Bush had issues, in phrases such as "the fact that we don't agree with the man on everything all of the time." As for those who believed that conservatives would withhold their support: "It isn't going to happen . . . at least not this time around." [Ellipsis in the original.]

The same day (May 18th) that Mr. Keene's column appeared, the *New York Times* ran an op-ed headlined, "For Conservatives, Mission Accomplished." The authors, John Micklethwait and Adrian Wooldridge, were identified as writers for The *Economist*, a fine British magazine, and authors of *The Right Nation: Conservative Power in America*.

Citing the ACU, the authors concluded:

> . . . *it is because of such groups that the right has out-organized, outfought and out-thought liberal America over the past 40 years. And the left still shows no real sign of knowing how to fight back.*

Now, birthdays are times of celebration. But a fortieth might also provide a moment for some honest reality-checking. Reading these two items, I got a whiff of delusion, of generals sitting in bunkers at the end of a losing war, moving nonexistent armies around . . . or of good, decent people watching their world fall apart and refusing to acknowledge the fact.

Good, decent people? Yes, even though I'd read, four days before, an ACU item that urged people to blast-fax their support for Defense Secretary Donald Rumsfeld, then under attack for the Abu Ghraib prison mess. The document asked:

"How do you think Osama bin Laden will feel if Rumsfeld is forced to resign?

"He'd dance for joy in the dark, damp cave where he's now cringing, hiding from our troops who are circling in on him."

The ACU also predicted that "These blood-thirsty goons will consider Rumsfeld's resignation an immediate affirmation of everything they've done, and they'd immediately double the shootings and triple the bombings."

But the ACU reserved its major vitriol for the liberals, arguing that "Partisan Politics Couldn't Get Any Dirtier Without Becoming Treason." The ACU item also noted that Democratic Senator Robert Byrd, a Rumsfeld critic, was a former Ku Klux Klan member who "recently used the 'n' word on national television"; that Senator Ted Kennedy had once been at Chappaquiddick; and that former attorney general Janet Reno had gotten a congressional "free pass after she admitted responsibility for over 80 American deaths at the siege of Waco." As for Abu Ghraib: It's only a little problem. Can't we just move on?

Good, decent people? Yes. But also desperate, angry, bitter, sad. It's hard to watch the success you never really had, evanesce.

Don Devine, ACU vice chair, is one of the good and decent, sad and angry conservatives. On May 20, 2004, syndicated columnist Robert Novak (he who, some months before, had published the name of Ambassador Joseph Wilson's "CIA operative" wife) did another number, this time on Don Devine. It seems that Don had remained seated and unapplauding throughout President Bush's speech, when most everyone else was getting into the standing applause. Mr. Novak also quoted Don's unfavorable off-the-record comments on the speech, classed him as representative of a growing Republican disenchantment, and suggested that he "feels betrayed." A couple days later, Don wrote the president, apologizing for any perception of disrespect, but in no way recanting or eliding their political differences.

I called Don to ask him if I could mention the letter in this book. He said yes, but demurred at direct quotation. We chatted a bit about the political situation, Iraq, his new book, the Catholic church, and some recent scholarly exegesis on Mary Magdalene. He muttered in his rich new York voice:

"You know, you still haven't told me what that damn book of yours is about."

"That's right."

★   ★   ★

For as long as I've been involved in think tanks, I've pondered starting my own. Somewhere around 1995, I did. Bruce was sensitive about the Discovery name appearing on articles that might offend real or potential funders and other supporters: a standard and justifiable concern. Nor was he willing to go the disclaimer "opinions expressed are his own" route. Not even when I suggested that we adopt an approach Mac Owens had pondered while working on the Hill: "The opinions expressed herein, although correct, are not necessarily those of the United States Government." Since I no longer taught at Georgetown, I couldn't identify myself as a professor. So I asked Bruce if he thought it would be OK for me to invent a think tank that I could be president of, for identification purposes only. He offered that it might be kosher, provided I didn't make any false claims about it, solicit funds without proper incorporation and IRS certification, lie to editors, or do anything else. If I wanted an imaginary empire, he concluded, he'd be the last to say no. And anyway, after pondering several of our conversations about religion, he'd decided that a faith with only one member would be ideal for me. A somewhat reduced danger of schism.

And so was born Aretéa, a modernization of the Greek *aretē*. What I wanted was a place given to recombinance.

Instead of homogeneity, I'd build conflict into the system. The basic unit would be a two-person team, one man and one woman, different backgrounds and perspectives. No requirement for consensus, no "agree to disagree" waffling—just turn them loose on whatever problems they might be pondering, see what they come up with. No restrictions on outside publication. The goal: On any given issue, first change the terms of debate. Then craft whatever solution might work, regardless of where the ideas came from. Then publicize it at a very high literary level, to engage both policy and general audiences, and especially those millions desperate for something, anything, to cut through the garbage and get their brains going again.

Those millions who want, once again, to be citizens: political, economic, and cultural citizens of a nation for which they are responsible, in virtue and in excellence and in humane regard.

There would be a PhD hanging by the door, that fellows without the degree could borrow as needed, then return. There would also be Thursday afternoon high teas, where fellows could present their works in progress. Aretéans are, by definition, fascinated by everything that everybody else is doing. Ultimately, we would have our own press, on-site day care, a gym, artists and poets in residence, and a hefty endowment. We would keep it small.

I worked up a prospectus. I got some people interested. Nothing happened, although one friend persuaded me that my preferred institutional motto, *Getting America Unfucked*, might not prove that effective a fund-raising tool. After 9-11, I despaired.

Then came Erin.

She was hard to know what to do with, at first. Anyone who can tear your opinions and your friends up one side and down the other, then sign her e-mail, V/R—Very Respectfully—

presents challenges. So did her way of describing herself as a radical feminist former Army reserve officer whose motto held, "Everything I need to know about life, I learned training Dobermans."

We e-mailed for a year or two, then started yakking on the phone. Soon it was daily. I learned that she'd forsaken her Army career at the outset, in order to marry a Marine. Eleven hard years later, there was a divorce. She'd gone back to school to get her master's at Norwich University, and was working as a secretary in order to avoid the impoverished postgraduate lifestyle. Her complaints about her thesis board led me to ask to read her project. It was a study of what happened to one World War II Army National Guard regiment when they failed to receive replacements in combat during the Buna campaign in New Guinea. It all sounds obvious, but it led her to a pair of conclusions that, when she presented them in military circles, got her hated and dismissed as a "feminazi" . . . no small accomplishment, since the feminists were calling her "fascist" and worse for her belief that civilization must be defended—and by women.

Specifically, she found that small unit cohesion, the emotional bonding of soldiers, does not necessarily produce combat effectiveness. She also realized: One of the reasons that the military places such high value on cohesion is that it's a dandy argument against inclusion of putative outsiders. Not so long ago, it was African-Americans who shouldn't serve because of how others might feel about them. Now it was women and gays.

I read her thesis with a professorial eye. It was terse and rough. But there were flashes of brilliance and she was not getting what she needed from a faculty board that might charitably be described as lazy, hostile, perhaps incompetent. I did what I could.

Soon we were talking about other things. Civic feminism, for one. Erin felt strongly that feminism had lost its way, indeed sold its soul, when it abandoned the quest for true and full equality and became an exercise in victimhood and hissy-fitting. I understood what she meant. Feminism had started out as a movement capable of aristocratic excellence and humane regard. She told me that the word I was looking for wasn't, "aristocrat." It was "citizen."

She asked me what I looked like. Not wishing to confess to middle age too early, I told her that I was a cross between Groucho Marx and Denzel Washington. She inquired no further. We coauthored some columns. She started writing on her own, including ahead-of-the-pack work on PMCs (Private Military Companies), sexual assault in the military, and the Pentagon's underreporting of American casualties. Within nine months, she'd completed her degree and published a half dozen significant and prescient pieces. She also agreed to be executive director of Aretéa, should we ever find a way to stand it up. We met for the first time in February 2004.

The Iraqi venture, which she'd opposed as imprudent, was starting to sour. She decided she had to go over. The subject of investigation: American military men and women operating together as honorable equals, and their impact on those who witness it. Abu Ghraib, with its images of men and women operating together in other ways, increased her resolve.

Erin got herself a travel grant and newspaper accreditation. We found her a book agent for *Second Class, Second Chance: American Women and Their Military in the World*. There was the matter of embedding. The 81st Armored Brigade of the Army National Guard jerked her around for two months, then said that they couldn't accommodate her during the dates she'd requested. She hadn't requested any dates. The Marines took two days to say yes. The Army's First Infantry Division, "The Big Red One," invited her out of the blue. I found that getting a woman ready to go to war when you're also talking about marriage—and pondering the neocons—can be challenging. I also found that shopping for wedding rings and body armor on the same day can be an experience with, shall we say, dimensions.

We're planning to coauthor a relationship manual when she gets back. My preferred title: *Mistress Erin's High-Discipline Weight Loss Program and Couth School.*

Hers: *The Younger Woman's Guide to Improving Older Men.*

Both work. And maybe some of the people who read the book will come away thinking, I knew that. Why didn't anybody ever tell me before? Thank you for saying it.

And we'll respond, You're welcome. The pleasure was ours.

Bibliography

Adams, Robert. *Decadent Societies*. San Francisco: North Point Press, 1983.

Albom, Mitch. *Tuesdays with Morrie*. New York: Doubleday, 1997.

American Conservative Union. "President Bush: Don't Throw Secretary Rumsfeld to the Wolves." http://conservative.org/rumsfeld.html.

American Psychiatric Association Diagnostic and Statistical Manual of Mental Disorders IV. Washington, DC: American Psychiatric Association, 1994.

Annas, Julia. *The Morality of Happiness*. New York: Oxford University Press, 1993.

Baritz, Loren. *Backfire: A History of How American Culture Led us into Vietnam and Made Us Fight the Way We Did*. New York: Morrow, 1984.

Baskir, Lawrence and William Strauss. "The Vietnam Generation," in A. D. Horne, ed. *The Wounded Generation: America after Vietnam*. Englewood Cliffs; Prentice-Hall, 1981.

Boorstin, Daniel. *The Image: A Guide to Pseudo-Events in America*. New York: Atheneum, 1961.

Boot, Max. "The Bush Doctrine Lives." *Weekly Standard*, February 16, 2004.

Brennan, Mary C. *Turning Right in the Sixties: The Conservative Capture of the GOP*. Chapel Hill: University of North Carolina Press, 1995.

Brooks, David. "A More Humble Hawk." *New York Times*, April 19, 2004.

———. "For the Iraqis to Win, the U.S. Must Lose." *New York Times*. May 11, 2004.

Bui Tin. *From Enemy to Friend: A North Vietnamese Perspective on the War*, tr. Nguyen Ngoc Bich. Annapolis: U.S. Naval Institute Press, 2002.

Bush, George W. "Remarks by the President to the American Conservative Union 40th Anniversary Gala," TK May 2004.

Clelak, Peter. *America's Quest for the Ideal Self: Dissent and Fulfillment in the 60s and 70s*. New York: Oxford UP, 1983.

Coram, Robert. *Boyd: The Fighter Pilot Who Changed the Art of War*. Boston: Little, Brown, 2002.

Decter, Midge. *Liberal Parents, Radical Children.* New York: Coward, McCann & Geoghegan, 1975.

Defense of Civilization Fund, a Project of the American Council of Trustees and Alumni. Pamphlet, "Defending Civilization: How Our Universities Are Failing America," details TK.

Della Femina, Jerry. *From Those Wonderful Folks Who Gave You Pearl Harbor: Front-Line Dispatches from the Advertising War.* New York: Simon and Schuster, 1970.

Devine, Don. "Torture facts and American Greatness." *Conservative Battle-Line,* May 19, 2004. http://acuf.org/issues/issue12/040519news.asp.

Drury, Allen. *Advise and Consent.* Garden City, NY: Doubleday, 1959.

Edwards, Lee. "The Origins of the Modern American Conservative Movement." Heritage Lecture #811. Washington, DC: Heritage Foundation, 2003.

Erikson, Kai. *A New Species of Trauma: Explorations in Disaster, Trauma, and Community.* New York: Norton, 1994.

Fallows, James. *National Defense.* New York: Random House, 1981.

Fallows, James. "What Did You Do in the Class War, Daddy?" in A. D. Horne, ed. *The Wounded Generation: America after Vietnam.* Englewood Cliffs: Prentice-Hall, 1981.

Free Congress Foundation. "A Brief History of Cultural Conservatism." http://freecongress.org/centers/cc/history.asp.

Friedman, Richard Elliott. *The Hidden Face of God.* (San Francisco: HarperSanFrancisco, 1995.

Fukuyama, Francis. "The End of History?". *National Interest* (Summer 1989).

Fussell, Paul. *Wartime: Understanding and Behavior in th Second World War.* New York: Oxford UP, 1989.

Gerson, Mark. *The Neoconservative Vision: From the Cold War to the Culture Wars.* New York: Madison, 1996.

Gitlin, Todd. *The Twilight of Common Dreams: Why America Is Wracked by Culture Wars.* New York: Metropolitan, 1995.

Gladwell, Malcolm. *The Tipping Point: How Little Things Can Make a Big Difference.* Boston: Little, Brown, 2000.

Glendinning, Chellis. *Waking Up in the Nuclear Age: The Book of Nuclear Therapy.* New York: Morrow, 1987.

Glendon, Mary Ann. *Rights Talk: The Impoverishment of Political Discourse.* New York: Free Press, 1991.

Glueck, Michael and Robert Cihak. "Conscience of a Former Conservative." *WorldNetDaily,* December 5, 2002. http://www.worldnetdaily.com/news/article.asp?ARTICLE_ID=29880

Gold, Philip. *Evasions: The American Way of Military Service*. New York: Paragon, 1985.

———. *Advertising, Politics and American Culture: From Salesmanship to Therapy*. New York: Paragon, 1987.

———. *Against All Terrors: This People's Next Defense*. Seattle: Discovery Institute Press, 2002.

———. "The Titanic Sails at 12." *New York Times*, March 4, 1980.

———. "Fruitful Fallout of 'Star Wars.'" *Insight*, October 3, 1988.

———. "A Think Tank that Treads New Ground." *Insight*, June 21, 1992.

———. "Peddling Ecstasy." *Seattle Weekly*, April 10, 1996.

———. "Has Judaism Lost Its Roots?" *Seattle Weekly*, June 12, 1996.

———. "At the Right Hand of God." *EastsideWeek*, October 8, 1997.

———. "Rule Number One: NEVER Write a Book with a Lawyer." *Washington Law & Politics*, July 1998.

———. "The education of Forbes." *Washington Times*, December 23, 1999.

———. "Report from the WTO frontier." *Washington Times*, November 30, 1999.

———. "Green burden." *Washington Times*, December 2, 1999.

———. "WTO consequences." *Washington Times*, December 14, 1999.

———. "New tactics needed for cultural wars." *Washington Times*, March 8, 2000.

———. "Jihadistan." *Washington Law & Politics*, June 2001.

———. "Jihadistan II." *Washington Law & Politics*. August 2001.

Goldwater, Barry. *Where I Stand*. New York: McGraw-Hill, 1964.

———. *Why Not Victory? A Fresh Look at American Foreign Policy*. New York: McGraw-Hill, 1962.

Gottfried, Paul and Thomas Fleming. *The Conservative Movement*. Boston: Twayne, 1988.

Halberstam, David. *The Best and the Brightest*. New York: Penguin, 1972.

Hawkins, David. "The David Frum Interview." *Right Wing News*, January 26, 2004. http://www.rightwingnews.com/interviews/frum/php.

Herbert, Bob. "Mistakes Will Be Made." *New York Times*, December 10, 2001.

Himmelstein, Jerome. *To the Right: The Transformation of American Conservatism*. Berkeley: University of California Press, 1990.

Hofstadter, Richard. *The Paranoid Style in American Politics and Other Essays*. New York: Knopf, 1965.

Hodgson, Godfrey: *The World Turned Right Side Up: A History of the Conservative Ascendancy in America*. Boston: Houghton Mifflin, 1996.

Hood, Michael. "Almost Famous." *Seattle Magazine*, June 2003.

Hughes, Robert. *The Culture of Complaint: The Fraying of America*. New York: Oxford University Press, 1993.

Hunter, James Davison. *Culture Wars: The Struggle to Define America*. New York: Basic, 1991.

———. *Before the Shooting Begins: Searching for Democracy in America's Culture War*. New York: Free Press, 1994.

———. *The Death of Character: Moral Education in an Age without Good and Evil*. New York: Basic Books, 2002.

———. "When Psychotherapy Replaces Religion." *The Public Interest* (Spring 2000).

Kagan, Robert. "Lowering Our Sights." *Washington Post*, May 2, 2004.

———and William Kristol. "Democracy Now." *Weekly Standard*, May 17, 2004.

Katz, Roberta with Philip Gold. *Justice Matters: Rescuing America's Civil Justice System for the Twenty-First Century*. Seattle: Discovery Institute Press, 1997.

Keene, David. "Bush Can Count on the Right." *The Hill*, May 18, 2004.

Kennan, George. "The Sources of Soviet Conduct." *American Diplomacy*. Chicago: University of Chicago Press, 1951,1979.

Keniston, Kenneth. *The Uncommitted: Alienated Youth in American Society*. New York: Harcourt, Brace & World, 1965.

———. *Young Radicals: Notes on Committed Youth*. New York: Harcourt, Brace & World, 1968.

Kernon, Alvin. *Crossing the Line: A Blue Jacket's World War II Odyssey*. Annapolis: U.S. Naval Institute Press, 1994.

———. *The Death of Literature*. New Haven: Yale UP, 1990.

———. *In Plato's Cave*. New Haven: Yale UP, 1997.

Kirk, Russell. *The Conservative Mind: From Burke to Santayana*. Chicago: Regnery, 1953.

Klatch, Rebecca. *A Generation Divided: The New Left, the New Right, and the 1960s*. Berkeley: University of California Press, 1999.

Krause, Sharon. *Liberalism with Honor*. Cambridge: Harvard University Press, 2002.

Kristol, Irving. "The Neoconservative Persuasion." *Weekly Standard*, August 25, 2003.

Kristol, William and Robert Kagan. "Toward a Neo-Reaganite Foreign Policy." *Foreign Affairs* (July/August 1996).

———. "Do What It Takes in Iraq." *Weekly Standard*, September 8, 2003.

Kuhn Thomas S. *The Structure of Scientific Revolutions*, 2nd ed., Chicago: University of Chicago Press, 1962, 1970.

Lasch, Christopher. *The Revolt of the Elites and the Betrayal of Democracy*. New York: Norton, 1995.

Ledeen, Michael. "The War on Terror Won't End in Baghdad." *Wall Street Journal*, September 4, 2002.

————. "The Mullahs Pray for President Bush's Defeat." *National Review Online*, January 26, 2004.

Leebaert, Derek. *The Fifty-Year Wound: The True Price of America's Cold War Victory*. Boston: Little, Brown, 2002.

Lifton, Robert Jay. *The Life of the Self: Toward a New Psychology*. New York: Simon and Schuster, 1976.

Lind, Michael. *Up from Conservatism: Why the Right Is Wrong for America*. New York: Free Press, 1996.

Lind, William S. *Cultural Conservatism: Toward a New Agenda*. Washington, D.C.: Institute for Cultural Conservatism, 1987.

————. "Victoria." http://freecongress.org/centers/cc/950430.asp. This originally appeared as William S. Lind. "Militant Musings: From Nightmare 1995 to My Utopian 2050." *Washington Post*, April 30, 1995.

————. "New Strategy for culture war already in place: A reply to Philip Gold." March 26, 2002. http://freecongress.org/commentaries/2002/020326wl.asp.

Link, Arthur S. and Richard McCormick. *Progressivism*. Arlington Heights: Harland Davidson, 1983.

Lippmann, Walter. *Drift and Mastery: An Attempt to Diagnose the Current Unrest*. New York: Kennerly, 1914.

Long, A. A. *Hellenistic Philosophy: Stoics, Epicureans, Sceptics*. Berkeley: University of California Press, 1986.

Macy, Joanna Rogers. *Despair and Personal Power in the Nuclear Age*. Philadelphia: New Society Publishers, 1983.

Marcus Aurelius. *Meditations*, ed. Maxwell Staniforth. London: Penguin, 1964.

Micklethwait, John and Adrian Wooldridge. "For Conservatives, Mission Accomplished." *New York Times*, May 18, 2004.

Miles, Jack. *God: A Biography*. New York: Vintage, 1995.

Nash, George. *The Conservative Intellectual Movement in America since 1945*. New York: Basic Books, 1976.

Novak, Robert. "Conservative base shows cracks." *Chicago Sun-Times*, May 20, 2004.

Nussbaum, Martha. *The Therapy of Desire: Theory and Practice in Hellenistic Ethics*. Princeton: Princeton University Press, 1994.

Oates, Whitney J., ed. *The Stoic and Epicurean Philosophers*. New York: Random House, 1940.

Ortega y Gasset, José. *The Revolt of the Masses*, authorized translation. New York: Norton, 1932.

Plant, Judith, ed. *Healing the Wounds: The Promise of Ecofeminism*. Philadelphia: New Society Publishers, 1989.

Project for the New American Century. "Letter to the Honorable William J. Clinton," January 26, 1998.

———. "Letter to the Honorable George W. Bush," September 20, 2001.

———. "Defense Planning Guidance," details TK

Reich, Charles. *The Greening of America*. New York: Crown, 1970.

———. *The Sorcerer of Bolinas Reef*. New York: Random House, 1976.

———. *Opposing the System*. New York: Crown, 1995.

Rieff, Philip. *Freud: The Mind of the Moralist*. Chicago: University of Chicago Press, 1959, 1979.

Rosenau, Pauline Marie. *Post-Modernism and the Social Sciences*. Princeton: Princeton University Press, 1992.

Rossiter, Clinton. *Conservatism in America: The Thankless Persuasion*. New York: Knopf, 1964.

Roszak, Theodore. *The Making of a Counter-Culture: Reflections on Technocratic Society and Its Youthful Opposition*: Garden City: Doubleday, 1969.

———, Theodore. *The Voice of the Earth*. New York: Simon and Schuster, 1992.

Santayana, George. "Reason in Common Sense," *The Life of Reason*, in *The Columbia World of Quotations*, http://www.bartleby.com/66/29/48129.html

Snell, Bruno. *The Discovery of the Mind in Greek Philosophy and Literature*. New York: Dover, 1982.

Sommers, Christina Hoff. *Who Stole Feminism? How Women Have Betrayed Women*. New York: Simon & Schuster, 1994.

Sorley, Lewis. *A Better War: The Unexamined Victories and Final Tragedy of America's Last Years in Vietnam*. San Diego: Harcourt, Inc., 1999.

Steinem, Gloria. *Revolution from Within: A Book of Self-Esteem*. Boston: Little, Brown, 1992.

Steinfels, Peter. *The Neoconservatives: The Men Who Are Changing American Politics*. New York: Simon and Schuster, 1979.

Stockdale, James B. *A Vietnam Experience: Ten Years of Reflection*. Stanford: Hoover Institution Press, 1984.

———. "Courage under Fire: Testing Epictetus's Doctrines in a Laboratory of Human Behavior." Hoover Essay #6. Stanford: Hoover Institution Press, 1993.

————. "Epictetus' Enchiridion: Conflict and Character." *Stoic Voice Journal* (November 2001).

————and Sybil Stockdale. *In Love and War: The Story of a Family's Ordeal and Sacrifice during the Vietnam Years.* New York: Harper & Row, 1984.

Summers, Harry. *On Strategy: A Critical Analysis of the Vietnam War.* Novato, CA: Presidio, 1982.

Sykes, Charles. *A Nation of Victims: The Decay of the American Character.* New York: St. Martin's, 1992.

Tierney, John. "The Hawks Loudly Express Their Second Thoughts." *New York Times*, May 16, 2004.

U.S. Department of Defense. "Excerpts from 1992 Draft Defense Planning Guidance."

White, Theodore H. *The Making of the President 1964.* New York: Atheneum, 1965.

Notes

49–50   "'Dad, am I . . . "I say?'": Quoted in Gold, *Advertising*, 68.

50   "Sanitized beyond recognition": Interview with the author.

51–52   "America's contribution . . . quarter reprints": Kirk, 426–428.

52   "how we have . . . of life": Daniel Boorstin, *The Image*, 3.

57   "The risks . . . everywhere": NSC-68, 53, 54, 79.

58   "Surely, there . . . to bear": George Kennan, "Sources of Soviet Conduct," 128.

60   "For me then. . . obligation": José Ortega y Gasset, *Revolt of the Masses*, 71.

61   "the free . . . existence" Ibid., 58. "If you . . . done" (Ibid. 88).

61–2   "The most important . . . spirit": Rossiter, ix, 48, 46.

62   "As the interest . . . many [ways]": Bruno Snell, *Discovery of the Mind*, 154, 170.

64   Then came. . . Party: Mary C. Brennan, *Turning Right*, 1.

64   "Forging . . . easy task.": Ibid., 3.

65   *"Extremism . . . virtue"*: Barry Goldwater, *Where I Stand*, 9–17. "lost . . . of ways" (Ibid.). "It has been . . . American people" (Ibid.).

66   "come late . . . entirely unreal": Theodore H. White, *Making of the President*, 208.

66–7   "profoundly undermined . . . of program": Ibid., 315.

CHAPTER 3: YALE

70   "Once it . . . the masses": Christopher Lasch, *Revolt of the Elites*, 25.

82   Demographically . . . draft-related offenses: Baskir and Strauss, "The Vietnam Generation," in Horne, 6.

88   "Alienation . . . toward society": Keniston, *Uncommitted*, 3.

89–90   "Central to . . . pessimism": Ibid., 56. "the scorn . . . themselves" (Ibid., 61). "But . . . self-serving defenses" (Ibid., 66). "What they want . . . creativity" (Ibid., 69). "With no . . . *a burden*" (Ibid., 74, 78, 186).

90   "To these . . . is underlined": Keniston, *Young Radical*, 36, 27.

92–4   "There is a revolution coming": Charles Reich, *Greening of America*, 2. "It will not . . . the land" (Ibid., 6). "This is . . . passing fad" (Ibid., 241). "Of all . . . new generation" (Ibid., 236). "a universal . . . obligations" (Ibid., 241–245).

94   "Because of . . . *factual truth*": Reich, *Sorcerer*, 245–246.

95   "We have . . . *self-knowledge*": Reich, *Opposing the System*, 3, 7, 12, 13.

CHAPTER 4: THE CORPS

97   "Rebels . . . weakness": Philip Rieff, *Freud*, 353.

98   "It is . . . with rebels": Tod Gitlin, *Twilight of Common Dreams*, 71.

103   "Truth claims . . . who disagree": Pauline Marie Rosenau, *Post-Modernism*, 78.

104   "The post-modern . . . him/her": Ibid., 54–55. "All readings are equivalent" (Ibid., 25).

107   "our national . . . "winning combination": Loren Baritz, *Backfire*, 54. "American nationalism . . . to instruct" (Ibid., 31, 39).

CHAPTER 5: GEORGETOWN

136   "The basic . . . established themes": Richard Himmelstein, *To the Right*, 88, 90.

137   "[T]he high road . . . court decisions": Mary Ann Glendon, *Rights Talk*, 6.

CHAPTER 6: CULTURE WAR

142   Five years . . . the seventies: William S. Lind, "New strategy for culture war," at freecongress.org, 26 Mar 02. My column, "New tactics needed for cultural wars," appeared in *Washington Times*, 8 March 00.

143   As a . . . mass destruction: The White House, *National Security Strategy of the U.S.*, Sep 02, at whitehouse.gov, cover letter of 17 Sep 02, 2; 6, 14.

145   *New York Times* . . . ran it: Philip Gold, "The Titanic Sails at 12," *New York Times*, 4 Mar 80.

151   "stringent language . . . of psychotherapy": Glendon, x, xi.

151–2   "Political correctness . . . therapeutic politics": Sykes, 164.

155–6   "justice in an . . . that justice.": Link, *Progressivism*, 70, 85.

159   *"At stake* . . . contemporary life": Hunter, *Culture Wars*, 34, 42, 44–5.

159   "base of . . . one another": Hunter, *Before the Shooting*, 9, 148.

159   "The moral . . . say, obligation": Ibid, 139, 137.

162–3   "Throughout the . . . is depression": Sommers, 20–1.

163   "I was . . . the world": Steinem, 8.

165   "We may . . . impact statement": Roszak, *Voice*, 38.

165   "truth must . . . content:" Roszak, *Counter-Culture*, 57.

165   "I carried . . . my chest": Macy, *Despair*,17.

165–6   "There is . . . of identity": Macy, "Awakening the Ecological Self," Plant, ed., *Healing*, 204.

166–7   "Before I . . . commitment and hope: Glendinning, 15–16, 81, 17.

168   "we are . . . as well": Lifton, 114.

168   "Did any . . . cheap shots?": Hughes, 24.

169   *Washington Times* . . . "Schlep Barocha": Three *Washington Times* columns ensued. "Report from the WTO frontier," 30 Nov 99; "Green Burden," 2 Dec 99; and "WTO consequences," 14 Dec 99.

171–2   "She was . . . our duty": William S. Lind, *Victoria*, at freecongress.org.

CHAPTER 7: THINK TANKS, ETC.

176   "The Progressives . . . public function": Link, 70.

196   "may . . . breast enhancements": Philip Gold, "Fruitful Fallout of 'Star Wars,'" *Insight*, 3 Oct 88, 18.

CHAPTER 8: JIM

202   "We have . . . for peace": "Defending Civilization," Defense of Civ. Fund, at goacta.org.

204   "[T]here is . . . be lost": "Short History," at freecongress.org.

210   "I came to . . . for years: Stockdale, "Courage," Hoover #6, 1.

211   "I just . . . with me?": Stockdale, "Epictetus' Enchiridion," *Stoic Voice Journal.*

211   "Sickness is . . . the will": Epictetus, "Arrian's Discourses," Oates, 228.

212   Colonel Bui . . . go along: Bui Tin, 54–7.

212   "the unpunished . . . man apart": Stockdale, "Epictetus' Enchiridion."

212–3   "For a good . . . the bullshit": Jim & Sybil Stockdale, *In Love and War*, 184, 175.

213   "My name . . . never utilized": Stockdale, "Epictetus' Enchiridion."

216   "To us . . . of answers?": Annas, 27.

216   "the answers . . . the theory": Ibid., 7.

216   "Ancient ethics . . . development": Ibid., 4.

217   "The idea . . . of society": Nussbaum, 12.

217   "My own . . . for me": Marcus Aurelius, 101.

218   "Yet I will . . . and reproach": *Arrian's Discourses*, Oates, 236.
218   "As far . . . since antiquity": Long, *Hellenistic Philosophy*, ix.
219   "Inside the office . . . Morrie nodded": Albom, 20.
220   "Four features . . . individual liberties": Krause, 23, 18.
220   "Those with . . . circumstances": Ibid., 26.

CHAPTER 9: NEOCONS

222   The story ran: Philip Gold, "A Think Tank That Treads New Ground," *Insight*, 21 Jun 92, 12–13, 28.
226   "The Sanhedrin . . . day": Gold, "Right Hand," *EastsideWeek*, 8 Oct. 97.
227   *Washington Times* . . . Culture War: Gold, "The Education of Forbes," *Wash. Times*, 23 Dec 99.
228   "Has Judaism Lost its Roots?": Gold, *Seattle Weekly*, 12 Jun 96.
228   I also . . . Harry Truman: Gold, "Peddling Ecstasy," *Seattle Weekly*, 10 Apr 96.
228   *Justice Matters*: Katz with Gold.
229   "Would you . . . with lawyers?": Gold, "Rule Number One," *Washington Law*.
238   "anybody . . . a hawk": Hawkins, "David Frum Interview," 26 Jan 04 at rightwingnews.com.
238   "I . . . hawk": Brooks, "A More Humble Hawk," *New York Times*, 19 Apr 04 at nytimes.com.
238   "intellectual . . . liberate": Brooks, "For Iraqis to Win," *New York Times*, May 11, 2004 at nytimes.com.
238   "All . . . now": Kagan, "Lowering Our Sights," *Washington Post*, 2 May 04, B-7.
239   "Instead . . . elections," Kagan and William Kristol, "Democracy Now," *Weekly Standard*, 17 May 04, at.weeklystandard.com.
239   "We should . . . popular support": Ledeen, "War on Terror," A-22.
239–40 "In short . . . embattled Iraqis": Michael Ledeen, "Mullahs Pray," National Rvw. Online, 26 Jan 04.
240   "Well, Lyndon . . . once": Halberstam, *Best*, 53.
241   "grand conservative destiny": Donald Devine, "Torture Facts," *ConservativeBattleline*, 19 May 04, at conservative.org.
242   "If the . . . not acceptable": William Kristol and Robert Kagan, "Do What It Takes in Iraq," *Weekly Standard*
243   "convert . . . a modern democracy": Kristol, "Neoconservative Persuasion," *Weekly Standard*.

245   "Few neoconservatives . . . be identified": Gottfried and
        Fleming, 69.
245   "conservative worthies . . . politely overlooked": Irving Kristol,
        "Persuasion," weeklystandard.com.
246–7   *"The current . . . manners corrupt"*: Peter Steinfels, *Neoconserva-*
        tives, 55. See also Gerson, *Neoconservative Vision. 275.*
248–9   "The number one . . . superpower":"Defense Planning Guidance."
249   The first letter . . . "the policy . . . from power": PNAC ltr. to
        Pres. Clinton, 26 Jan 98, at phal.org.
250   "It may . . . international terrorism": PNAC ltr. to Pres. Bush, 20
        Sep 01, at phal.org.
251–2   "What should . . . and watch": Kristol and Kagan, "Neo-Rea-
        ganite Foreign Policy," *Foreign Affairs*, at ceip.org.

CHAPTER 10: THE WORLD AS IT IS
256   "Here's a . . . just begun": Max Boot, at weeklystandard.com.
259   "Those who . . . repeat it": George Santayana. Chapter 12.
260   "The end . . . history existed": Fukuyama, 18.

AFTERWORD
217   "The conservative . . . politics": George Bush, remarks to ACU, 2.
272   "The fact . . . around": David Keene, at conservative.com.
272   "It is . . . back": John Micklethwait and Adrian Wooldridge.
272–3   "How . . .Waco": ACU, at conservative.com.
273   "feels betrayed": Robert Novak, at washingtonpost.com.

Index